THE
GREAT
COWBOY
STARS
OF MOVIES &
TELEVISION

THE GREAT COWBOY STARS

OF MOVIES & TELEVISION

LEE O. MILLER

Introduction by
Joel McCrea

ARLINGTON HOUSE·PUBLISHERS
165 HUGUENOT STREET • NEW ROCHELLE, NEW YORK 10801

Manufactured in the United States of America

Library of Congress Cataloging in Publication Data

Miller, Lee O.   1922-
  Great cowboy stars of movies and television.

  1. Western films—United States. 2. Westerns (Television pro-
grams)—United States. 3. Actors—United States. I. Title.
PN1995.9.W4M57   791'.092'2   79-12361
ISBN 0-87000-429-8

To

My wife Charlotte and our four children: Carolyn, Marina, Wade, and Laurie. Today's younger generation, which is without cowboy heroes to look up to and emulate, and the older generation, which still idolizes the heroes in this book and respects them. Three great cowboy stars: Tim McCoy, Ken Maynard, and Johnny Mack Brown, whom I interviewed just before they died. And all the other great stars I interviewed to make this book possible.

Key to Abbreviations

All.—Allied Pictures
AA—Allied Artists Pictures
Bat.—Batjac Productions
BV—Buena Vista
CBS—Columbia Broadcasting System
CD—Chas. Davis
Col.—Columbia Pictures
Dis.—Walt Disney Productions
Emb.—Embassy Pictures
FBO—Film Booking Offices
FD—First Division
FN—First National Pictures
Fox—Fox Film Corp.
GN—Grand National
Ince—Thomas H. Ince
It.—Italian
Lib.—Liberty Pictures
Lip.—Lippert Pictures
LSP—Lone Star Productions
Mas.—Mascot Pictures
Met.—Metropolitan
MGM—Metro-Goldwyn-Mayer
Mon.—Monogram Pictures
Mona.—Monarch

NBC—National Broadcasting Company
NGP—National General Pictures
Par.—Paramount Pictures
Pathé—Pathé Studio
PDC—Producers Distributing Corp.
PRC—Producers Releasing Corp.
Pur.—Puritan Pictures
Rel.—Reliable Pictures
Rep.—Republic Pictures
RKO—RKO Radio Pictures
SG—Screen Guild
Sup.—Supreme Pictures
Syn.—Syndicate Pictures
Tif.—Tiffany
Tri.—Triangle
TS—Tiffany-Stahl
20th—Twentieth Century-Fox
UA—United Artists
UI—Universal-International
Univ.—Universal Pictures
Vic.—Victory Pictures
WB—Warner Brothers
WW—World Wide Pictures

SPECIAL ACKNOWLEDGMENT

I want especially to thank the following stars, agents, and agencies for their splendid cooperation and extra efforts to help me make this book a reality . . .

George O'Brien, Tim McCoy, Gene Autry, Roy Rogers, Joel McCrea, Randolph Scott, Charles Starrett, Noah Beery, Jr., Ken Maynard, Johnny Mack Brown, John Wayne, Bob Steele, Dennis Weaver, James Arness, "Lash" LaRue, Sunset Carson, Tommy Scott, Clint Eastwood; Joan Hanson (Screen Actors Guild); Lee Roy Willis; Art Rush Agency, Ted Wilk Agency, Mishkin Agency, Famous Players Agency, Milton Grossman Agency, Gordean-Friedman Agency; Warner Bros. Studios, Universal-International Studios, Paramount Pictures, Inc., Wide World Photos, Film Favorites; Larry Edmunds Bookstore, Bill Black, Robert R. Michelson, James Bellah, and "Skip" Heinecke.

—Lee O. Miller

Contents

Part Three: Ghost Riders in the Sky

Foreword

THE WESTERN PICTURE has been a staple of the American movie industry almost from the beginning. *The Great Train Robbery* (1903) is a landmark of the film industry; it was a Western, and since then moviegoers have watched the sagebrush genre expand along with filmmaking in general.

There are probably few people who, at one time or another, have not fallen under the spell of Western movies that depicted a time when life was a lot simpler; the good guys were good and the bad guys were bad; right was right and wrong was punished with a six-gun, or a trial (sometimes), or a hanging, or the restitution of ill-gotten property.

Whether the story was based on fact or fiction was hardly important; what was important was the struggle between virtue and evil. It was wrong for the bad guy to steal the beautiful widow's homestead. It was right for the hero to get it back for her by *any* means, and it stood to reason that the good guy was quicker on the draw because his heart was pure. Later on, I recall, Tom Mix adequately summed it up on a radio show when he said, "Straight shooters always win. Those who can't shoot straight always lose."

As a Western film actor, when I saw audiences leaving theaters across the country content that I had done in the bad guy, won the girl, and rode off peacefully into the sunset, I *knew* I'd done a good job.

But a good job doesn't just stop there, pleasing adult audiences. A really good job as a Western actor is when you realize that kids in the country are emulating you, playing as if they're the hero riding herd on the bad guy—just as they saw you do it in films. The super job of acting, to me, is when you thrill young and old alike, and get top notices in film box-office reviews and polls.

Unfortunately, kids today don't play cowboys and Indians as much; King Kong, Godzilla, Dracula, and other movie monsters and ghouls occupy them more, as do police and detective shows in movies and on TV. Many times I've heard parents ask: Where are the heroes our children used to look up to? Where are the models they used to copy as their lifestyle?

I can answer the questions rather simply. The heroes the kids used to look up to were the cowboy stars. Why? Because they were Americana and stood for American heroes at their level best. What youngster wouldn't use a cowboy star as a model to live up to, myths though all of us truly were?

A few years ago Westerns, like cops-and-robbers pictures, sort of got out of hand, went too far, in the realism factor. That is, they portrayed too much violence when much of it wasn't really necessary. But it was a trend—the more realistic, the better—and it left its brand on the Western in films and on TV. Antiviolence groups of parents organized and brought pressure to bear upon Hollywood, to such an extent that an intangible "antiviolence code" was effected. And though it was not fully implemented at the time, it forced producers to shy away from making films that contained too much violence.

Whereas the theme of the antiviolence code was proper at the time, it produced disastrous effects. Producers of movie and TV Westerns panicked, thereby hurting production of staid old films because of their natural tendency toward violence. It got so a hero couldn't shoot the bad guy without pressure against such "violence," an integral part of good Westerns. Producers thus overreacted and shied away from making Westerns, forcing such good TV series as "Bonanza" and "Gunsmoke" to bite the dust because plots could not be done plausibly without some violence in them.

However, and thank God, most of the panic of a few years ago is gone and once again the Western is returning to the screen and TV. And with the return of Westerns, maybe the youth of this country can again have heroes to look up to—heroes that represent Americana and *mean American*—and the world will be better again.

I am proud to have been a Western actor; would be proud to act again in any good Western, as long as it represents what the Westerns of old represented: Americana.

I am proud to do this foreword, not only because I personally knew, worked with, and respected many of the stars profiled herein, but also because this work represents a genre I'm sure every American loves and will continue to cherish: the Western movie-TV star.

—Joel McCrea

The Way a Cowgirl Sees Things

What's the use to try and try
Cause trouble don't seem t' pass y' by,
You try t' smile till you're plumb
Wore out, take life's kicks and try
Not to doubt,
If it's not one thing, well then it's three,
I'm tellin' you—it beats hell outta me;
The sun won't shine in your back door,
You make some money but always need more,
The rent's high and the house is cold,
Guess that's all in makin' us old;
So if I die, don't y'all feel sad,
Cuz I think I'll be kinda glad,
And I just hope everything's not high,
In that Glory Land of sweet bye and bye.

Ovella Machen (Maxie)
Former rodeo trick rider

Gilbert M. "Broncho Billy" Anderson—first Western motion picture star.

Prologue

THE SHORT HAPPY life of the B-Western closely paralleled that of a man. It was born, suffered growing pains, matured, reached peaks of outstanding success and sank into valleys of utter failure, grew senile, and died prematurely after a lifespan of approximately fifty-two years.

The birth of the Western genre took place in 1903 when, after a few short experimental films were made featuring brief scenes of fictionalized historical incidents, the Edison Company made *The Great Train Robbery*. The film ran for only ten minutes, but in that timespan it told a complete story of a robbery, with a chase and final action-packed showdown.

The film wasn't much but it was a beginning, and other studios promptly made copies to cash in on the original's success.

In 1908 G. M. Anderson, who played several roles in *The Great Train Robbery,* made a short Western entitled *Broncho Billy and the Baby.* Its interesting plot line had Anderson playing the role of a "good" badman who sacrifices himself to save a child. The name Broncho Billy stuck with Anderson like glue and he went on to develop the character in a score of two-reeler Westerns. He had, in fact, become the cinema's first Western hero.

Development of the B-Western format was furthered between 1908 and 1913 by pioneer directors D. W. Griffith and Thomas H. Ince, who cranked out one- and two-reelers featuring silver-screen notables like Lillian Gish and Blanche Sweet as the feminine leads.

Unlike *The Great Train Robbery,* which was filmed in the "wilds" of New Jersey, Griffith shot many of his motion pictures in and around Hollywood, at that time still fairly primitive country containing vast stretches of uncluttered natural scenery. Film titles such as *The Goddess of Sagebrush Gulch, The Battle of Elderbush Gulch,* and *The Last Drop of Water* came forth. The films were action-packed and had moments of striking visual beauty. It was another big step in the B-Western's ever-maturing process.

Two men who were to contribute enormously to the genre began their film careers at the same time, in 1914. They were William S. Hart and the late film director John Ford.

Hart had a distinguished background of theatrical experience already behind him when he began appearing in one-reelers. He rapidly caught on to the new art and soon graduated to full-length feature pictures. Before long he was turning out minor classics like *Hell's Hinges* and *The Aryan,* both filmed in 1916. By the twenties Bill Hart had perfected his role of the "good" badman and went on to do pictures like *The Testing Block, Three Word Brand,* and *Wild Bill Hickok* for Paramount Studios. He starred in his final film in 1925, the epic *Tumbleweeds,* which noted Western authority William K. Everson ranks with *The Covered Wagon* and *The Iron Horse,* two of the best Western motion pictures ever made.

Hart, in addition to starring in *Tumbleweeds,* codirected the picture with King Baggott. He then retired from the screen and wrote his autobiography. Many years later, in 1939, *Tumbleweeds* was reissued and Hart made a ten-minute introduction to the film in which he told the audience some facts about the opening of the Cherokee Strip, and then concluded with personal comments of his own.

John Ford began in films as an actor and a stuntman in 1914, and by 1917 Universal had signed him to direct some two-reel Westerns which featured, among other stars, Hoot Gibson and Harry Carey. Unfortunately, most of these films have been lost or accidentally destroyed and are thus unavailable to historians and scholars for study, creating a noticeable gap in the record of John Ford's early career.

Motion picture companies were then, and unfortunately continue to be, fearfully shortsighted. Early films made on nitrate stock were allowed to decompose, or were simply junked, since it was felt there would be no future use for them after their initial screenings.

Rumors still persist that Universal, while filming a spectacular fire sequence for a later feature film, used hundreds of rare original negatives as fuel, thus forever destroying many of their great silent classics.

Happily, John Ford's very first feature film, *Straight Shooting,* made in 1917 and starring Hoot Gibson and Harry Carey, is one that has managed to survive. In 1924 Ford made his epic *The Iron Horse,* and thereafter was the dean of Western filmmaking until his death in 1973.

As the B-Western grew in popularity and actors like Hart, Carey, and Gibson prospered, it was only natural there would be a rush to bring new faces to the screen in outdoor action dramas. Men like William Desmond, Roy Stewart, Dustin Farnum, and William Farnum were all big box-office favorites, but a great many others have long since been forgotten.

The twenties brought more than a score of new stars into the B-Western fold. A few like Buck Jones, Ken Maynard, Tim McCoy, Bob Steele, and Hoot Gibson continued to be popular for years to come (a few are still performing on TV today, as we'll note in upcoming chapters). Others like Ted Wells, Fred Thomson, Jack Hoxie, Fred Humes, and Leo Maloney became character actors, faded into oblivion, or died (as did Thomson in 1928 and Maloney in 1929).

Of all the great stars who achieved enormous popularity in the twenties, none ranked higher than Tom Mix, who was rated by his fans *the* most popular Western film star ever to appear on the silver screen.

The twenties offered more new cowboy faces to Western fans than any other decade. Besides those already mentioned, there were Wally Wales (later known as Hal Taliaferro), Art Acord, Edmund Cobb, Buddy Roosevelt, Buffalo Bill, Jr. (real name Jay C. Wilsey), Bob Custer, Bill Cody, Lane Chandler, Jack Perrin, Jack Luden, Gary Cooper, Jack Holt, Richard Dix, Bill Boyd (later known as Hopalong Cassidy), Warner Baxter (the original Cisco Kid), Bob Steele, and Tom Tyler.

The thirties ushered in a few more new faces: Johnny Mack Brown, Charles Starrett, Joel McCrea, Gene Autry, Roy Rogers, John Wayne, Randolph Scott, Guinn "Big Boy" Williams, and Noah Beery, Jr.

Came the forties and Western fans saw Sunset Carson, Tim Holt, Don "Red" Barry, Chill Wills, William "Wild Bill" Elliott, Allan "Rocky" Lane, Al "Lash" LaRue, Rod Cameron, and Clayton Moore (the Lone Ranger).

The fifties marked finis to fifty-two years of B-Western moviemaking because of a rising newcomer—television. TV spawned its own B-type Western heroes (many former stars making the transition from big screen to tube): Autry, Rogers, James Arness, Richard Boone, Clint Walker, Robert Blake, Robert Fuller, Lorne Greene, Michael Landon, Dan Blocker, Ward Bond, Dennis Weaver, Bob Steele, Fess Parker, Ben Murphy, Hugh O'Brian, Lee Majors (ABC's "Six Million Dollar Man"), Peter Deuel, James Drury, Chuck Connors, Jock Mahoney, Dick Jones, Dean Martin, Glenn Ford, Terry Wilson, Dale Robertson, Rod Taylor, Gene Barry, John McIntire, and Edd Byrnes (who made the transition to Westerns after his success on "77 Sunset Strip" waned).

The purpose of this book is to pay proper tribute to all the great Western superstars—those who have ridden off to their final roundup in the sky, and those still alive and kickin' today—and to air their opinions, many for the first time, about the Western films of yesterday as compared with movies and TV today; about the so-called non-violence code, which many assert is ruining the making of Westerns for movies and TV; and about the outlook for the future. The oldtimers have a lot of savvy to relay to our youngblood about these matters and about what being a Western superstar really means.

PART ONE

Salute to
the Living Legends

George O'Brien, as he appeared in Western film roles in the late thirties.

George O'Brien

("Mr. Atlas" to his fans)

Born: April 19, 1899, San Francisco, Calif.
Married: Marguerite Churchill (1933);
  divorced (1950); children: Orin, Darcy

WHEN THE LATE director John Ford made his second great Western epic, *The Iron Horse* (1924), he cast in one of the leading roles a handsome, well-built young man who had personality, get-up-and-go, and the promise of becoming a big star if he stayed in the business.

The young man was George O'Brien, who proved himself worthy of Ford's estimation of him and went on to become one of the biggest outdoor and Western stars in Hollywood. His step was lithe, and when he expanded his barrellike chest to a maximum forty-four inches and flexed his muscular arms and torso in films, females in the audience oohed and aahed, and swooned their bedazzled hearts out. To females he was Rudolph Valentino, Gary Cooper, Tom Mix, and Buck Jones all wrapped up in one muscular package. To males he was a tough good-guy hero with lots of charm and witty remarks, who with apparent ease could handle *any* bad guy that came along.

George O'Brien skyrocketed to fame, and then, a couple of years before Pearl Harbor, he suddenly began to fade, until he was lost to oblivion. Or so it seemed to his worldwide public.

"Where's George O'Brien? Where's our lover boy, our man?" cried females at home and abroad.

"How about it, Hollywood? Where's our hero, George O'Brien?" demanded the male audience.

Hollywood had only one logical answer: George O'Brien had given up his screen career to enter again naval service in behalf of his country.

But this was not quite accurate. O'Brien had only *interrupted* his screen career to rejoin the navy because he sensed, more than knew, that America would sooner or later be plunged headlong into war with Japan and Nazi Germany.

Hollywood's answer to O'Brien's fans brought a flood of irate letters demanding a better explanation of what had happened to their favorite star. O'Brien himself was contacted by his studio (RKO) and read many of those letters. To aid in getting his studio off the hook and let his fans know the truth, he composed a press release explaining all. RKO's publicity department mimeographed the release and sent it to every major newspaper in the country, along with a photo of George. The fans read the truth, but were not happy. Many to this day feel that O'Brien was handled shabbily and that the enlisting-in-the-navy bit was strictly Hollywood's way of covering up the real truth of how it mistreated him.

"Dammit, George *do* something!" O'Brien recalls his producers saying.

"What could I do that wasn't already done?" he says, shrugging. "I suppose it was *I* who treated my studio shabbily, cutting off my career like that by enlisting in the navy, but at the time I felt enlisting was the right thing to do, what with the situation abroad so sticky. I could offer neither my studio nor my fans anything beyond the press release I composed, and at the time accepted whatever fate the future held for me."

O'Brien served in the navy from 1939 to 1945 and again from 1950 to 1963, when he retired as a full captain. But his naval service began long before he gave up his movie career to reenlist in 1939.

George O'Brien was reared in San Francisco. His father was a journalist and his mother an accomplished pianist. An older brother, James, later managed his business affairs while he was away at war.

George's early stage appearances were with the Columbia Park Boys' Club in San Francisco, where he performed in a variety of things— acrobatics, tumbling, and plays. "We were strictly a boys' club," he recalls proudly, "and on summer vacations from school we went hiking all through northern California, earning our keep, camping out, doing all the camp work, cooking, and sleeping on the ground. We swam in the lakes and rivers and whenever we happened to stop in a town we'd challenge the boys' club there to boxing matches, swimming meets, baseball, or whatever.

"We also had a boys' band at our club in San Francisco. None of the things we did netted us any money; any donated money left over from our summer camping trip went to support our club during the winter. But we had fun, loads of it. And we learned a lot of things too. Like how to compete, how to win, and how to be a good loser. How to get along with one another, how to make good and useful citizens of ourselves and not statistics down at police headquarters. I was eight when I went on the first camping trip, and was twelve when I went for the last time."

During his high school days, when he wasn't swimming or practicing or playing football, basketball, or baseball, he was studying.

"My father wanted me to become a professional man, preferably a doctor, not a journalist like himself. He liked being a journalist and respected his work, but found little solace in the low pay it rendered for his long hours of endeavor. I wanted to please my father because I both loved and respected him, so I studied hard to become the doctor he wanted me to be.

"I was in my freshman year of college [University of Southern California] when we were plunged into the first war with Germany. I was eighteen at the time. I could have remained in college and obtained my degree and then gone into medical school, but decided to enlist and serve my country instead. I tried to enlist in the Marine Corps but they wouldn't accept me because their quotas at the time were full. So I tried the navy and they accepted me."

After boot training O'Brien went on to seaman's training and then was sent to radio school and became a radioman-signalman. This was a far cry from the medical career he had been so diligently studying for, so once he got the chance he transferred from his ship to the Marine Corps as a medical attendant (stretcher-bearer).

"I saw the terrible cost of what steel does to human flesh and bone by the time I was nineteen," recalls George. "My first action assignment was with the marines at Belleau Wood, and I was scared stiff all the time. But not so badly that I wasn't mindful of my duties or trying to save a life. I saved many a marine from dying, and luckily didn't wind up a casualty myself."

George is modest about his bravery. He received five decorations—two French and three U.S.—for bravery under fire in World War I. He was discharged as a navy pharmacist's mate when the war ended.

"A civilian again, I returned to college to resume my studies to become a doctor. I'd had plenty of firsthand experience by then, so I was eager to accomplish my objective.

"However, another 'deviation' was just ahead to sway me from my proposed medical career. I had long been a movie nut, even when my father took me to films and read me the words on the screen and whisperingly told me what the film was all about. Later, when I could read and understand for myself, I became a fan of the first Western action films of Broncho Billy Anderson, Bill Hart, and Tom Mix. Fox Studios was not far from the college, so I used to spend a lot of time there, watching them make the Western films I would later see on the screen.

"I became good friends with a lad named Charles Gebhart, who was an army veteran and hailed from Vincennes, Indiana. Charley was a rugged individual, who'd been, besides a soldier in the war, a cowboy, race driver, and boxer. At the time, he was a double and stuntman for Tom Mix. He later became a big Western star under a different name—Buck Jones.

"Anyway, Charley soon learned how interested I was in breaking into the movies, so he talked to Mix and got me a job as a stuntman. I'll state here and now I never was the stuntman Charley Gebhart was, but was good enough to play tough-guy parts and play Indian parts, that sort of thing, and make good deathfalls, when 'shot.' I got bunged up several times, but nothing serious. But I learned to ride horses and this later came in handy when I also became a Western star."

Buck Jones was instrumental in obtaining a ten-year contract for George with Fox.

As he appeared in a boxing film.   *The star.*

On the Navajo Indian Reservation, Monument Valley, Arizona, while filming Zane Grey's The Lone
Star Ranger *(1930).*

24

"My big break came when my late and dearest friend John Ford cast me, through Charley's persuasion, in *The Iron Horse*. I had had prior experience as a stuntman—incidentally, I also was Buck Jones' stuntman—and was good enough to make Ford notice me. He asked Charley about me, or maybe it was vice versa; anyway I got the part in *Iron Horse*.

"Obviously I was good enough in my part in the film, because it not only launched my screen career, but got me a ten-year contract with Fox as well. I remained with that studio most of my career.

"When I returned from naval service after World War II, I found one helluva lot of changes had taken place in Hollywood—especially with the making of Westerns. New techniques, better sound equipment, better everything seemed to predominate. Mostly the pay was much more generous than I recalled. For example, I was usually paid $2,000 to $3,000 per film, pretty standard for the leading star in my time, and $500 extra if I did most of my own stunts in the film to cut down on production costs. When I returned to Hollywood after the war it was to find lead Western stars getting anywhere from $15,000 to $25,000 per film, plus what they called 'residuals' every time a new print of the film was made and it was re-released.

"Also a new industry, called television, was looming in the immediate future, and had everyone, including even the big stars, pretty worried. Later, after TV became so popular and movies all but ceased to exist for years, the worrisome fears of those I mentioned proved well founded.

"Another thing I noticed was the absence of many former Western film stars. Charley had been killed trying to save lives in the Cocoanut Grove fire in Boston, during a war-bond tour during the war, but stars like Tim McCoy, John Mack Brown, Chuck Starrett, Ken Maynard, Hoot Gibson, etc., were no longer popular. Many in fact, like Maynard, had tried to 'drown' their sorrows and it only proved their undoing in the years to come.

"I'd had a fairly versatile experience in my film career, meaning I hadn't played a Western hero all the time. Like Tim McCoy and Charley Gebhart—pardon, Buck Jones—I had been cast in roles as reporter, detective, campus athlete-hero-lover, and even as a mountie in *O'Malley of the Mounted* . . . so you see, I didn't have to depend on just Western roles to earn a living.

"My versatility led to jobs in films of various kinds, not in the leading roles, mind you, but in roles that paid me as much as I had earned as a big star in my early films. I also made the transition into TV films, along with my old friend Tim McCoy, who won several awards.

"I was slowly but surely rebuilding my second career in films, when the trouble in Korea started. Maybe it was my inner sense of patriotism, or loyalty, I don't exactly know, but whatever it was forced me to again abort my career in films and again resume the life of an officer in the navy."

Just before the Korean conflict began in the summer of 1950, George left his wife and two children and horse ranch in the Malibu Mountains and went to San Diego to report for active duty in the navy. He was in Naval Intelligence and operated many times behind Red lines in North Korea, but to this day cannot reveal exactly what he did.

"My biggest sorrow and disappointment came when my wife Margie filed for divorce. I'd married Margie prior to World War II and she had stuck with me during the long, lonely years of absence, so, when the Korea mess happened and I again returned to duty, she couldn't take it. Nor, she said, could the kids take it. So she divorced me and kept Orin and Darcy. We're still good friends today, and the children—hell, they're grown now—and I get together often when I'm not traveling, which is usually constantly, between the States, Europe, and the Orient producing and directing my own TV film specials. 'Windjammer' is a good example, and it was on in prime time with the NBC network in 1973."

George's second naval career lasted until his retirement from the Navy in 1963 with the rank of captain. His service in duty stations took him all over the world, even as a naval attaché to the NATO conferences in France, Italy, Turkey, Greece, and England.

During World War II he saw active duty in many combat areas: Attu, Kiska, Adak, Great Sitkin, Dutch Harbor, Kodiak, Anchorage, White Horse—all in the Aleutians and Alaska; in the Pacific: Saipan, Guam, Kwajalein; in the Philippines: Leyte, Samar, Panay, Majuro, San Fernando, Mindanao, Manila, Cavite, Cebu, Zamboanga, Mindoro, Subic Bay, and Luzon. He was also at Pearl Harbor when the Japanese attacked on December 7, 1941.

His navy decorations include: World War I—Navy Commendation Medal, Marine Corps Commendation Medal, Silver Star (plus two French medals); World War II—Navy Commendation Medal (with pendant), Presidential Citation for North Pacific duty, American medal, South-Central Pacific campaign medals, also ribbons with four battle stars, Philippine government ribbon with battle star, pre-Pearl Harbor medal; post-Korean awards—Department of Defense special citation and Special Projects medal for duties rendered in eight Southeast Asian countries from 1957 to 1961: Taiwan, Japan, Korea, Okinawa, Philippines, Vietnam, Cambodia, and Thailand.

What does this naval hero and former Western star think of today's Western filmmaking efforts?

"I think movie and TV Western films are today in one big colossal rut. What's more, I'm not alone in thinking this. Other good friends and former actors think as I do. And if you don't believe me, ask Joel McCrea, Gene Autry, and Randy Scott what they think of the matter and they'll tell you the same—if not more vehemently.

"Hollywood used up most of what I term the good Western plots years ago," George continues. "Today, they have a fresh bunch of young

26

writers who are trying to take these old plots and reshape them into something more contemporary for use today. The result is chaotic. The result is utter failure.

"They don't have the same types of Western stars today as they used to have during my career in films. Today the Western film heroes are too tinselly; that is to say, they use violence to portray their toughness and virility instead of the old way we used to act out roles. I personally feel that John Wayne is more the living legend of the way a Western star should act, instead of what they're turning out today.

"Very few actors today do their own stunts, and that was half the fun in my day—the rough-and-tumble part—in films. I doubt seriously if you will find today a Western star who will leap from his horse into a moving wagon and do a fight scene, or onto a train for the same thing, or knock another rider from his horse and get up and fight it out with him. If this is still done, I have yet to see it on TV or in a movie. Tom Mix, you know, was the actor responsible for most of the daring stunts all of us used to do in our own pictures. Tom is credited with doing more for the industry, I suppose, than anyone except John Wayne. And Duke, well, like the rest of us—he got his start through Mix, and learned practically everything he knows from him. All in all, they just didn't come bigger or greater than Tom Mix."

Asked what he thought of the antiviolence code forced upon Hollywood by pressure groups, he says:

"First, let me say that Westerns, as a whole, I feel, captivate most young audiences today just as they used to during my day, with one exception, however—lack of hero identification in today's Western star. Today, there are no Western movie-star heroes for the youth of our country to identify with. I don't believe the antiviolence code, if that's what it's called, had anything to do with this initially, but now it most certainly does.

"My own children—grown up now—and their kids get a big charge out of watching oldtime Westerns rerun on TV. And they all agree that the kind of action they had in my day was much better than the gory type they see in today's TV Westerns and movie 'spaghetti' films. What they actually like better is to identify with the hero in the old films, a hero they can feel and be part of from the beginning to the slam-bang chase and fight sequence of the hero-wins-over-the-bad-guy at the end, a hero that finally wins his sweetheart and rides off on his horse with her into the sunset. I know this all sounds pretty corny, but I believe it's the main element—identity—that Western TV and movie producers lost somewhere between my day and now. And if our children need any one single thing today from TV or movies, it's a *hero* to identify with and respect."

What films did he enjoy making most of all?

"Oh, God, they're so many—over sixty—it's hard to say. However, I did enjoy doing the Zane Grey series and the *O'Malley of the Mounted* series about as much as any of the rest. Except of course those I've appeared in since World War II . . . *Fort Apache, She Wore a Yellow Ribbon, Gold Raiders, My Wild Irish Rose,* and *Cheyenne Autumn.* . . . And I was with such a group of talented actors I probably will never again appear with, I naturally cherish these films best of all."

Who are his favorite Western actors today?

"That's very easy. There are three. They are Duke Wayne for movies, and James Arness and Richard Boone for TV. These three top honchos make the West come alive again and make Western characters act like they're supposed to."

Western Film Credits

The Iron Horse (Fox, 1924)
Rustling for Cupid (Fox, 1926)
Three Bad Men (Fox, 1926)
The Lone Star Ranger (Fox, 1930)
A Rough Romance (Fox, 1930)
Last of the Duanes (Fox, 1930)
Fair Warning (Fox, 1931)
A Holy Terror (Fox, 1931)
Riders of the Purple Sage (Fox, 1931)
The Rainbow Trail (Fox, 1931)
The Gay Caballero (Fox, 1932)
Mystery Ranch (Fox, 1932)
The Golden West (Fox, 1932)
Robbers' Roost (Fox, 1933)
Smoke Lightning (Fox, 1933)
Life in the Raw (Fox, 1933)
The Last Trail (Fox, 1933)
Frontier Marshal (Fox, 1934)
The Dude Ranger (Fox, 1934)
When a Man's a Man (Fox, 1935)
The Cowboy Millionaire (Fox, 1935)
Hard Rock Harrigan (Fox, 1935)
Thunder Mountain (Fox, 1935)
Whispering Smith Speaks (Fox, 1935)
O'Malley of the Mounted (Fox, 1936)

The Border Patrolman (Fox, 1936)
Daniel Boone (RKO, 1936)
Hollywood Cowboy (RKO, 1937)
Gun Law (RKO, 1938)
Border G-Man (RKO, 1938)
The Painted Desert (RKO, 1938)
The Renegade Ranger (RKO, 1938)
Lawless Valley (RKO, 1938)
The Arizona Legion (RKO, 1939)
Trouble in Sundown (RKO, 1939)
Racketeers of the Range (RKO, 1939)
Timber Stampede (RKO, 1939)
The Fighting Gringo (RKO, 1939)
The Marshal of Mesa City (RKO, 1939)
Legion of the Lawless (RKO, 1940)
Bullet Code (RKO, 1940)
Prairie Law (RKO, 1940)
Stage to Chino (RKO, 1940)
Triple Justice (RKO, 1940)
Fort Apache (RKO, 1948)
She Wore a Yellow Ribbon (RKO, 1949)
Gold Raiders (UA, 1951)
Cheyenne Autumn (WB, 1964)

Bob Steele, Western star.

Bob Steele

(The Fightin' Kid)

Born: January 23, 1907, Pendleton, Ore.
Married: Rowina Mix (1932); divorced
  (1945); children: Robert, William

WHEN ROBERT NORTH BRADBURY, JR. (better known to his many
Western film fans as Bob Steele) and his younger brother Bill were about
twelve and eleven years old respectively, they were already headed for
moviedom.

Their famous father, Robert N. Bradbury, was a motion picture producer-director, having started out as an actor in early two-reelers starring
Broncho Billy Anderson. He later directed Broncho Billy in three of his
longer films, and then directed William S. Hart in several pictures. But
most of his popularity came from directing Tom Mix films, after which he
began producing and directing his own, starring his son Bob.

But in the beginning it was Bobby and Billy the ambitious father
filmed and directed in episodes he named *The Adventures of Bill and Bob.*
He showed the two-reelers (and longer features) of the boys to friends, and
one of his producer friends suggested he adjoin the reels and produce
them as an adventure series for children. Bradbury thought this a
splendid idea.

The Adventures of Bill and Bob was produced and screened for theater
audiences. It met with very modest success, however. And since the series
was designed for children and not adults, screenings were withdrawn
from theaters and confined largely to school and Sunday-school groups
and classes around the country. The series proved embarrassing to both
brothers.

During his high school years Bob was a superb athlete who participated in every sport and excelled in boxing and wrestling. He also took
part in several junior and senior class plays. He decided he liked acting
and wanted to make acting in films a career.

After graduation from high school, Bob enrolled as a freshman at the
University of Oregon. He intended to pursue a degree in physical education, but his father soon changed his mind for him. Dad offered him the
opportunity of coming to Los Angeles to learn the moviemaking business, and Bob immediately—and eagerly—accepted.

He accompanied his father to work every morning and throughout

31

each working day sat and observed his father's directing techniques and how the actors responded. Bob was convinced he could become a good Western cowboy star if given the chance. However, his father insisted that he enroll in the University of Southern California and pursue his new objective more thoroughly.

Yielding to his father's wishes, he studied acting and drama, besides working part-time on his father's Western sets as an extra and a stuntman. Finally tiring of college and the routine of part-time work in films, Bob confronted his father, insisting he could carry the load of a star if given a chance to do so.

In 1927 Robert Bradbury (who now became Bob Steele) appeared as the young hero and leading man in his first major Western film, entitled appropriately *The Mojave Kid*. The film was silent, but young Steele put his college learning and apprenticeship to work; by a little innovation, he subdued the villain strictly with his fists instead of a six-gun.

The Mojave Kid was a tremendous success. Hollywood did not hesitate to announce that a new Western star had been born, that Bob Steele would "exemplify himself as a hero to males and win the hearts of females with his good looks, charisma, and physical prowess."

The new Bob Steele lived up to the publicity. He starred in thirteen

With Joan Barclay, Budd Buster, Hal Price, and Frank Ball in The Trusted Outlaw *(1934).*

more silent feature films and, with his pleasant speaking voice, easily made the transition to sound.

Steele appeared in his first Western talkie in 1930, *Near the Rainbow's End*. He followed this with an additional thirteen major features, with attention-getting action titles like *The Ridin' Fool* (1931), *Fighting Champ* (1932), *Breed of the Border* (1933), *The Gallant Fool* (1933), and *Trailing North* (1933).

He made thirty-five more features between 1934 and 1939, his biggest being the famous *Powdersmoke Range* (1935), with its all-star Western cast. Featured with Steele were Hoot Gibson, Harry Carey, Tom Tyler, Guinn "Big Boy" Williams, William Farnum, William Desmond, Buzz Barton, Wally Wales, Art Mix (no relation of Tom's), Buffalo Bill, Jr., and Buddy Roosevelt.

To try his luck at dramatic acting, Steele accepted in 1939 a leading role opposite Betty Field in *Of Mice and Men*. His acting was superb and this versatility later brought him a leading role in the detective thriller *The Big Sleep* (1946). From *Of Mice and Men* Bob could have gone upward as a major star, but for reasons of his own he decided to return to Westerns.

He starred in the famous "Mesquiteer" series for Republic Studios and later in the "Trail Blazers" series with Ken Maynard, Hoot Gibson, and Chief Thundercloud.

He was drafted into the army and served at Fort Bliss, Texas, until the war ended. He then returned to Hollywood to resume his career but, like so many other former Western stars, found important changes had been made in his absence. Roy Rogers was now the top box-office star in Hollywood and the "King of the Cowboys." So Steele took character and bit parts, without really scoring big on the screen again.

In television he has played a badman and a cavalryman in Westerns, a gangster, the fatherly type in such TV series as "The Fugitive," and an oldtime star in Brian Keith's "Family Affair," in which he paid a visit to Keith's house and sat with Keith and the children watching one of his old films on TV. In the segment the children were disappointed to find their cowboy hero an elderly has-been, but they were eventually won over by his charm and personality. His last movie appearance was in *Charley Varrick* (Univ., 1973), which starred Walter Matthau.

Meanwhile, Steele is available for work and doesn't let the word *age* bother him one bit.

"It don't help any of us older actors to be classed as oldtimers or the like around Hollywood these days," Steele says. "They get a notion you're too old, a has-been, and you've sure enough had it, here. I still get enough work and make enough to support me like I'm accustomed to living . . . which is a far sight removed from the way I lived when I was a big star. But, that's the breaks. You win a few, you lose a few. You roll with the punches, but you stay in there and survive.

In Kid Courageous *(1935) with Vane Calvert and Renee Borden.*

In 1939.

At age 67, semi-retired.

"Would I pursue a career in physical education if I could live my life again? No, I'm afraid I'd do about the same as I did the first time. Except . . . maybe I'd go on to bigger things, instead of Westerns, if I got a big role like I had in *Of Mice and Men.*

"Regrets? Just one. That times changed so drastically with the advent of TV, that it killed Western filmmaking. But, well, that's how it goes. That's the breaks in this game.

"My favorite cowboy star actors? Well, there are several, I guess. I liked Buck Jones, Ken Maynard, and Tim McCoy. I sort of at one time fancied myself as a combination of all three. Today, I think Jim Arness and Dick Boone best personify the Western actors as I knew them, as I was part of. The rest fall far short."

Western Film Credits

The Mojave Kid (FBO, 1927)
The Bandit's Son (FBO, 1927)
Breed of the Sunsets (FBO, 1928)
Driftin' Sands (FBO, 1928)
The Riding Renegade (FBO, 1928)
Man in the Rough (FBO, 1928)
The Trail of Courage (FBO, 1928)
The Invaders (Syn., 1929)
The Amazing Vagabond (FBO, 1929)
Near the Rainbow's End (Tif., 1930)
Texas Cowboy (Syn., 1930)
Breezy Bill (Syn., 1930)
Cowboy and the Outlaw (Syn., 1930)
Western Honor (Syn., 1930)
Hunted Men (Syn., 1930)
Man from Nowhere (Syn., 1930)
The Oklahoma Sheriff (Syn., 1930)
Land of Missing Men (Tif., 1930)
Headin' North (Tif., 1930)
Oklahoma Cyclone (Tif., 1930)
The Nevada Buckaroo (WW, 1931)
The Ridin' Fool (Tif., 1931)
The Sunrise Trail (Tif., 1931)
Son of Oklahoma (WW, 1932)
South of Santa Fe (WW, 1932)
Texas Buddies (WW, 1932)
Riders of the Desert (WW, 1932)
The Man from Hell's Edges (WW, 1932)

The Fighting Champ (Mon., 1932)
Law of the West (WW, 1932)
Hidden Valley (Mon., 1932)
Young Blood (Mon., 1932)
Trailing North (Mon., 1933)
The Gallant Fool (Mon., 1933)
Breed of the Border (Mon., 1933)
Galloping Romeo (Mon., 1933)
The Ranger's Code (Mon., 1933)
Brand of Hate (Sup., 1934)
A Demon for Trouble (Sup., 1935)
Kid Courageous (Sup., 1935)
Tombstone Terror (Sup., 1935)
Western Justice (Sup., 1935)
Smoky Smith (Sup., 1935)
Big Calibre (Sup., 1935)
Powdersmoke Range (RKO, 1935)
Trail of Terror (Sup., 1935)
Rider of the Law (Sup., 1935)
The Law Rides (Sup., 1936)
The Kid Ranger (Sup., 1936)
Alias John Law (Sup., 1936)
No Man's Range (Sup., 1936)
Sundown Saunders (Sup., 1936)
Brand of the Outlaws (Sup., 1936)
The Last of the Warrens (Sup., 1936)
Cavalry (Rep., 1936)
The Border Phantom (Rep., 1936)
The Gun Ranger (Rep., 1936)

Doomed at Sundown (Rep., 1937)

Gun Lords of Stirrup Basin (Rep., 1937)

Arizona Gunfighter (Rep., 1937)

The Trusted Outlaw (Rep., 1937)

Lightnin' Crandall (Rep., 1937)

Ridin' the Lone Trail (Rep., 1937)

The Red Rope (Rep., 1937)

The Colorado Kid (Rep., 1937)

Paroled—to Die (Rep., 1938)

Thunder in the Desert (Rep., 1938)

Desert Patrol (Rep., 1938)

Durango Valley Raiders (Rep., 1938)

The Feud Maker (Rep., 1938)

Feud on the Range (Met., 1939)

El Diablo Rides (Met., 1939)

The Pal from Texas (Met., 1939)

Smoky Trails (Met., 1939)

Mesquite Buckaroo (Met., 1939)

Riders of the Sage (Met., 1939)

Wild Horse Valley (Met., 1940)

Pinto Canyon (Met., 1940)

The Carson City Kid (Rep., 1940)

Billy the Kid in Texas (PRC, 1940)

Billy the Kid's Gun Justice (PRC, 1940)

Billy the Kid Outlawed (PRC, 1940)

The Trail Blazers (Rep., 1940)

Under Texas Skies (Rep., 1940)

Lone Star Raiders (Rep., 1940)

Billy the Kid in Santa Fe (PRC, 1941)

Billy the Kid's Range War (PRC, 1941)

The Great Train Robbery (Rep., 1941)

Prairie Pioneers (Rep., 1941)

Pals of the Pecos (Rep., 1941)

Saddlemates (Rep., 1941)

Gangs of Sonora (Rep., 1941)

Outlaws of Cherokee Trail (Rep., 1941)

Gauchos of El Dorado (Rep., 1941)

West of Cimarron (Rep., 1941)

Billy the Kid's Fighting Pals (PRC, 1941)

Code of the Outlaw (Rep., 1942)

Riders of the Range (Rep., 1942)

Westward Ho! (Rep., 1942)

The Phantom Plainsmen (Rep., 1942)

Shadows on the Sage (Rep., 1942)

Valley of Hunted Men (Rep., 1942)

Thundering Trails (Rep., 1943)

The Blocked Trail (Rep., 1943)

Santa Fe Scouts (Rep., 1943)

Riders of the Rio Grande (Rep., 1943)

Death Valley Rangers (Mon., 1943)

Westward Bound (Mon., 1944)

The Outlaw Trail (Mon., 1944)

The Utah Kid (Mon., 1944)

Marked Trails (Mon., 1944)

Trigger Law (Mon., 1944)

Arizona Whirlwind (Mon., 1944)

Sonora Stagecoach (Mon., 1944)

Wildfire (SG, 1945)

Northwest Trail (SG, 1945)

The Navajo Kid (PRC, 1945)

Thunder Town (PRC, 1946)

Ambush Trail (PRC, 1946)

Six-Gun Man (PRC, 1946)

Sheriff of Redwood Valley (Rep., 1946)

Rio Grande Raiders (Rep., 1946)

Twilight on the Rio Grande (Rep., 1947)

Cheyenne (WB, 1947)

Bandits of Dark Canyon (Rep., 1947)

South of St. Louis (WB, 1949)

The Savage Horde (Rep., 1950)

Cattle Drive (UI, 1951)

Silver Canyon (Col., 1951)

Fort Worth (WB, 1951)

The Lion and the Horse (WB, 1952)

Rose of Cimarron (20th, 1952)

San Antone (Rep., 1953)

Savage Frontier (Rep., 1953)

Column South (UI, 1953)

The Outcast (Rep., 1954)

Drums Across the River (Univ., 1954)

Last of the Desperados (Associated, 1955)

Pardners (Par., 1956)

Decision at Sundown (Col., 1957)

Duel at Apache Wells (Rep., 1957)

Gun for a Coward (Univ., 1957)

The Parson and the Outlaw (Col., 1957)

Band of Angels (WB, 1957)

Once upon a Horse (Univ., 1958)
Rio Bravo (WB, 1959)
No Name on the Bullet (Univ., 1959)
Hell Bent for Leather (Univ., 1960)
The Comancheros (20th, 1961)
The Wild Westerners (Col., 1962)
Six Black Horses (Univ., 1962)
McLintock! (UA, 1963)
Bullet for a Badman (Univ., 1964)

Taggart (Univ., 1964)
The Bounty Killer (Emb., 1965)
Requiem for a Gunfighter (Emb., 1965)
Town Tamer (Par., 1965)
Shenandoah (Univ., 1965)
Hang 'em High (UA, 1968)
Rio Lobo (NGP, 1970)
something big (NGP, 1971)

John Wayne, Western star.

John Wayne

(From Singin' Sandy to just plain Duke)

Born: May 26, 1907, Winterset, Iowa
Married: Josephine Saenz (1933); divorced
   (1943); children: Antonio, Melinda,
   Michael, Patrick; remarried: Esperanza
   Bauer (1946); divorced (1953); remarried:
   Pilar Palette (1954); children: Aissa,
   Marisa, Ethan; separated (1977)
Died: June 11, 1979

(Author's note: John "Duke" Wayne passed away on June 11, 1979, before he could read this work. His memory is still vividly alive in our minds. And so, in his honor and as a final tribute, we let The Legend remain up front where he belongs. It is this writer's deep regret that this great actor could not have lived long enough to be presented his Gold Medal by the President of the United States.)

IT'S EASY TO SEE how John Wayne won his Best Actor Oscar for his performance in *True Grit* (1969). The past two years offer more than adequate proof of his courage. He had open heart surgery at a hospital in Boston in 1978, wherein the valve of a pig's heart was implanted in Duke's heart to replace an "old" valve that had stopped working. Before he was fully recovered from heart surgery, he was doing television specials and making special appearances—against doctors' orders. For this, he suffered a bout with hepatitis.

    January of this year Duke was under the scalpel once again, this time in Los Angeles, for what was at first believed to be the removal of his gall bladder. However, surgeons discovered the Duke had carcinoma of the stomach and removed his stomach during a nine-hour operation. Cancer was later detected in the Duke's lymph glands. Despite the odds, he again made a gallant stand against what he long ago termed the "Big C" (when he won his fight against lung cancer in 1964).

    Despite all that beset him medically, Duke endured. His grit held fast to the very end. His many fans never stopped rooting for him to come through and swing back into the saddle for another film. If heroes are to be awarded medals for bravery, Duke Wayne certainly deserves his country's highest.

    Conversely, what is not easy to understand is why, at the outset of his career, he was billed as "Singin' Sandy" in a film titled *Riders of Destiny*

(1933). Of course an old professional singer named Smith Ballew actually sang the songs while Wayne pantomimed them, but the Duke gets credit nevertheless as the first saddle-burning songbird. In an interview Duke confessed it still embarrassed him for anyone in jest to refer to him as Singin' Sandy.

"They really used t' pour it on about that sissified moniker I was tabbed with," said Wayne, "and it took me a good many years, plus a few fights, t' outlive it." He ruefully added, "If y' don't mind, kindly drop th' whole thing an' forget it ever happened t' me, okay?"

No argument. Subject dropped (but not forgotten). Besides, who in his right mind would have wanted to tangle with big John Wayne?

John Wayne (real name Marion Michael Morrison) was an All-American football player—right end—for the University of Southern California (1925-28) and might have gone on to become a great pro star had it not been for two men: Tom Mix and John Ford. But Wayne tells it better himself:

"I was attendin' th' University of Southern California, playin' right end on th' football team. My father was havin' a pretty rough time of things—he simply was not a very good businessman. We had opened a new drugstore in Glendale, and it'd failed.

"Howard Jones, th' Trojan football coach at th' time, heard that I needed a job if I intended stayin' in school and playin' football. It seems that Coach Jones was a very close friend of film star Tom Mix, a great sports enthusiast, and he arranged for Mix t' get some box seats at one of our big games. For the favor, Mix showed his appreciation by promisin' Coach Jones t' give any of his football boys a good job durin' th' summer if they wanted one.

"That summer I was given a job at Mix's studios with th' 'swing gang,' a sort of utility work outfit. My wages were $35 a week; my job was t' lug furniture and props around t' arrange them on th' sets. I didn't particularly like th' hard work, but th' pay wasn't bad and besides I was learnin' a lot about th' motion picture business and what all goes into makin' a big movie. I also learned a bit about actin', too, and doin' some stunts for an extra $50 a stunt.

"Then a director named Ford, John Ford, who was later t' become my best friend, gave me my first actin' chance. It was in a film titled *Mother Machree*. But I goofed up so badly that John Ford cussed hell outta me right in front of everybody. Talk about embarrassin'! Man! I was th' most downtrodden, whipped cur in th' whole world. Or at least I felt like it. And I guess it showed, 'cause th' next thing I knew Ford was smilin' and apologizin' and even invited me t' have lunch with him.

"But I didn't get another chance t' act for quite a while, and had t' be content bein' a propman and part-time stuntman.

"I finally got bit parts in a few other films. Ham Hamilton was th' director of those films. He was a friend of Ford's and th' latter asked

Hamilton t' give me a chance at actin' if he had any bit parts t' cast me in.

"I played bit parts in *Hangman's House* [1928], *Salute* [1929], which also starred an old pal of mine, George O'Brien, and *Men Without Women* [1930].

"In *Men Without Women*, bein' made off th' California coast near Catalina Island, John Ford, directin' th' film, ran into a little difficulty. Th' script called for a professional stuntman to perform feats of heroism in the rough, high waters, which got rougher by th' hour. Noticin' th' stuntman balkin', John proceeded t' call on me.

" 'Hey, Morrison,' he called t' me—he called me by my real name then. 'Show 'em up!' Me? Hell, I acted like an obedient dog of some kind and jumped inta th' water, clothes, workin' tools, everything, and damned near drowned doin' th' stunt th' damned stuntman was afraid t' do. In fact, after they hauled me back aboard ship I was so cold and near drowned they took pity on me and let me stay in John Ford's stateroom t' recuperate.

"John acted sincerely worried about me, and even gave me several shots of his best bourbon t' warm up by. Then once he knew I was okay, he smiled and told me what a good job I'd done. He said courage like I'd showed had to be rewarded, and he proved it by gettin' me my first real break into films in Raoul Walsh's film, *The Big Trail*. And I haven't been idle since."

With Rock Hudson in The Undefeated *(1969).*

The Big Trail (1930) was, on most counts, a true epic Western filled with wonderfully cinematic tableaux filmed in picturesque locations. Pictorially it holds up as a classic today, but in acting talent it was sadly lacking.

Duke Wayne simply wasn't ready for the big push upward to stardom. He was young, handsome, athletic, and virile—in fact, he possessed all the leading-man qualities for a star except one: experience. His lack of experience made him appear awkward in the film, and his delivery of lines was far from satisfactory. With Wayne matched against such notables as Tyrone Power, Sr., and Ian Keith, the Duke's shortcomings stood out plainly. On the plus side, though, he photographed well, and was more than convincing in the film's action sequences.

At a time when sound pictures were just beginning to make themselves felt, Wayne certainly should have made enough impression to launch himself in a less routine way, but the powers at Fox Studios failed to capitalize on the young star's potential. They threw him into a couple of straight roles as a follow-up to *The Big Trail,* and both Duke and the studio were disappointed.

Wayne left Fox and went over to Columbia Pictures, where he played lesser roles in routine pictures with big-name Western stars like Tim McCoy and Buck Jones. The following year, 1932, he went to Warner Bros. Studios to make a series of B-Westerns, in which he was the star, and ground them out for the next two years.

Actually he had little to do in most of the films as far as the hard-riding action sequences were concerned. Old Ken Maynard silent-film footage was used for these scenes, with long shots of Ken and a music-sound background duping the audience into believing John Wayne was the film hero doing everything.

"Ol' Ken and I became good friends," recalled Wayne. "He was always obligin' t' help me out any way he could, so long as I didn't step on his toes. We went ridin' t'gether many times, up in th' hills behind th' sound stages, and I learned one helluva lot from Ken that I put t' good use in many of my future pictures."

In the latter part of 1933 Wayne signed up to star in a long series of B-Westerns for Lone Star Productions and released through Monogram Pictures. It was by then a field day for the young leading man as he rode, fought, and "sang" his way through sixteen riproaring Westerns with titles like *Riders of Destiny* (his Singin' Sandy venture), *Blue Steel, Randy Rides Alone, The Star Packer, Rainbow Valley,* and, the last in the sequence, *Paradise Canyon.* These films offered viewers more than just a pleasing new leading man. Supporting the Duke was a superb collection of character actors who were to form a kind of Western stock company. Heading the list was George Hayes, who alternated between playing good guys, villains, and oldtimers. He had not as yet tacked on the famous "Gabby" nickname and often appeared on the screen clean-shaven.

Appearing in nearly three-quarters of the action titles was Yakima Canutt, who became Duke's friend for life and the top stuntman in Hollywood (it was Canutt who later staged the realistic stunt scenes for the epic *Ben-Hur*). Canutt taught Duke all the tricks he used in later pictures, including the great fight scenes and stunt falls from horses.

"I even copied ol' Yak's smooth-rollin' walk," Wayne said, "and th' way he talks—kinda low and with that quiet strength. I kinda think of Yak as bein' a brother t' me, and I'll respect him as such until th' ornery old cayuse cashes in his chips."

In 1935 Monogram, Mascot, Liberty, and Consolidated merged to form Republic Studios. Having hit a small bonanza with the Gene Autry features, the new company decided to give Wayne a little bigger boost up the ladder of success and spend a little more time, money, and effort on a new series of feature films. Duke was excellent as the lead in all his assignments and rapidly became a top-notch box-office favorite with Western fans.

But his wanderlust surfaced again, and Duke left the increasingly wide-open spaces of Republic's back lot for the soundstages of Universal Pictures, where he starred in a series of six entertaining non-Western films. In 1936 and 1937, his films included *Sea Spoilers*, a Coast Guard adventure; *Conflict*, an involved prizefighting yarn; *California Straight Ahead*, a race between trucks and a train; *I Cover the War*, a story about newsreel cameramen; *Idol of the Crowds*, a tale about an ice-hockey player; and *Adventure's End*, a story about a pearl diver involved in a ship's mutiny.

Wayne made a very brief journey to Paramount Pictures to costar with Johnny Mack Brown in one of that studio's short Zane Grey features, *Born to the West* (1937, reissued later under the title *Hell Town*), but the film was noteworthy only because it starred two great Western actors.

One of the most popular Western series that ran for a long duration was *The Three Mesquiteers*, starring at the outset Robert Livingston, Ray "Crash" Corrigan, and Max Terhune (who replaced Syd Saylor in the first film). When Republic decided to withdraw Livingston from the series and star him in straight dramatic roles in high-budgeted pictures, it had a willing replacement in John Wayne, who was only too happy to board a horse again after the unpleasantness he suffered doing adventure roles.

Beginning as Stony Brook in *Pals of the Saddle* in 1938, Wayne soon shot to the top as the most popular Western star at the box office. He was succeeded in popularity only once, by his old pal Buck Jones; but after John Ford gave him a starring role as Ringo in *Stagecoach* (1939), Duke regained the top spot on the box-office list of Western stars and wasn't ousted again.

Describing his launch into stardom in *Stagecoach,* Duke explained things this way:

"I worked on and off in menial jobs for years for John Ford. I developed a kinda hero worship, which lasted till he died in 1973. But when I got stuck in three-and-one-half-day Westerns, Ford passed me by without speaking. This went on for, oh, three years at least. He just plain wouldn't look *my* way.

"Then one day I was at a waterfront bar kinda drownin' my sorrows, y' might say, when Ford's daughter came in and said her papa wanted t' see me—pronto—aboard his yacht.

"Hell, I didn't know what t' do. So I kept right on drownin' my sorrows after first tellin' Ford's daughter I didn't feel like bein' chewed out by her papa at that time.

"But later when Ford's wife, Mary, showed up and said, 'He wants to see you,' I went with her. Aboard his yacht Ford sat me down in a corner, ignored me for a few minutes, then said, 'You're going to have a starring role in my new picture, *Stagecoach*.'

As Rooster Cogburn in True Grit *(1969).*

"Well, th' rest is film history, I guess. Th' role of Ringo in *Stagecoach* made a big star of me, and I'll forever be grateful to my friend John Ford for it—wherever he is now.

"But y' know somethin'? I don't think John had any kinda real respect for me as an actor until I made *Red River,* for Howard Hawks, ten years later. And even then, I was never quite sure just what ol' John Ford did think of me as an actor. I know now, though. Because when I finally won an Oscar for my role as Rooster Cogburn in *True Grit,* Ford shook my hand and said th' award was long overdue me as far as he was concerned. Right then, I knew he'd respected me as an actor ever since *Stagecoach,* even though he hadn't let me know it. He later told me his praise, earlier, might've gone to my head and made me conceited, and that was why he'd never said anything to me. Until th' right time."

What did superstar—legend—Duke Wayne think about Western filmmaking today?

"Don't ever for a minute make th' big mistake of lookin' down your nose at Westerns. They're art—the good ones, I mean. They deal in life and sudden death and primitive struggle, and with th' basic emotions—love, hate, and anger—thrown in. In other words, they're made outta th' same kinda raw material that Homer once used. In Europe, they understand that better'n we do over here. They recognize their relationship t' th' old Greek stories that are classics now, and they love 'em. But I don't think that's th' real reason they love 'em.

"We love 'em too, but not because of anything we stop t' think about. A horse is th' greatest vehicle for action there is. Planes, automobiles, trains, they're just great, but when it comes t' gettin' th' fans' hearts t' pumpin' with excitement—hell, they can't touch a horse for action.

"He's basic too. Put a man aboard a horse, and right off you've got th' makin's of somethin' magnificent. Physical strength, speed where you can see and feel it, plus heroism. And th' hero, he's big and strong. You pit another big strong man against him, with both their lives at stake, and right there's a simplicity of conflict y' just can't beat.

"Maybe we don't exactly tell it with poetry like ol' Homer once did, but in one way we've got him beat. We never once let Hector turn tail and run from Achilles. There's just *gotta* be a showdown. And my recent *Shootist* picture's a good example of what I mean.

"Westerns're folklore, th' same as th' *Iliad* is. And folklore's international. But don't for a minute ever think they're foolproof, either. It takes damn good men t' make Westerns. And besides that, they're fun t' make. Hell, I'd rather make a good Western picture'n anything else!

"We'll have Western films as long as th' cameras keep turnin'. Th' fascination that th' Old West has will never die. And as long as people wanta pay money t' see me act, I'll keep right on makin' Western pictures until th' day I cash in my chips."

In Chisum *(1970).*

Asked about two breakaway films from his regular Westerns—*McQ* (1974) and *Brannigan* (1975)—Wayne had this to say:

"Hell, it's just in me t' try somethin' different, now and then. It ain't anything unusual for me, 'cause I've done it lots of times in th' past. It's just that, well, every once in a while I feel like I'm gettin' in a rut and, well, that's when I start t' look at other scripts. Then, once I do a couple adventure or detective pictures I'm ready to get back in th' saddle again and grind out more Westerns. But I just gotta have a little versatility, now and then, t' keep my head on straight." He chuckled and added, "Neither of th' two detective pictures I made amounted t' anything, which is why I sold 'em t' TV. Maybe th' vast audience on TV'll enjoy 'em more'n movie audiences did."

In a way, it was the same old Duke Wayne of yesteryear talking, much older and more mature, but still possessing that urge now and then to rebel, pull away from the norm, make different pictures before vaulting into the saddle again to make more Westerns.

Now the Duke's hair was nearly gone—though he did his best to cover up this deficit with an expensive toupee—his face was leathery and lined, his oft-broken nose more prominent than ever. (Wayne got his nose broken by Randolph Scott during a fight sequence in *The Spoilers* [1942], the longest and roughest sequence ever filmed, according to experts. Both actors landed a few punches that were too hard and both became angry and really fought, resulting in a broken nose and bruises for Wayne, and contusions, bruises, and a chipped hipbone for Scott. After 1942, neither actor appeared in a film with the other again, yet both became friends again and held great respect for each other.)

But on the screen, Wayne, over six feet tall and stereophonic, resumes his rightful dimensions as a superstar and the last of the great celluloid cowboy stars. We see him dressed in the old, sweat-stained brown Stetson, the double-breasted blue flannel shirt, and the tan vest and know he will always be "the Duke."

Tall in the saddle, strong and silent, the traditional American hero, the inexorable force behind a soft, slow voice, sex appeal submerged by a reverence for good women, cunning and ruthless in the cause of right, the Duke embodies the lore of what people, especially those who prefer illusion to the reality of history, like to think of as the Old West.

The frontier is gone, but the image John Wayne left us in his films remains—like the Alamo—an American legend, a landmark for all to see.

Western Film Credits

A Rough Romance (Fox, 1930)
The Big Trail (Fox, 1930)

Range Feud (Col., 1931)
Two-Fisted Law (Col., 1932)

Texas Cyclone (Col. 1932)
Haunted Gold (WB, 1932)
Ride 'Em Cowboy (WB, 1932)
The Big Stampede (WB, 1932)
The Telegraph Trail (WB, 1933)
Man from Monterey (WB, 1933)
Somewhere in Sonora (WB, 1933)
Riders of Destiny (Mon., 1933)
Sagebrush Trail (Mon., 1933)
The Lucky Texan (Mon., 1934)
West of the Divide (Mon., 1934)
Blue Steel (Mon., 1934)
The Man from Utah (Mon., 1934)
Randy Rides Alone (Mon., 1934)
The Star Packer (Mon., 1934)
The Trail Beyond (Mon., 1934)
'Neath Arizona Skies (Mon., 1934)
Texas Terror (Mon., 1935)
Lawless Frontier (Mon., 1935)
Rainbow Valley (Mon., 1935)
The Dawn Rider (Mon., 1935)
Paradise Canyon (Mon., 1935)
Westward Ho! (Rep., 1935)
The Desert Trail (Mon., 1935)
The New Frontier (Rep., 1935)
Lawless Range (Rep., 1935)
Lawless Nineties (Rep., 1936)
King of the Pecos (Rep., 1936)
The Oregon Trail (Rep., 1936)
Winds of the Wasteland (Rep., 1936)
The Lonely Trail (Rep., 1936)
Born to the West (Par., 1937)
Pals of the Saddle (Rep., 1938)
Overland Stage Raiders (Rep., 1938)
Red River Range (Rep., 1938)
Santa Fe Stampede (Rep., 1938)
Stagecoach (UA, 1939)
The Night Riders (Rep., 1939)
Three Texas Steers (Rep., 1939)
Wyoming Outlaw (Rep., 1939)
New Frontier (Rep., 1939)
Allegheny Uprising (RKO, 1939)

Dark Command (Rep., 1940)
Three Faces West (Rep., 1940)
Lady for a Night (Rep., 1941)
Lady from Louisiana (Rep., 1941)
In Old California (Rep., 1942)
The Spoilers (Univ., 1942)
In Old Oklahoma (Rep., 1943)
Tall in the Saddle (RKO, 1944)
Flame of Barbary Coast (Rep., 1945)
Dakota (Rep., 1945)
Angel and the Badman (Rep., 1947)
Three Godfathers (MGM, 1948)
Red River (UA, 1948)
Fort Apache (RKO, 1948)
The Fighting Kentuckian (Rep., 1949)
She Wore a Yellow Ribbon (RKO, 1949)
Rio Grande (Rep., 1950)
Hondo (WB, 1953)
The Searchers (WB, 1956)
Rio Bravo (WB, 1959)
The Horse Soldiers (UA, 1959)
The Alamo (UA, 1960)
The Comancheros (20th, 1961)
The Man Who Shot Liberty Valance (Par., 1962)
How the West Was Won (MGM, 1963)
McLintock! (UA, 1963)
The Sons of Katie Elder (Par., 1965)
El Dorado (Par., 1967)
The War Wagon (Univ., 1967)
True Grit (Par., 1969)
The Undefeated (20th, 1969)
Chisum (WB, 1970)
Rio Lobo (NGP, 1970)
Big Jake (NGP, 1970)
The Cowboys (WB, 1972)
The Train Robbers (WB, 1973)
Cahill, U.S. Marshal (WB, 1973)
Rooster Cogburn (Univ., 1975)
The Shootist (Par., 1976)

Joel McCrea, at his ranch.

Joel McCrea

(From blue serge to Levi's)

Born: November 5, 1905, Los Angeles, Calif.
Married: Frances Dee (1933);
  children: David, Jody, Peter

JOEL McCREA IS one of the movies' few male stars to rise from the ranks of screen extras. He is also one of the few Western stars who has appeared successfully in a variety of other starring roles, including comedies and spy films. In the Western genre he never starred in anything but a high-quality production, and his radio and television Western work was always high caliber as well.

Today a wealthy rancher near Camarillo, California, McCrea is in excellent health and still has the good looks of a leading man that he had in his Westerns in the forties and fifties. For a fact, he surprised everyone in 1976 by returning to the screen to star in Universal's big *Mustang Country,* which had good ratings after its release.

McCrea's ancestry dates back to California's earliest settlers. As a boy Joel worked as a ranchhand, sold newspapers (William S. Hart was one of his customers), and later was an extra in films. He graduated from Hollywood High School and attended the University of Southern California, later switching to Pomona College. There he became interested in acting and went to the Pomona Community Playhouse.

Determined to have a career in films, Joel continued working as an extra. From the ranks he was picked for a feature role in *The Jazz Age* (1929). Next he obtained a bit part in Greta Garbo's *The Single Standard* (1929), and then was employed by Cecil B. DeMille for a bit part in *Dynamite* (1929). During the production of *Dynamite* the young man became good friends with this important industry figure, and the friendship lasted until DeMille's death.

In 1930 Joel supported Will Rogers in *Lightnin'* and had his own leading role in *Silver Horde.* By now the young performer was developing into an important screen property, as well as cultivating an active social life—dating, among others, Constance Bennett, whom in 1931 he played opposite in *Born to Love.* In 1933 he concluded his life as a bachelor by marrying screen actress Frances Dee—later his costar in many Westerns.

The early thirties found McCrea working at RKO where his screen image was the typical clean-cut American young man. In *The Lost*

51

With Ivan Triesault in Border River *(1954)*.

Squadron (1932) he was a movie stunt flyer; in *Bird of Paradise* (1932) the young man in love with Dolores Del Rio; and he was the hunted prey in the horror classic *The Most Dangerous Game* (1932). *Barbary Coast* (1935) proved to be a turning point for Joel. In this vehicle about California's gambling quarters, in which he costarred with Miriam Hopkins and Edward G. Robinson, he first worked for producer Samuel Goldwyn and director Howard Hawks.

McCrea's stock rose with his performance in *These Three* (1936), Sam Goldwyn's laundered version of Lillian Hellman's *The Children's Hour*. He was in the frontier melodrama *Come and Get It* (1936), and for 20th Century-Fox he joined Barbara Stanwyck in *Banjo on My Knee* (1936). The next year Joel and Stanwyck worked at Paramount in *Internes Can't Take Money*, the first of the Dr. Kildare films (which would star Lew Ayres at MGM). Also in 1937 he and Frances Dee costarred in *Wells Fargo* and he joined with Sylvia Sidney in the impressive slum drama *Dead End*. Although many critics were branding Joel's acting style as stodgy, fans insisted he was handsome, sincere, and energetic.

By the late thirties Joel, along with Gary Cooper and James Stewart,

At his ranch.

was stereotyped as the All-American performer. Cecil B. DeMille enhanced this image by starring Joel with Barbara Stanwyck in *Union Pacific* (1939). The next year Joel asked to be let out of the leading role in DeMille's *Northwest Mounted Police* because he felt uncomfortable in the part; he was immediately replaced by Gary Cooper. Since Joel had played the lead in *Espionage Agent* (1939), Alfred Hitchcock called upon his services the next year for the superior *Foreign Correspondent*.

The war years found Joel at the top of his popularity. He joined Jean Arthur for the splendid comedy *The More the Merrier* (1943), and also did more films for Preston Sturges. In *Sullivan's Travels* (1941) he was the

As he appears today.

54

well-intentioned film director who set out to find out about life in the real America. For *The Palm Beach Story* (1942) he and Claudette Colbert performed dual roles. *The Great Moment* (1944) dealt with the pathfinding practitioner who first used ether as an anesthesia, but the film was a big letdown. Fortunately for McCrea's career he made *Buffalo Bill* (1944), which restored his popularity.

After the eerie *The Unseen* (1945) Joel worked almost exclusively in Westerns. Perhaps it was McCrea's love of the great outdoors that kept him constantly active in this specialty. It should also be noted that in the Western genre aging leading men (Gary Cooper, Randolph Scott, Joel McCrea) could still maintain a good following with action stories calling for rugged looks and adventure.

Beginning with *The Virginian* (1946), in which he had the title role, Joel averaged nearly two horse operas a year until 1960. Among the best were the pacifistic *Four Faces West* (1948), with Frances Dee; the brawling cattle-drive story *South of St. Louis* (1949); *The Outriders* (1950), a Civil War story; and *Trooper Hook* (1957), which reunited him with Babs Stanwyck. Along the way Joel portrayed several historical figures: Wyatt Earp in *Wichita* (1955), Sam Houston in *The First Texan* (1956), and Bat Masterson in *Gunfight at Dodge City* (1959).

During the late forties and early fifties, Joel starred in the radio series "Tales of the Texas Rangers" (later on TV, with Willard Parker and Harry Lauter featured). In 1959 Joel abandoned films to coproduce and star in the NBC-TV series "Wichita Town," which featured his son Jody. The series, however, lasted only one season. Not long after, Joel accepted the role of the villain in Sam Peckinpah's *Ride the High Country*. But after reading the script, Joel and costar Randolph Scott (an old friend) agreed to switch roles, leaving Joel with the sympathetic part.

McCrea might have played unassuming Americans oncamera, but in real life he proved to be a very astute businessman. He was one of the partners in the formation of Four Star (TV) Productions. From Will Rogers he had acquired some knowledge of real estate, and in 1931 he purchased a 1,200-acre ranch near Moorpark, California, for $19,500 (by the early seventies he could sell it for $1.3 million). Son David managed his dad's Shandon, California, ranch until he recently moved to New Mexico, near Roswell. Both he and Jody reside there now; both are graduates of New Mexico Military Institute.

Joel has long been interested in the plight of the American Indian. In 1970 he emerged from retirement to do the documentary *Sioux Nation*, which was filmed in South Dakota at the Pine Ridge Indian Reservation. The same year he appeared briefly in *Cry Blood, Apache,* which starred son Jody. In 1974 he narrated the Academy Award-winning documentary *The Great American Cowboy.* In 1975, besides starring in *Mustang Country,* he was honored by the National Cowboy Hall of Fame and is at present chairman of its board of directors.

Joel McCrea can look back on a long illustrious Hollywood career, but none of his many roles becomes him better than the one he enjoys today—Western rancher.

Western Film Credits

The Silver Horde (RKO, 1930)
Scarlet River (RKO, 1933)
Wells Fargo (Par., 1937)
Union Pacific (Par., 1939)
The Great Man's Lady (Par., 1942)
Buffalo Bill (20th, 1944)
The Virginian (Par., 1946)
Ramrod (UA, 1947)
Four Faces West (UA, 1948)
South of St. Louis (WB, 1949)
Colorado Territory (WB, 1949)
Stars in My Crown (MGM, 1950)
The Outriders (MGM, 1950)
Saddle Tramp (UI, 1950)
Frenchie (UI, 1951)
Cattle Drive (UI, 1951)
Lone Hand (UI, 1953)
Black Horse Canyon (UI, 1954)

Border River (UI, 1954)
Stranger on Horseback (UA, 1955)
Wichita (also TV series) (AA, 1955)
The First Texan (AA, 1956)
The Oklahoman (AA, 1957)
Trooper Hook (UA, 1957)
Gunsight Ridge (UA, 1957)
The Tall Stranger (AA, 1957)
Cattle Empire (20th, 1958)
Fort Massacre (20th, 1958)
Gunfight at Dodge City (UA, 1959)
Ride the High Country (MGM, 1962)
Sioux Nation (documentary, 1970)
Cry Blood, Apache (Golden Eagle Int'l, 1970)
The Great American Cowboy (narrator) (Sun Int'l, 1974)
Mustang Country (Univ., 1976)

Randolph Scott, in one of his favorite poses (1957).

Randolph Scott

(Gentleman cowboy from Virginia)

Born: January 23, 1903, Orange County, Va.
Married: Marianna DuPont Somerville
(1936); divorced (1939); remarried: Marie
Patricia Stillman (1944); children:
Christopher, Sandra

IF YOU BELIEVE it impossible for a screen performer to attain stardom merely on the strength of a remarkably virile appearance, a code of ethics that identifies him as a gentleman, and an image that personifies pioneer America, consider George Randolph Scott, better known as Randolph Scott, Western superstar, whose action films are still thrilling millions of TV viewers nightly.

Director Michael Curtiz, famous for a paucity of kind words about performers, once said: "Randy Scott is a complete anachronism. He's a real fine gentleman. And so far he's the only one I've met in this business full of self-promoting sons-o'-bitches!"

Curtiz's blunt appraisal accurately characterizes Scott, who for years was listed with the top box-office actors and who rightfully deserves the kind of acclaim enjoyed by the late Gary Cooper and ever-popular John Wayne. It does not, however, account for the present public indifference to a man who, in a very special way, contributed substantially to the art and history of films and probably did more than anyone else to keep the medium-budget Western film alive during the troublesome, transitional fifties. Even with the avalanche of TV sagebrush yarns, Scott was able to retain high quality in his theatrical releases; in retrospect it is evident that he made some of the finest genre films of the decade.

It might have been a different story, however, if he had been cast as Ashley Wilkes in *Gone with the Wind,* a role which he was born to play and which an actor even as good as Leslie Howard could not make wholly believable. Why he was denied this opportunity after author Margaret Mitchell personally tried to promote him for the part (until Selznick's publicity flacks advised her against it) is a question that cannot now—or ever—be answered, for David O. Selznick is dead.

George Randolph Scott was born in Orange County, Virginia, where his father, George G. Scott, a descendant of the first settlers of Virginia, was an administrative engineer with a textile firm. His mother, Lucy

Crane Scott, was the daughter of an old-guard Charlotte, North Carolina, family, and it was in Charlotte where the Scotts eventually lived. George, always called Randy or Randolph, was an only son with five sisters.

Scott was educated at private schools, and at Woodberry Forest Prep School he excelled in sports, played a piano in the school orchestra, and sang with the glee club. He then entered Georgia Tech and played football. He appeared a sure bet to make All-American but sustained in his junior year a back injury which ended his gridiron career (and much later prevented his being accepted for military duty during World War II).

Since his prime reason for attending Georgia Tech was to play football and attain All-American status, he transferred for his last two years to the University of North Carolina, where he concentrated on studying textile engineering and manufacturing.

After graduation he induced his father to let him tour Europe a year before settling down. But when he did return to Charlotte and began his apprenticeship with the textile firm with which his father was associated, he seemed to have little interest in it. When his parents expressed their concern, Randy startled them by saying he was really interested in an acting career.

Scott's mother, who seldom denied her only son anything, was deeply disappointed, but his father handled the situation by advising him to try out for theatrical work and get it all out of his system. The only person the elder Scott knew who was even remotely connected with show business was Howard Hughes, so he gave his son a letter of introduction. Scott decided to look Hughes up and talked his best friend, Jack Heath, into going to California with him.

When they arrived in Hollywood, they soon learned that Howard Hughes was an extremely elusive character, in no hurry whatever to return Scott's phone calls. While waiting to be summoned for an introduction, Randy and Heath became tourists and took in the sights.

"My friend Jack Heath and I finally met Howard Hughes," Scott said, "and we played a lot of golf with him." (Scott shoots in the low 70s, and is still an avid golfer.) "We'd been acting like a couple of hick tourists itching to see the inside of a big studio, so I asked Hughes if he could get us on a movie set so we could see just how films were made. Instead of doing that, he got us jobs as extras working four days on a George O'Brien-Lois Moran film. I think it was one of the last silent pictures ever made."

The film was *Sharp Shooters* (1928), and they did their bit in a sequence which ostensibly takes place in a Moroccan saloon.

Randy liked Southern California's climate, and now decided that movies, rather than the stage, might be his true métier. He stood six feet two inches, was muscular without being muscle-bound, and possessed a great American face. Howard Hughes, who looked at the rushes of *Sharp Shooters*, agreed that the newcomer had potential but sorely lacked experience. He arranged for Scott to meet Cecil B. DeMille, then preparing his first talking picture, *Dynamite*.

DeMille, needing an actor with exactly the sort of college-boy looks Scott had, gave him a screen test but the results were somewhat disappointing.

"C.B. suggested I join the Pasadena Playhouse group (then called the Pasadena Community Playhouse). I did and stayed there two years. C.B. also gave me an extra bit in *Dynamite* before the film was ever released. The same thing happened on that picture to Carole Lombard," Scott recalled.

At the Pasadena Community Playhouse, under Gilmore Brown's direction, Randy got to move scenery around, paint flats, run errands, and read lines at rehearsals when someone was late. He also got a walk-on bit in a production of Shaw's *Man and Superman*, in which Robert Young also appeared.

Scott finally resigned himself to being less than a big success in Hollywood and decided to take an extended vacation in Hawaii before returning to Charlotte and textiles. But the day before his departure, Margaret Fawcett, daughter of actor George, ran into him and told him that she had been looking for him everywhere.

Her mother was putting on a production of Kenneth Cole's *Under a Virginia Moon* at the Vine Street Theatre and she wanted Randy to read for the juvenile lead. Randy showed Miss Fawcett his ticket to Hawaii and reservations, but she talked him into walking over to the theater and at least rejecting the offer in person.

Mrs. Fawcett, however, ignored everything he tried to say. She handed him a script, ordered him to read, and then told him to report the following day for rehearsals. Randy, the perfect gentleman, looked at her disbelievingly, muttered something politely, walked out, and canceled his ticket and reservations to Hawaii.

Fortunately, one of the few people to see the farce was Leo Carrillo, who liked Scott's looks and good manners and cast him as the romantic juvenile in *The Broken Wing*. The play opened at the El Capitan Theatre and brought Scott, Carrillo, and leading lady Dorothy Burgess some good notices—so good, in fact, that talent scouts showed up nightly to offer Randy a screen test.

Years later Carrillo said, "I think Scott turned down four offers of screen tests. Finally, one night, after a scout from Warners had talked to him for about an hour and still got a rejection, I asked Scott what he was waiting for. I can still remember him giving me that famous grin and saying, 'A *Paramount* scout—they're the ones who didn't want me two years ago.'"

A Paramount scout finally did show up, and Randy's screen test resulted in a seven-year contract.

But between the test and signing the contract, he accepted a role in a poverty-row quickie, *The Women Men Marry* (1931), in which he and Sally Blane played honeymooners fleeced by Natalie Moorhead and Kenneth Harlan. No one was surprised when the distributing company, Headline Pictures, declared bankruptcy.

While waiting at Paramount for the allegedly promised "star buildup," Randy was given a small role in *Sky Bride* (1932), which Howard Hughes financed and produced; he also did an unbilled extra bit, along with Alan Ladd, in a horror film, *The Island of Lost Souls* (1932). This was just about the low point in Randy's screen career.

Then Paramount, true to its word, did feature him in an important role in Nancy Carroll's *Hot Saturday* (1932). On its release, several critics said Scott and not Cary Grant, the romantic lead, should have won the heroine. It was during the filming of *Hot Saturday* that Scott and Grant became lifelong friends.

Cary, having already acquired his habit of thrift, suggested that he and Scott share quarters and expenses. Carole Lombard later defined what Grant meant by sharing expenses: "Cary opened the bills, Randy wrote the checks, and if Cary could talk someone out of stamps, he would mail them."

With Scott's good reviews in *Hot Saturday*, Paramount found itself in a dilemma over how best to use him. He obviously had stardom stamped all over him. But the studio already had Gary Cooper for its top-notch action films, Cary Grant for romantic leads, and Buster Crabbe for action programmers.

Because of script difficulties and author arbitration over what was scheduled to be Scott's next film, *The Lusitania Secret*, Paramount loaned him to Warners for a small romantic part in George Arliss' *A Successful Calamity* (1932). When Scott returned to Paramount, author and magazine illustrator Will James, who had just signed a contract with the studio, chose Randy to star in *Lone Cowboy*, an autobiographical film to be made on James' 1,500-acre ranch in Montana. He never got to do the film, however.

Scott did get some national publicity when, early in 1932, the volatile Lupe Velez told her producer she needed the afternoon off to rest because late that night she was getting married. When queried about who the groom might be, Miss Velez smiled and said, "Randolph Scott. He'll make an ideal husband and I'm tired of working."

The following day Miss Velez showed up for work and said she had changed her mind. "Maybe I won' marry heem, Randee Scott, after all, even though he ees zuch a sweet person. Marriage ees a ver' seerious beezness and soo permanent, and perhops . . . walll . . . maybee I'm not ready to set-tle down, no?"

When a columnist asked Scott about Miss Velez' rejection, he looked

In 1947.

Ready for action.

dumbfounded. "Lupe Velez? Gosh, she's a pretty woman. I saw her once when I was in the Brown Derby."

Miss Velez' joke made Paramount realize what the ideal Scott image was: a man appreciative of women's charm but aware of their guile, and too much a gentleman to object. The ideal vehicles in which Scott could convey that image were a series of Zane Grey Westerns which Paramount owned and had made before.

The first was *Heritage of the Desert* (1932), which was also Henry Hathaway's first film as a full-fledged director. Their subsequent joint venture, *Wild Horse Mesa* (1932), was released first in most parts of this country. Both films proved so popular that within the next two years Randy made seven additional films based on Zane Grey novels and stories.

Scott got to work again with Sally Blane, Loretta Young's sister, in *Hello, Everybody!* (1933). The film was intended to turn radio star Kate Smith into a film luminary. But Miss Smith was slightly ill at ease in front of the camera and fans seemed to prefer her as a radio personality.

Other 1933 films saw Randy as a stock leading man in *Murders in the Zoo* (wherein Lionel Atwill madly runs around knocking off every male who admires his wife, Kathleen Burke) and merely on hand to comfort his friend Carole Lombard when she emerges from one of her trances in *Supernatural.*

On loanout to Columbia for Victor Schertzinger's *Cocktail Hour,* Randy was just a foil for adventuress Bebe Daniels. Except for another loanout to Monogram for *Broken Dreams,* Scott's other films that year were all Westerns. In all, he had eleven films in release in 1933.

Randy's 1934 films were Westerns, but in 1935 he made three change-of-pace films for RKO. "It's wonderful to get away from cowboy roles and into *Roberta,*" he said, "but I don't know chiffon from chiffonier." The musical also starred Irene Dunne, who sang "Smoke Gets in Your Eyes," Fred Astaire, and Ginger Rogers. A year later Randy teamed up with Astaire-Rogers in *Follow the Fleet* and has since remained one of Astaire's closest friends, occasionally playing golf with him. Besides *Roberta, So Red the Rose, Home on the Range,* and a curious drama John Cromwell directed (immediately after *Of Human Bondage*) called *Village Tale,* Scott's other 1935 film was the spectacular but juvenile *She,* produced by Merian C. Cooper, who hoped for another *King Kong.*

In King Vidor's top-budgeted production of Stark Young's Civil War novel *So Red the Rose,* Scott was well cast, though the film was a financial disaster, making one Paramount executive quip: "So red the ink!"

Scott was regarded by most critics as the best star in the film. One said: "When you watch Randy Scott in *So Red the Rose,* you suddenly realize how right he was for the role of Ashley Wilkes in *Gone with the Wind,* as was Clark Gable as Rhett Butler."

Besides roles in *Follow the Fleet* and a programmer called *And Sud-*

den Death, Randy was ideally cast as Hawkeye in George B. Seitz's excellent production of *The Last of the Mohicans.* That year (1936) Scott and Grant rented Constance Talmadge's oceanside house and moved bachelor hall to the beach. Earlier, on March 23, at the home of his parents, Scott married Marianna Du Pont Somerville, the sister of William Du Pont, Jr., of *the* Delaware Du Ponts. The previous October Mrs. Scott had divorced her sportsman-millionaire husband, Thomas Somerville, in Reno. Her marriage to Scott was not publicly announced until August 2, 1936, and from newspaper accounts very few people were aware that the groom, George R. Scott, was Hollywood movie star Randolph Scott.

The marriage was of short duration. Early in June 1938 Randy made the announcement: "Our separation is entirely friendly. It's merely a case of being separated too much, which did not prove compatible to marriage." Hollywood friends, many completely ignorant of Scott's marriage, expressed surprise. But others intimated that Scott was a born bachelor.

Scott completed his Paramount contract by making *The Texans* (1938), a largely disappointing Western in which Joan Bennett costarred. Instead of negotiating a new contract with Paramount, Randy signed a nonexclusive pact with Darryl F. Zanuck. His first 20th Century-Fox film, a very loose remake of *Rebecca of Sunnybrook Farm* (1938), united him with Shirley Temple. Randy also negotiated to make one film a year at Universal and his first one there, *Road to Reno* (1938), had him stooging for a hopelessly hammy Hope Hampton.

In 1939, Zanuck put Scott in his first Technicolor film, *Jesse James,* which starred Tyrone Power and Henry Fonda, and he followed that triumph with a good role in the sepia-toned *Susannah of the Mounties,* in which he did not let Shirley Temple have everything her way. He then freelanced one film for Columbia, *Coast Guard,* a low-budgeted action picture which gave him a chance to play opposite actress Frances Dee, wife of his old friend Joel McCrea, whom he regards as a close personal friend to this day.

He then played Wyatt Earp to Cesar Romero's Doc Holliday in Allan Dwan's action-packed *Frontier Marshal,* which John Ford admired so much that seven years later he remade it as the classic *My Darling Clementine,* starring Henry Fonda.

Randy got another Ashley Wilkes type of role in *Virginia City,* which starred Errol Flynn, Miriam Hopkins, and an outrageously miscast Humphrey Bogart. The same year, 1940, he teamed a second time with Cary Grant and Irene Dunne, in the farce *My Favorite Wife,* a moneymaker.

Scott's adventures at Universal, which started off so badly, improved slightly in 1940 with *When the Daltons Rode,* an action-packed programmer redeemed by spectacular stunt work and obviously designed to cash in on the popularity of *Jesse James.*

Four of his other Universal films were all big moneymakers. *The Spoilers* (1942) teamed him with John Wayne (in the roughest onset fight ever filmed, which left both men enemies for years) and Marlene Dietrich. Scott confesses, even today, that when *Spoilers* was cast he did not particularly like Wayne, who he said was uncouth and very ungentlemanly. "We actually fought it out, for real, on the set, and the cameras unfortunately kept rolling and got every punch, show of blood, and fall. Duke Wayne and I sustained injuries from the brawl, scars I still carry on me today. However, we eventually became good friends [ten years later], and today are on the best of terms." *Pittsburgh*, made right after *The Spoilers*, was the last film Wayne and Scott starred in together.

In 1941, while playing a tight-lipped stalwart in Fritz Lang's *Western Union*, Randy found himself listed among the top moneymaking stars. And his 1942 Fox flagwaver *To the Shores of Tripoli*, a tribute to the Marine Corps costarring John Payne and Maureen O'Hara, was one of that year's box-office hits. It is also the film, said Randy for many years afterward, that contained his best performance.

Corvette K-225 and *Gung Ho!*, produced respectively by Howard Hawks and Walter Wanger in 1943, were action-packed, top-budgeted, well-made wartime epics which President Roosevelt cited as important contributions to the film industry's war efforts.

In addition to continual film work during World War II, Scott toured military hospitals and other U.S. installations in the South Pacific and entertained servicemen. He worked up an act with nightclub comic Joe DeRita, signed autographs, answered questions about the film stars he knew, and passed out pinups.

In March 1944 Scott married Marie Patricia Stillman in Riverside, California. The ceremony was performed by Justice of the Peace R. A. Moore. Witnesses included the bride's mother, Mrs. Marie Stillman, her brother, Dixwell, and Walter Van Pelt. Scott had met Miss Stillman three years earlier at the home of Townsend Fletcher. Not a few of his fans, to say nothing of seasoned newsmen, were slightly confused about the identity of the bride, for Scott had also dated another girl, Priscilla Stillman, who in some reports was mistakenly identified as his bride.

The marriage has produced two children, Christopher and Sandra, and is still regarded as one of Hollywood's happiest.

Immediately after Randy's second marriage Louella Parsons said: "Scott's marriage to the Du Pont heiress was always a mystery to Hollywood. She was years older than Scott and completely disinterested in the theater." Nor had Randy's closest friends ever understood.

Scott has since maintained a total blackout with the press, particularly regarding his personal life. On one rare occasion when he did discuss his family, he said of his father, "He went to see all of my films, not because he had a son starring in them, but because he thought I looked and acted like Wallace Reid, his favorite actor."

Of his mother who died in 1958, Scott once said, "She was an old-fashioned southern lady who always contended movies were not here to

In Riding Shotgun *(1954)*.

stay. My five sisters took her to see me in a film, and the first time she saw me on the screen she said, 'Oh, no! That can't be Randolph! This fellow's older than Randy and not nearly as good looking.' I'm not sure she ever saw another one of my films."

Scott's first venture into film production, in collaboration with William A. Seiter, got off to a shaky start with an oddball Western, a musical, called *Belle of the Yukon* (1944). An attempt had been made to interest Mae West in it, but all that appealed to her was the fact that it was to be filmed in Technicolor. After Miss West's wise decision, Gypsy Rose Lee took the role. But *Belle* never got off the ground, despite the presence of Scott, Dinah Shore, Florence Bates, and Charles Winninger.

Scott's 1945 film, *China Sky,* showed him as a newly married doctor running an American hospital in a small Chinese village at the outbreak of World War II. In 1945 he coproduced (with Nat Holt) and starred in *Abilene Town,* which United Artists released in early 1946. He also made *Badman's Territory,* which, like RKO's follow-up film, *Return of the Badmen,* rallied virtually every outlaw immortalized in Old West legends for an action-packed shoot-'em-up.

Except for *Home Sweet Homicide* (1946), *Christmas Eve* (1947), and a guest appearance in Warners' 1951 musical *Starlift,* Randy's films since 1945 have been Westerns.

Nat Holt, who died in 1971, coproduced many of these with Scott. In 1949 Holt and Scott formed their own production unit and made *Canadian Pacific* on exterior locations in western Canada, with interiors at General Service Studio in Hollywood. It was photographed in Cinecolor and distributed by Fox, which wanted more of the same. And with good reason: *Canadian Pacific* proved a big box-office hit and was named by film exhibitors in this country as one of the top ten moneymakers.

Holt followed through with such other moneymakers as *Fighting Man of the Plains* (1949), *The Cariboo Trail* (1950), and *Rage at Dawn* (1955). Of Randy, Holt said: "Scott is a superb actor, no temperament . . . and he's always a gentleman. Customers come to see him knowing exactly what to expect. And they are never disappointed. It used to be the same with Bill Hart."

Later, while Scott was still among the top ten moneymaking stars in America, Hedda Hopper asked him if he ever intended trying roles other than Westerns. "No, I don't," came Scott's firm reply. "I believe in letting well enough alone. I'm no longer looking for new fields to conquer, Hedda, and I'm also afraid of saturation. And that's why I'm going to lay off of television."

Upon completion of a very good minor Western, *The Walking Hills* (1949), Scott formed another production company, Scott-Brown, with Harry Joe Brown, who died early in 1972. Brown eventually became a partner in an exceedingly lucrative corporation which produced superior Westerns, all starring Scott. *Man in the Saddle* (1951) anticipated *High Noon* with an over-the-credits and throughout-the-action title song (sung by Tennessee Ernie Ford) and a script that was somewhat superior to the one Stanley Kramer used in his Academy Award-winning film and that did not need the genius of an editor like Elmo Williams to make it succeed.

Another element behind the overall success of Scott's Westerns has been the writers. Among them were Kenneth Gamet, a truly unsung genius, and Burt Kennedy, in his predirector days.

Seventh Cavalry (1956), based on a Glendon Swarthout novel, was another big hit. Scott followed that gem with *The Tall T*, for which Burt Kennedy did the screenplay and which Bud (Oscar) Boetticher directed. It can also be called a classic. Boetticher, who directed seven of Scott's superior Westerns, can justly take pride in every one of those films. The last Scott opus Boetticher directed was *Comanche Station* (1960). Soon after that, Randy announced his retirement and was off the screen for nearly three years.

Scott returned for one last film, *Ride the High Country*, starring his good friend Joel McCrea and directed by another friend, Sam Peckinpah. *Ride the High Country* proved to be the *chef d'oeuvre* of Scott's film career. A year after its release, on the lower half of a double bill, it won a prize at the Venice Film Festival. *Newsweek* named it 1962's best film, as did the editor of *Film Quarterly*.

Said Peckinpah: "MGM saw *Ride the High Country* as a low-budget quickie they could throw away in the summer double features, and if I'd tried to talk to them about the basic theme, which was salvation and loneliness, they'd have fired me on the spot. Even so, they hated what I'd done and threw me out before I could finish cutting, dubbing, and scoring. It had originally been a package deal, handed to me, completely cast. But, after reading the script, Randy Scott and Joel McCrea got together and came up with the idea of switching roles, which I thought brilliant. And that's exactly what they did. Scott wound up playing the bad guy!"

Ride the High Country was Scott's last film.

In 1971 Scott underwent chest surgery, called a hernia operation, at Mayo Clinic in Rochester, Minnesota. His condition was never deemed serious and he was soon back on the links at the Los Angeles Country Club, where he is still a member although show-biz people generally are not on its roster.

Randy seldom mentions he was one of the original sponsors of a long-range Mayo Clinic plan to extend its research activities and develop a feasible training program, aimed at offering the public free medical and health-care education.

The late Mike Connolly, a columnist for the *Hollywood Reporter*, said in 1965 that Randolph Scott was one of the wealthiest actors in the world, having real estate holdings in the San Fernando Valley and Palm Springs alone worth over one hundred million dollars.

"I've always been a fatalist about my career," said Scott recently. "What was to be was to be. At least it worked out that way in my case. My retirement from films is both voluntary and involuntary. One reason, and

*Scott is "mauling"
John Ireland
with convincing
realism in*
The Walking Hills
*(1949) as
Charles Stevens
watches.*

*At 75, he
plays the role of
a newspaperman.*

this is voluntary, is the impact of television. All old movies are turning up on TV these days, and, frankly, making pictures doesn't interest me too much anymore. Another reason is that the motion picture industry is in a steadily declining state, what with nudity and the like flagrantly displayed in films today."

Randolph Scott's credo might well be taken from *Ride the High Country:* "All I want to do is enter my own house justified."

He's one actor who can do just that.

Western Film Credits

The Virginian (Par., 1929)
Wild Horse Mesa (Par., 1932)
Heritage of the Desert (Par., 1932)
Man of the Forest (Par., 1933)
To the Last Man (Par., 1933)
Sunset Pass (Par., 1933)
The Thundering Herd (Par., 1933)
The Last Roundup (Par., 1934)
Wagon Wheels (Par., 1934)
Rocky Mountain Mystery (Par., 1935)
Home on the Range (Par., 1935)
The Last of the Mohicans (UA, 1936)
Go West, Young Man (Par., 1936)
High, Wide and Handsome (Par., 1937)
The Texans (Par., 1938)
Jesse James (20th, 1939)
Susannah of the Mounties (20th, 1939)
Frontier Marshal (20th, 1939)
Virginia City (WB, 1940)
When the Daltons Rode (Univ., 1940)
Western Union (20th, 1941)
Belle Starr (20th, 1941)
The Spoilers (Univ., 1942)
The Desperadoes (Col., 1943)
Belle of the Yukon (RKO, 1944)
Abilene Town (UA, 1946)
Badman's Territory (RKO, 1946)
Trail Street (RKO, 1947)
Gunfighters (Col., 1947)
Albuquerque (Par., 1948)
Return of the Badmen (RKO, 1948)
Coroner Creek (Col., 1948)
Canadian Pacific (20th, 1949)

The Walking Hills (Col., 1949)
The Doolins of Oklahoma (Col., 1949)
Fighting Man of the Plains (20th, 1949)
The Nevadan (Col., 1950)
Colt .45 (WB, 1950)
The Cariboo Trail (20th, 1950)
Sugarfoot (WB, 1951)
Santa Fe (Col., 1951)
Fort Worth (WB, 1951)
Man in the Saddle (Col., 1951)
Carson City (WB, 1952)
Hangman's Knot (Col., 1952)
Man Behind the Gun (WB, 1952)
The Stranger Wore a Gun (Col., 1953)
Thunder over the Plains (WB, 1953)
Riding Shotgun (WB, 1954)
The Bounty Hunter (WB, 1954)
Rage at Dawn (RKO, 1955)
Ten Wanted Men (Col., 1955)
Tall Man Riding (WB, 1955)
A Lawless Street (Col., 1955)
Seven Men from Now (WB, 1956)
The Seventh Cavalry (Col., 1956)
The Tall T (Col., 1957)
Shoot-out at Medicine Bend (WB, 1957)
Decision at Sundown (Col., 1957)
Buchanan Rides Alone (Col., 1958)
Ride Lonesome (Col., 1959)
Westbound (WB, 1959)
Comanche Station (Col., 1960)
Ride the High Country (MGM, 1962)

Charles "Durango Kid" Starrett, one of the all-time greats.

Charles Starrett

(Alias the Durango Kid)

Born: March 28, 1904, Athol, Mass.
Married: Mary McKinnon (1927);
   children: Charles, David

FROM 1935 TO 1952, the longest reign for any movie cowboy star at a single studio (in this instance Columbia), Charles Starrett rode the range triumphant. He brought fast action and well-plotted stories and a fresh character in Western acting (the Durango Kid) to a new pinnacle on the silver screen. And even today, the Durango Kid is being enjoyed in far-off places—Africa, New Zealand, Australia, South America, to name a few—via special arrangements with Screen Gems' television releasing company.

Starrett was the youngest of nine children. His father, Frank Starrett, was a prominent precision tool and die maker and provided for his children the best education possible. Charles' mother Lena rode herd on her brood and brought them up strict and proper. His birthplace on Old Main Street was later used as a convent; then was torn down in 1969. Survivors of the Starrett family today are Charles, his brother Philip, who runs an antique shop in Charlestown, Rhode Island, and their sister Mrs. Mildred Garrett of London, England.

Charles attended Athol High School, Billerica (Massachusetts) Military School, Worcester Academy, and Dartmouth College. He was always an outstanding athlete, and it was during his tenure on the varsity football team at Dartmouth that his future career was determined.

In 1926 Starrett and other members of the Dartmouth eleven were used in the Richard Dix programmer *The Quarterback.* Small as his part was, it was enough to convince Charles that he wanted to become an actor. After graduation from college, he began the long uphill climb toward stardom, fame, and success.

Charles' first professional work consisted of writing and producing one-act plays for foot-weary shoppers in Wanamaker's department store in New York City. He then joined the Stewart Warner Stock Company and toured with it for three years in New England, Ohio, and Indiana. One of his early motion pictures, made in New York, was a sound film entitled *Damaged Love* (1931) with June Collyer and Eloise Taylor (Mrs. Pat O'Brien). "I clicked," says Charles, "and my agent rushed me right over to take a screen test for Paramount." That test also proved fruitful and Charles Starrett's acting career was under way.

He did not, however, start by making Westerns. His tall, well-muscled physique and handsome looks made him dramatic star material, and he was thus cast in films like *The Sweetheart of Sigma Chi* (1933), *Murder on the Campus* (1933), and *So Red the Rose* (1935).

He ran the gamut from drawing-room frolics to jousting with Fu Manchu and his equally rotten daughter, Fah Lo Suee, in *The Mask of Fu Manchu* (1932). This film was and is a wonderful excursion into thrilling hokum on a grand scale. But Charles entered into the spirit of it all and made a believable hero stand out.

In 1935 the Columbia executives selected Starrett from among their contract players to replace the then departing Tim McCoy as the star of a series of action Westerns. It proved a wise selection, for Charles Starrett was the most durable Westerner that any studio had the good fortune to employ.

Although best remembered today for the sixty-five Durango Kid films he starred in, Charles' best movies were made between 1937 and 1941. These featured many of the outstanding supporting actors of the period as well as the top musical group, the Sons of the Pioneers.

Charles' first screen outfit seemed to be inspired by those of his Columbia predecessor, Tim McCoy. Though somber, the attire befit a frontier crusader. Topped off with a large white Stetson hat and white scarf or neckerchief to lighten the mood, the ensemble was neat without seeming too flamboyant.

Starrett played a likable cowpoke, slow to anger. When his ire was provoked, however, he demonstrated on many a screen villain that he was no drugstore cowboy. He engaged the most malevolent of screen villains in a no-holds-barred manner. His most frequent opponent was Dick Curtis. "Dick was a wonderful fellow and dear friend, off the screen," recalls Charles, "but onscreen—he was a real problem. That is to say, a problem to me as my 'archenemy.' We had so many screen fights, Dick and I, that we had the routine down perfectly. When we started off, they would change the camera speed from twenty-four frames per second to twenty-two. But later we got so good at fighting they shot us at regular speed. Dick was a perfectionist at timing, his reflexes always perfect. Every screen brawl we had he made me look good. Some of the other young actors I fought onscreen I had to be alert and watch out for. They didn't have their timing right lots of times, and more than once I caught a left jab or right hook that really hurt and shook me up. So I learned to keep alert and be wary with young actors as my villains. But with Dick, no sweat at all. We staged some of the roughest brawls ever shot in a Western, and though tired from the physical exertion it was all in a day's work for the two of us."

Several actors appeared as Starrett's sidekick during his sixteen years of stardom, but only two are generally remembered and identified with

Starrett gets the winning edge on Art Mix and Dick Curtis in Outlaws of the Prairie *(1937).*

As "The Durango Kid" with Jock Mahoney (right) and badmen Dan Sheridan, Jason Robards, Sr., and John Dehner in Horsemen of the Sierras *(1949).*

him: Dub "Cannonball" Taylor and Smiley Burnette. Burnette appeared in fifty-six films with Charles as the Durango Kid. He aided immeasurably when the later Starrett films bogged down with stock shots and budget cuts.

Although not exactly a sagebrush troubadour, Starrett liked musical interludes as a change of pace from the action sequences. His first Western films benefited from the addition of a group known as the Sons of the Pioneers. Roy Rogers was still with the Pioneers in the first two films, *Gallant Defender* (1935) and *The Mysterious Avenger* (1936). The Sons of the Pioneers stayed with Starrett until Rogers was established and strong enough at the box office to request them to leave Columbia and join him at Republic.

The absence of the best Western vocal group didn't deter Starrett long. Other groups eagerly flocked to strengthen his entourage. Spade Cooley is one recalled today, as are the Cass County Boys, Pee Wee King and his Golden West Cowboys, Merle Travis and his Bronco Busters, Jimmy Wakely and his Saddle Pals, and Bob Wills and his Texas Playboys. These and similar groups delivered the tuneful melodies pleasing to fans of country and western music.

Charles Starrett was fortunate in having many of the finest Western character actors in his casts—names like Dick Curtis, Kenneth MacDonald, Hank Bell, Edward Le Saint, Charles Middleton, Jack Ingram, Edmund Cobb, Art Mix, Alan Bridge, George Chesebro, Noah Beery, Jr., Lon Chaney, Jr., Jack Rockwell, and Hal Taliaferro. Comics and singers like Cliff Edwards, Frank Mitchell, Jimmy Davis, and Donald Grayson appeared many times.

In 1940 Starrett starred in *The Durango Kid* in which he played a masked crusader for law and order. Although this was the first of what was to become one of the most popular and longest Western series ever, it did not, like many other series, immediately proliferate. For reasons unknown even today, Starrett continued doing regular Westerns until 1945, when the Durango Kid was resurrected and took off in a big way for moviegoers and masked star alike. Until his retirement, Starrett played the Durango Kid.

Asked who first came up with the idea of starring him as a masked crusader, Starrett replied: "I'm not sure who first came up with the idea of the Durango Kid, but the movie was written by Paul Franklin."

Queried about being in any series besides Durango, Starrett said, "Yes, I was in a series entitled *The Medico*. The studio shot three of them, then scrapped the whole idea. They decided 'formula' Westerns paid off and not wild ventures like *Medico*."

Once *Return of the Durango Kid* was released in 1945, the series became a top box-office success. It kept Charles Starrett's name among the top ten Western stars until his retirement in 1952.

What was the typical formula for a Durango Kid movie?

"I'd come riding in as Steve, hear some gunshots over the hill, and take off," said Starrett. "I'd find that the stagecoach had been robbed, or something of that sort (a ranch had been burned down, or rustlers had run off with the cattle). Any sort of a plot to get the action going. I'd come into it. Why? I honestly don't know. Really. I'd come out of nowhere and suddenly I'd become involved. I'd help get the wounded driver and stagecoach, or whatever else have you, back to town. After I got involved in the plot of the thing, I had to change into Durango. I had to change into my disguise as the Durango Kid."

How many Durangos were made in a year?

"Ten, I believe, were made each year. We made sixty-five Durangos in all."

A desirable asset of the Durango Kid series lay in the fact that it was easy to use stuntmen. What better way to disguise a double than behind a black bandana mask? Jock Mahoney, stuntman extraordinaire, created the perfect illusion. The falls and stunts accomplished by Durango/Mahoney gave Durango/Starrett wide audience acclaim and approval.

What did he think of Jock Mahoney as his double?

"I can't say enough good words to describe my feelings for Jock Mahoney," said Starrett. "He was superb. Excellent. He was perfect, in all respects. He was a fine athlete, a fine stuntman, a perfect double for me. He turned into quite a star himself, and all deserving. I personally can't praise Jock enough."

Asked how he got along with his Durango sidekick Smiley Burnette, who was rumored to be the opposite of funny offscreen, Starrett said, "Smiley's another fine comic actor and gentleman I cannot say enough good words about. We worked together for a long time. I found it fun to work with him. He always had a new story for me. If I felt a little down, he could pick me up. By the same token if he felt a little down, I could pick him up. We really got along fine and worked well together. I was both shocked and saddened at his sudden death from a heart attack. He was only fifty-five or fifty-seven. But he always worked hard, much too hard. And he was constantly overweight. The combination finally proved too much for him and killed him, I guess. I felt very bad about the news of his death."

In 1952 Columbia Studios announced that Starrett had not renewed his contract and that a new series starring his former stuntman and double, Jock Mahoney, would be forthcoming. But the series never materialized and Columbia had to rely on Gene Autry to fill the void left by Starrett.

Why did he retire in 1952 when he was only forty-eight?

"Lee, to be honest, back in 1952 when the TV monster was threatening the industry like sound did twenty years earlier, I was positive I saw the writing on the proverbial wall . . . and wanted out without a big hassle. Besides, I'd been in the business a long time, had become a success as a

With "Raider," one of the horses he rode as the "Durango Kid."

With another "Raider," the horse he terms "the best of the thirty-three that I rode."

78

Lee — Don't be afraid of this hombre — I know the gun's not loaded!

Charles Starrett

Ready for action.

An action pose.

With badman Kenneth MacDonald (left) in The Durango Kid *(1940).*

top Western star and, also, I was cognizant more than anybody else that action Westerns are for young men and not old ones. Kind of like pro football today. The game is for young men, not old. When old pros continue to hang in there, stubbornly, they either wind up getting badly hurt or shamed and disgraced by several lousy seasons. They sooner or later have to retire; thus it's best to do it, retire, while on top rather than backsliding or at the bottom.

"Too, after making over a hundred action Westerns with all the riding and fighting—a lot of long, hard work—you don't come out all the time without your share of bumps and bruises. I landed in a hospital quite a few times from doing my own stunts when I was younger, which is why I accepted Jock Mahoney as my double later on. Anyway, the bugaboo of TV was upon us in the early fifties and I decided to retire and did."

Has he ever regretted retiring so early? "At first I did, I suppose. I didn't feel right about not working when other men my age were going to work every day and all. I like to watch TV and often caught myself reacting to various Westerns . . . and wondering how I would have made out had I not retired and hung in there another ten years or so. Who knows? I might have starred as Cheyenne Bodie, or Matt Dillon, in the beginning, or even Paladin. However, I finally put all thoughts of acting out of my head, and with my wife Mary set out on a world-sightseeing trip. Mary and I did a lot of traveling and saw all the things we couldn't see when I was working so hard at Columbia.

"Truly, though, I have no regrets about retiring. Our twin boys, Charles and David, are both married and successful businessmen in California. Mary and I own two nice homes, one we call our winter home at Laguna Beach, and the other at June Lake, in the high Sierras, near the Nevada state line. We're our own bosses, Mary and I, and we like it just fine."

Asked to name the title of one of his favorite films, Starrett said, "Lee, that's a good question. You see, we never put a title on the pictures. It was always production number 356 or number 1009, or the like. Or they would have a temporary shooting title.

"Columbia was quite well known for gathering all the stenographers and the help together to run the new film for them after it was cut. Then they would all submit a name for the picture. Somebody would win the prize and get $15 for naming it *South of the Border,* or *North of Arizona,* or *West of Tombstone.* I often made the comment: 'What are they doing, boxing the compass?'"

What does he regard as the two most important talents necessary to become a top Western star?

"That's simple," said Starrett. "The first talent is a fast draw of the six-shooter; the second is a good mount to ride. The way a Western star draws his gun, fans the hammer, spins it back into his holster goes a long way in ringing up points for himself at the box office; the same applies to a good horse. The way you mount it, the way you sit in the saddle, the way

81

In 1975.

you alight—all bear on audience reaction and your popularity as a star. Really. So I would consider those two talents beneficial to any Western actor's success, then or today."

Does he by chance still have his old Durango Kid outfit?

"As a matter of fact, yes," mused Starrett, "I do still have the outfit, which I'm sure I couldn't get into today. I try to watch my health and keep trim, but as one ages he gets more fleshy, or portly, whichever term you prefer, and puts weight on in the wrong places. But I will keep the Durango Kid outfit and hat as lasting mementos of my career as a star."

Who is his favorite cowboy star today, in movies or on TV?

Without hesitation he said, "Duke Wayne. There is nobody else who can compete with the Duke. As for TV cowboys, I'd have to put my money on Bob Fuller, formerly star of 'Laramie' and 'Wagon Train,' who's now a doctor in 'Emergency' [subsequently canceled]. Bob looks and acts like the movie cowboy should, and he's in excellent physical condition and loves action in his films. He also rides a good horse, and, well, is an expert in drawing a six-gun. Give Bob Fuller a Western movie to make, and then sit back and watch *real* entertainment."

The demise of the B-Western has left a deep void in movies. Only those fortunate few film collectors and their families and friends have the opportunity once again to view a film genre that is long gone but not forgotten by middle-aged folks.

In a moment of reverie, one sees Charles Starrett as the Durango Kid still riding endless dusty trails. . . .

Western Film Credits

Gallant Defender (Col., 1935)
The Mysterious Avenger (Col., 1936)
Stampede (Col., 1936)
Secret Patrol (Col., 1936)
Code of the Range (Col., 1936)
The Cowboy Star (Col., 1936)
Dodge City Trail (Col., 1936)
Two-Gun Law (Col., 1936)
Two-Fisted Sheriff (Col., 1937)
Westbound Mail (Col., 1937)
Trapped (Col., 1937)
One-Man Justice (Col., 1937)
The Old Wyoming Trail (Col., 1937)
Outlaws of the Prairie (Col., 1937)
Cattle Raiders (Col., 1938)
Law of the Plains (Col., 1938)
West of Cheyenne (Col., 1938)

Colorado Trail (Col., 1938)
Call of the Rockies (Col., 1938)
South of Arizona (Col., 1938)
Rio Grande (Col., 1938)
West of the Santa Fe (Col., 1938)
Spoilers of the Range (Col., 1939)
Western Caravans (Col., 1939)
The Man from Sundown (Col., 1939)
Riders of Black River (Col., 1939)
Texas Stampede (Col., 1939)
Outpost of the Mounties (Col., 1939)
The Stranger from Texas (Col., 1939)
The Thundering West (Col., 1939)
North of the Yukon (Col., 1939)
Bullets for Rustlers (Col., 1940)
Blazing Six-Shooters (Col., 1940)
Two-Fisted Rangers (Col., 1940)

Texas Stagecoach (Col., 1940)
West of Abilene (Col., 1940)
The Durango Kid (Col., 1940)
Thundering Frontier (Col., 1940)
Outlaws of the Panhandle (Col., 1941)
The Pinto Kid (Col., 1941)
The Medico of Painted Springs (Col., 1941)
The Prairie Stranger (Col., 1941)
Thunder over the Prairie (Col., 1941)
Riders of the Badlands (Col., 1941)
The Royal Mounted Patrol (Col., 1941)
West of Tombstone (Col., 1942)
Lawless Plainsmen (Col., 1942)
Down Rio Grande Way (Col., 1942)
Riders of the Northlands (Col., 1942)
Bad Men of the Hills (Col., 1942)
Overland to Deadwood (Col., 1942)
Riding Through Nevada (Col., 1942)
Pardon My Gun (Col., 1942)
The Fighting Buckaroo (Col., 1943)
Cowboy in the Clouds (Col., 1943)
Robin Hood of the Range (Col., 1943)
Frontier Fury (Col., 1943)
Hail to the Rangers (Col., 1943)
Law of the Northwest (Col., 1943)
Riding West (Col., 1944)
Cowboy Canteen (Col., 1944)
Sundown Valley (Col., 1944)
Cowboy from Lonesome River (Col., 1944)
Cyclone Prairie Rangers (Col., 1944)
Saddle Leather Law (Col., 1944)
Rough Ridin' Justice (Col., 1945)
Return of the Durango Kid (Col., 1945)
Both Barrels Blazing (Col., 1945)
Blazing the Western Trail (Col., 1945)
Rustlers of the Badlands (Col., 1945)
Lawless Empire (Col., 1945)
Outlaws of the Rockies (Col., 1945)
Texas Panhandle (Col., 1945)
Sagebrush Heroes (Col., 1945)
Frontier Gun Law (Col., 1946)
Gunning for Vengeance (Col., 1946)
Roaring Rangers (Col., 1946)

Galloping Thunder (Col., 1946)
Two-Fisted Stranger (Col., 1946)
Desert Horseman (Col., 1946)
Heading West (Col., 1946)
Landrush (Col., 1946)
Terror Trail (Col., 1946)
Fighting Frontiersman (Col., 1946)
South of the Chisholm Trail (Col., 1947)
West of Dodge City (Col., 1947)
The Lone Hand Texan (Col., 1947)
Law of the Canyon (Col., 1947)
Prairie Raiders (Col., 1947)
Stranger from Ponca City (Col., 1947)
The Buckaroo from Powder River (Col., 1947)
The Last Days of Boot Hill (Col., 1947)
Riders of the Lone Star (Col., 1947)
Phantom Valley (Col., 1948)
West of Sonora (Col., 1948)
Whirlwind Raiders (Col., 1948)
Six-Gun Law (Col., 1948)
Blazing Across the Pecos (Col., 1948)
Trail to Laredo (Col., 1948)
El Dorado Pass (Col., 1948)
Quick on the Trigger (Col., 1948)
Challenge of the Range (Col., 1949)
The Blazing Trail (Col., 1949)
Desert Vigilante (Col., 1949)
South of Death Valley (Col., 1949)
Horseman of the Sierras (Col., 1949)
Laramie (Col., 1949)
Bandits of El Dorado (Col., 1949)
Renegades of the Sage (Col., 1949)
Frontier Outpost (Col., 1949)
Outcasts of Black Mesa (Col., 1950)
Texas Dynamo (Col., 1950)
Trail of the Rustlers (Col., 1950)
Streets of Ghost Town (Col., 1950)
Across the Badlands (Col., 1950)
Lightning Guns (Col., 1950)
Raiders of Tomahawk Creek (Col., 1950)
Prairie Roundup (Col., 1951)
Riding the Outlaw Trail (Col., 1951)
Fort Savage Raiders (Col., 1951)
Snake River Desperadoes (Col., 1951)

Bonanza Town (Col., 1951)
Cyclone Fury (Col., 1951)
The Kid from Amarillo (Col., 1951)
Pecos River (Col., 1951)
Smoky Canyon (Col., 1952)

The Rough Tough West (Col., 1952)
Junction City (Col., 1952)
Laramie Mountains (Col., 1952)
The Hawk of Wild River (Col., 1952)
The Kid from Broken Gun (Col., 1952)

Gene Autry, star.

Gene Autry

(Cowboy Horatio Alger)

Born: September 29, 1907, Tioga, Tex.
Married: Ina Mae Spivey (1932)

GENE AUTRY, FORMER King of the Cowboys in the late thirties and early forties, is now a retired multimillionaire who keeps active with his vast empire of profitable enterprises and doesn't let the "old rockin' chair" catch up with him. He says he owes his film and business success to "a lotta luck, prayers, and plain good old horse sense."

Autry is well known in Hollywood as a cowboy Horatio Alger with the Midas touch in business. His film career as a singing cowboy started with a bit part in a Ken Maynard movie, *In Old Santa Fe* (1934). Autry became an overnight success. Between 1934 and 1942 he starred in fifty-five feature films and a thirteen-part serial, and by the time World War II began he had parlayed the $5 per day bit-actor salary he earned for his first film into a yearly salary of over $600,000.

"In 1941," Gene recalls in his familiar southwestern drawl, "I made $600,000—a small fortune in those days—with pictures, radio, records, and personal appearances. Suddenly, I found myself in uniform [Army Air Corps] makin' $115-$125 a month as a tech sergeant.

"It started me t' thinkin'. If it hadn't been for royalties from items such as sweatshirts, toy pistol sets, boots, hats, and records, I would've been in a real mess.

"I knew I could make good money as long as I could work. But supposin' I was incapacitated? What then? Where would I get my income? So I decided I'd better start makin' my hard-earned bucks pay off for me. I started by investin' in some business enterprises."

Now, thirty-eight years later, the blond-haired, blue-eyed, smiling Texas troubadour sings only at birthday parties and occasionally as a guest on a TV variety show. His voice sounds much the same as always, belying his seventy-one years. He rides in chauffeured limousines, mainly, having put Champion out to pasture when he officially hung up his white hat, spurs, and guitar in 1960.

Autry's holdings now include a majority interest in the Golden West Broadcasting Company (four radio stations and a TV station), the California Angels baseball team, CBS television and radio outlets in Phoenix, the Gene Autry Hotel in Palm Springs, and ranches in Arizona, Nevada, and southern Colorado, plus a minority interest in the Los Angeles Rams football team.

In the mid-1960s the Autry empire also included an impressive string of hotels—including the Mark Hopkins in San Francisco, the Continental Hotel in Hollywood, the Ocotillo Lodge in Palm Springs, and the Sahara Lodge in Chicago.

He has since dissolved the Gene Autry Hotel Company and disposed of all hotels, except the Gene Autry Hotel, which he has always owned independently of the others in the chain, and where he often resides for relaxation—swimming and golf—in the warm desert sunshine.

But what of Gene's Horatio Alger-like rise to fame?

Born Orvon Gene Autry, he grew up in Tioga, Texas. His father was the minister of the Baptist church there and young Gene spent many a Sunday singing in the church choir.

As he matured, Gene worked for everything he got. He never once wanted "anything just handed to me" without having earned it. Upon graduation from high school, he decided to leave home and find his niche in life.

He got a job as a telegrapher for the railroad and, after some schooling at operating the key, was sent to Chelsea, Oklahoma. While working there Gene found time to sing in a variety of places: from a local restaurant on Saturday nights to carny shows, where those famous patent medicines seen in so many B-Westerns were actually huckstered.

Gene bought his first guitar for $20 (a dollar down and fifty cents a month until paid). His combined income from singing, guitar playing, and telegraphy enabled him to pay for a correspondence course in business administration. Then the owner of a Chelsea radio station heard Gene singing in a local restaurant and offered him a spot of air time. Gene accepted the generous offer and the moment the citizenry of Chelsea heard him he was a success.

A monumental decision now faced Gene. Should he continue his career as a railroad telegrapher or pursue a singing career? The humorist Will Rogers helped him to decide. Gene was strumming his guitar and singing quietly one evening during a lull in telegraphy chores, when Will Rogers, whom he recognized instantly, came into the station. Rogers told Gene he liked his singing and encouraged him to "keep up th' good work, son." Gene sincerely assured Rogers he would, and did.

A short time later—and Gene still suspects Will Rogers had a lot to do with it—a Columbia Records scout, Jimmy Long, "discovered" the Texas troubadour and immediately signed him to a contract.

"Along with Jimmy Long," says Gene, "I wrote 'That Silver-Haired Daddy of Mine' and the tune became an instant hit. I was on my way."

Gene next became a regular featured star on NBC's "National Barn Dance" radio program. Film producer Nat Levine then "discovered" the

In Mexicali Rose *(1939) with Luana Walters and William Farnum.*

With Champion, in 1950.

talented young Texan and offered him his first role in a film—the minor role of a cowboy-singer with Ken Maynard in *In Old Santa Fe* (1934).

"I was honored t' appear in a film with such a big box-office Western star as Ken Maynard was in those days. But I had t' let no hero worship stand in my way and work hard t' both act and sing right," says Gene.

"I sang only a few brief tunes in th' picture, but they were good enough t' encourage Mascot Pictures t' sign me as th' star of a way-out serial entitled *The Phantom Empire* (1935). I played th' part of a singin' cowboy who discovered a mysterious underground city called Murania and had numerous adventures and escapades. Mainly, I got th' chance t' sing 'That Silver-Haired Daddy of Mine' every few chapters, and the die for my movie career was cast, so to speak."

Autry was then put into his own series of starring vehicles released by Republic Pictures, which was a new studio formed by an amalgamation of Mascot, Monogram, Liberty, and Consolidated Studios, and became a smash hit in his very first feature film, *Tumbling Tumbleweeds*, released in 1935. Then followed in the same year *Melody Trail, Sagebrush Troubadour,* and *The Singing Vagabond.* But according to many of his fans (including this author) his best films were released between 1937 and 1942, films like *Mexicali Rose, Blue Montana Skies, Gold Mine in the Sky, Melody Ranch, Springtime in the Rockies,* and *Home in Wyomin'.*

World War II was declared and Gene enlisted in the U.S. Army Air Corps as a technical sergeant.

When he was honorably discharged and returned to Hollywood to pick up his film career again, he found that his own studio had built young Roy Rogers into its new King of the Cowboys.

"I kinda felt let down, hurt, at first," Gene admits even today, "but Roy was young, eager, and ambitious and worked hard to achieve his fame and fortune, just the same as I had done. So I kinda bowed outta th' picture, so t' speak, and let Roy have his chance t' make good too."

Shaking off the effects of having been dethroned, Gene made five more films for Republic in 1946-47 and then left the studio he had once helped to build. He went into independent production and turned out numerous films that were released by Columbia Pictures.

In addition he had a popular radio show, sponsored by Wrigley's Gum, which ran for years, and when television came into its own in the late forties and early fifties, Gene produced several series which featured not only himself but also Jock Mahoney (the Range Rider), Dick Jones (Buffalo Bill, Jr.), Gail Davis (Annie Oakley), and even his famous wonder horse Champion.

Gene had many shortcomings, and he frankly admits most of them. For example, he was not a good horseman and found himself falling out of the saddle in his early film days. One of the most embarrassing incidents in his life occurred during one of his famous Madison Square Garden rodeo appearances right after his discharge from the Air Corps; in front of

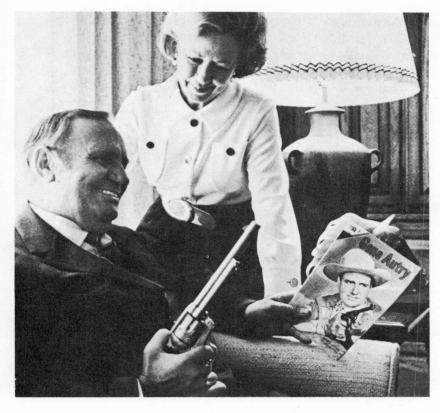

a packed house, he slipped off Champion and landed without ceremony on his *comosiama*. He also admitted it took years to learn how to throw a stage punch so that a double would not have to be used. But despite his shortcomings, Gene was one of the most successful and pleasing Western stars in film history.

Everything that Gene set out to do in life he has accomplished in orderly and successful fashion. As he climbed the ladder of success—from railroad telegrapher to King of the Cowboys to multi-millionaire—each rung seemed to be where it should be when his boot arrived.

In his entire movie career as a singing, fighting cowboy of the West, Gene appeared in ninety-five feature films. He gained his box-office prominence despite the fact that his early pictures did not meet with great success in metropolitan areas.

As his wife, the former Ina Mae Spivey, says, "Gene had a vast audience in small towns, and his pictures were the backbone of so many small theaters."

Rural America, the heart of Autry's fandom, could see its hero in person at the county or state fairs as well as on film. Gene would ride Champion as guest of honor in rodeo-opening parades, after which he would autograph a hundred or so photos of himself he happened to bring along.

"It's a good thing I took that correspondence course in business administration when I was a railroad telegrapher," says Gene, "because what I learned about handlin' money and investin' wisely sure came in handy. Of course, my luckiest break came when I married Ina Mae, because she's got a good business head on her shoulders and—well, lookit what all I've got today!"

Ina Mae Autry says this of her famous husband: "I think Gene's a wonderful example of what this country of ours is all about. He's a perfect example of what you can do if you go forth with the talent God gave you and make the most of it."

Gene's own movie rules confirm his wife's proud statement—he always wore a white hat, for he was the good guy; he never shot an adversary first, never hit one first, never hit a man smaller than he was, never smoked or took a drink of beer or booze. "I kinda borrowed most of my roles from Ken Maynard," Gene says, "but I stuck to them consistently, which, unfortunately, he didn't."

Gene now has sold close to forty million records, nine of them being golden records. The latter are: "That Silver-Haired Daddy of Mine," "Rudolph the Red-Nosed Reindeer," "Peter Cotton-Tail," "Here Comes Santa Claus," "Tumbling Tumbleweeds," "Back in the Saddle Again" (his film theme song), "You Are My Sunshine," "South of the Border, Down Mexico Way," and "Mexicali Rose."

Small wonder Gene Autry is known as the "Cowboy Horatio Alger with the Midas touch."

And despite all the fame and fortune he earned by hard work, Gene never once regarded himself as a movie star. "I just tried to be myself, a typical Westerner, t' add realism t' my pictures," he says.

Which means multimillionaire Gene Autry is basically just himself—about as American as apple pie. And that's the secret of his fame and fortune.

Western Film Credits

In Old Santa Fe (Mas., 1934)

Mystery Mountain (serial) (Mas., 1934)

The Phantom Empire (serial) (Mas., 1935)

Tumbling Tumbleweeds (Rep., 1935)

Melody Trail (Rep., 1935)

The Sagebrush Troubadour (Rep., 1935)

The Singing Vagabond (Rep., 1935)

Red River Valley (Rep., 1936)

Comin' Round the Mountain (Rep., 1936)

The Singing Cowboy (Rep., 1936)

Guns and Guitars (Rep., 1936)
Oh, Susanna! (Rep., 1936)
Ride, Ranger, Ride (Rep., 1936)
The Big Show (Rep., 1936)
The Old Corral (Rep., 1936)
Round-up Time in Texas (Rep., 1937)
Git Along, Little Dogies (Rep., 1937)
Rootin' Tootin' Rhythm (Rep., 1937)
Yodelin' Kid from Pine Ridge (Rep., 1937)
Public Cowboy No. 1 (Rep., 1937)
Boots and Saddles (Rep., 1937)
Springtime in the Rockies (Rep., 1937)
The Old Barn Dance (Rep., 1938)
Gold Mine in the Sky (Rep., 1938)
Man from Music Mountain (Rep., 1938)
Prairie Moon (Rep., 1938)
Rhythm of the Saddle (Rep., 1938)
Western Jamboree (Rep., 1938)
Home on the Prairie (Rep., 1939)
Mexicali Rose (Rep., 1939)
Blue Montana Skies (Rep., 1939)
Mountain Rhythm (Rep., 1939)
Colorado Sunset (Rep., 1939)
In Old Monterey (Rep., 1939)
Rovin' Tumbleweeds (Rep., 1939)
South of the Border (Rep., 1939)
Rancho Grande (Rep., 1940)
Shooting High (20th, 1940)
Gaucho Serenade (Rep., 1940)
Carolina Moon (Rep., 1940)
Ride, Tenderfoot, Ride (Rep., 1940)
Melody Ranch (Rep., 1940)
Ridin' on a Rainbow (Rep., 1941)
Back in the Saddle (Rep., 1941)
The Singing Hill (Rep., 1941)
Sunset in Wyoming (Rep., 1941)
Under Fiesta Stars (Rep., 1941)
Down Mexico Way (Rep., 1941)
Sierra Sue (Rep., 1941)
Cowboy Serenade (Rep., 1942)
Heart of the Rio Grande (Rep., 1942)
Home in Wyomin' (Rep., 1942)

Stardust on the Sage (Rep., 1942)
Call of the Canyon (Rep., 1942)
Bells of Capistrano (Rep., 1942)
Sioux City Sue (Rep., 1946)
Trail to San Antone (Rep., 1947)
Twilight on the Rio Grande (Rep., 1947)
Saddle Pals (Rep., 1947)
Robin Hood of Texas (Rep., 1947)
The Last Round-Up (Col., 1947)
The Strawberry Roan (Col., 1948)
Loaded Pistols (Col., 1949)
The Big Sombrero (Col., 1949)
Riders of the Whistling Pines (Col., 1949)
Rim of the Canyon (Col., 1949)
The Cowboy and the Indians (Col., 1949)
Riders in the Sky (Col., 1949)
Sons of New Mexico (Col., 1950)
Mule Train (Col., 1950)
Cow Town (Col., 1950)
Beyond the Purple Hills (Col., 1950)
Indian Territory (Col., 1950)
The Blazing Hills (Col., 1951)
Gene Autry and the Mounties (Col., 1951)
Texans Never Cry (Col., 1951)
Whirlwind (Col., 1951)
Silver Canyon (Col., 1951)
Hills of Utah (Col., 1951)
Valley of Fire (Col., 1951)
The Old West (Col., 1952)
Night Stage to Galveston (Col., 1952)
Apache Country (Col., 1952)
Barbed Wire (Col., 1952)
Wagon Team (Col., 1952)
Blue Canadian Rockies (Col., 1952)
Winning of the West (Col., 1953)
On Top of Old Smoky (Col., 1953)
Goldtown Ghost Raiders (Col., 1953)
Pack Train (Col., 1953)
Saginaw Trail (Col., 1953)
Last of the Pony Riders (Col., 1953)

Roy Rogers and Trigger, in Springtime in the Sierras *(1947).*

Roy Rogers

(King of the Cowboys)

Born: November 5, 1912, Cincinnati, Ohio
Married: Arlene Wilkens (1936); died (1946);
  children: Cheryl, Darlene, Linda, Roy,
  Marion; remarried: Dale Evans (1947);
  children: Robin, John, Deborah, Mary
  Little Doe

IT IS DOUBTFUL that anyone in the world is unfamiliar with the name Roy Rogers. It is equally doubtful that any of Roy's many friends and fans would not argue that their hero is still the undisputed King of the Cowboys.

"History informs us," one of Roy's ardent fans said recently, "that one of the most important functions of a king is that of conquering. Roy Rogers has calmly been conquering show business for over thirty years, confidently accepting each new challenge it has presented and emerging the victor."

Actually, Roy Rogers' first conquest took place before he came to Hollywood in the mid-1930s. His name was Leonard Slye then and he had a cheap guitar slung over his shoulder, a good voice, and the deep driving desire to become a name singer of Western music.

He left hometown Cincinnati and set out for the West, with little money but much musical talent and personality. He landed jobs in Western bands—playing at dances, barn dances, and sometimes on the radio—in Kansas (thirty days) and Oklahoma (ninety days) before turning southward to New Mexico. In Roswell he befriended radio station KGFL owner Walter E. Whitmore and was given a regular job of singing Western music on the air three times a week. Whitmore didn't like Roy's real name, so Len Slye temporarily became Dick Weston, the Texas Troubadour.

Response was instantaneous. Radio listeners in the Pecos Valley for miles around Roswell wrote their praises of Weston to Whitmore and demanded more. The popular young singer also received numerous invitations to area shindigs and barn dances, rodeos, etc., and his voice never failed to thrill the male set and cause the females to swoon.

Another group of Western music singers was touring the Pecos Valley at that time. They were headed by a young man named Bob Nolan and called themselves the Four Tumbleweeds. Len and Bob and his group were predestined to meet, and did, whereupon they formed a lasting friendship, one they cherish even today. Len joined the group and they became known as Dick Weston and the Tumblin' Tumbleweeds.

Fan mail at KGFL in Roswell got heavier and heavier. For a while, the boys tried to answer the many letters personally, but they agreed a secretary would have to be hired to free their time for singing and making more guest appearances.

Whitmore had long known what a find he had in Len and Bob and their group, but also knew his good fortune would be of short duration. His fears were soon realized. A Hollywood talent scout who happened to be passing through Roswell heard about KGFL's singing group and listened to them himself. He instantly liked what he heard and made an appointment to meet them.

Through Whitmore, Len and the Tumblin' Tumbleweeds met the talent scout and learned his studio (Columbia) was planning soon to launch a search for a singing talent to compete against Gene Autry. Would they, Len and Bob and their boys, be interested?

Would they? They were ecstatic!

Accompanying Whitmore and the talent scout, Len and Bob Nolan and his band went to Hollywood. They were screen-tested as a group, then Len was tested separately. The results were sensational.

Len and Bob signed contracts with Columbia. (Len legally changed his name to Roy Rogers in 1938 at Republic.) Bob Nolan and his boys became known as the Sons of the Pioneers and guested in a number of Western musical films while Roy was in Montana on a producer's ranch learning how to ride a horse well and how to shoot, rope, and crack a bullwhip. He also learned how to box and rough-and-tumble, careful at all times not to mar his face and his future as a movie star.

Republic Studios launched him on his career, later starring him in such Western musical extravaganzas as *Idaho* (1943) and *Cowboy and the Senorita* (1944). World War II took many Western stars into the armed forces, including Gene Autry. The draft somehow overlooked Roy. With Autry gone from Republic, that studio promoted Roy to "King of the Cowboys." He then "carried the ball" at Republic during the war years, happily and profitably.

Roy was soon number one box-office star of all Western motion pictures and remained there for the next twelve consecutive years, and was number three for two years after that.

In addition to his eighty-five feature films at Republic, Roy starred in *Melody Time* (1948), for Walt Disney, and costarred with Bob Hope and Jane Russell in Paramount's *Son of Paleface* (1952). In the film *Hollywood Canteen* (1944), Roy and the Sons introduced the Western song "Don't Fence Me In," and it became a smash success.

While at Republic, Roy teamed with Dale Evans in thirty-five feature films. She had been the featured singer on the highest-rated radio show in history, "The Chase & Sanborn Coffee Hour." Roy and Dale married in

The star.

With Dale Evans.

Cowboy singing star.

1947 and their family life has become a model of the American lifestyle they have been so instrumental in promoting.

Roy's second big challenge in postwar years was television. But the King of the Cowboys took it in stride. The fourteen specials he did for NBC-TV under the sponsorship of General Motors were never once out-rated by the competition. General Foods sponsored the Roy Rogers half-hour series on NBC for six years. As part of its promotional campaign for the show, General Foods placed Roy's picture on two and one-half billion Post cereal packages.

The Nestle Company sponsored the repeats of the 104 Roy Rogers half-hour shows in syndication through 130 markets for two and one-half years and then took the same series and repeated it on the CBS network for four more years. The same series is today being repeated in both American and foreign markets.

When "Hollywood Palace" was dropped from ABC network programming, the "Roy Rogers-Dale Evans Country & Western Special" was rated by Nielsen as the number one show during the seven-year tenure of that series. Other network shows that have featured Roy and Dale include the Nashville-based "Johnny Cash Show" and "Hee Haw."

The effect of the King of the Cowboys on the consumer has been attested by the more than one billion dollars spent on the name Roy Rogers.

Four hundred products and 150 licenses have been issued during Roy's career, resulting in $300,000,000 in retail sales alone. Roy Rogers Western Corrals were in all Sears Roebuck stores for over twenty years. Currently, the Roy Rogers Family Restaurants, in association with the Marriott Corporation, have 138 units open for business and more scheduled for opening soon.

A recent challenge confronting Roy has been contemporary music. Under the expert direction of producer Bill Walker, Roy has recorded three albums and many singles in Nashville for Capitol Records. His hit records have been "Money Can't Buy Love" and "Lovenworth." Roy's two Capitol albums currently in release are "The Country Side of Roy Rogers" and "A Man from Duck Run."

The honors bestowed upon Roy and his beautiful wife Dale are too numerous to mention. But they are indicative of the worldwide affection the couple garners. Ralph Edwards said that, during his many years of hosting the "This Is Your Life" television show, he had more requests to do the life of Roy Rogers than any other person in the world. And by popular demand the show depicting Roy's life has been repeated four times.

The 1972 schedule for Roy and Dale covered many major appearances in state fairs and rodeos—Illinois State Fair, State Fair of West Virginia, Ohio State Fair, Nebraska State Fair, Eastern States Exposition, and the Oklahoma State Fair.

That schedule prevailed for Roy and Dale in 1973, with the New

In 1976.

Mexico and Arizona state fairs being added. The same schedule held for 1974-75. In 1976 Roy attempted a comeback in movies in the film *Mackintosh and T.J.*, and therefore curtailed many state fair appearances. At present, he is hard at work on a sequel to his latest movie, the title not yet decided.

In between making movies and personal appearances at state fairs and rodeos (and guesting on TV shows), Roy and Dale will be doing recording sessions for their respective labels.

What does Roy think of his good friend and former competitor Gene Autry?

"Shucks, I think ol' Gene is one o' th' best ol' boys in th' whole wide world. Sure, we were competitors, but that was show biz, th' name of th' game. And thanks to th' good Lord, I came out on top. Yep, I've done mighty well for myself. Oh, sure, me and Dale have had our ups and downs, our share of tragedy and grief, over th' years, but we try t' let Him keep us sensible and calm when things like that happen. Because if He's for you, who's against you? Even ol' Gene agrees t' that, because he told me so many times."

Has he ever been back to Roswell, where he got his real start as a big film star?

"Heck, yes. I've been back t' Roswell a lotta times in past years, and I never fail t' pay my proper respects t' ol' Walt Whitmore's grave. I just wish Walt'd lived long enough to see me become a big success in show business. He used t' say how it gave him a big thrill t' see any o' his protégés make it t' th' top."

Was Montana the only place he learned to ride a horse, shoot, rope, and crack a bullwhip well?

"Truthfully, no. I used t' go up t' Ruidoso, back when I used t' live in Roswell, and I learned t' ride rent-hosses up there long before I went to that ranch in Montana. I also went out t' th' King Ranch, near Roswell, in th' old days and learned things there, too. So I pretty well knew what t' and not t' do when I went t' Montana."

What does Roy think of the new breed of cowboy stars on TV?

"Now, that's a real good question, y' better believe. I know a lotta ol' boys, like me, don't exactly like what we see in th' new breed of TV cowboy star, mostly because they aren't serious about becoming cowboy stars. They soon get tired of playin' cowboy and want t' transition into somethin' else, like detective or police series, for example. They don't want t' get what they call stereotyped in a cowboy role.

"Guys like me made a professional livin' bein' cowboy stars, and liked it. We wouldn't have what we have today if we didn't like bein' cowboy stars. So that lack of dedication in t'day's TV cowboy stars is what we ol'timers kinda resent."

How many movies does he plan to make in his newly launched comeback career in films?

"Shucks, I can't rightly say. I reckon th' public'll decide what I'll do by their attendance at my new films. I just hope they like me as Mackintosh, 'cause it's a lot different 'cowboy' role than anything I ever played before."

But as Roy said, if *He* is for you, who can be against you?

Western Film Credits

As Len Slye:
The Gallant Defender (Col., 1935)
The Mysterious Avenger (Col., 1936)
Rhythm on the Range (Par., 1936)
The Big Show (Rep., 1936)
The Old Corral (Rep., 1936)
The Old Wyoming Trail (Col., 1937)

As Dick Weston:
Wild Horse Rodeo (Rep., 1937)
The Old Barn Dance (Rep., 1938)

As Roy Rogers:
Under Western Stars (Rep., 1938)
Billy the Kid Returns (Rep., 1938)
Come on Rangers (Rep., 1938)
Shine on Harvest Moon (Rep., 1938)
Rough Riders Round-Up (Rep., 1939)
Frontier Pony Express (Rep., 1939)
Southward Ho! (Rep., 1939)
In Old Caliente (Rep., 1939)
Wall Street Cowboy (Rep., 1939)
The Arizona Kid (Rep., 1939)
Saga of Death Valley (Rep., 1939)
Days of Jesse James (Rep., 1939)
Young Buffalo Bill (Rep., 1940)
Dark Command (Rep., 1940)
The Carson City Kid (Rep., 1940)
The Ranger and the Lady (Rep., 1940)
Colorado (Rep., 1940)
Young Bill Hickok (Rep., 1940)
The Border Legion (Rep., 1940)
Robin Hood of the Pecos (Rep., 1941)
In Old Cheyenne (Rep., 1941)
Sheriff of Tombstone (Rep., 1941)
Nevada City (Rep., 1941)
Bad Man of Deadwood (Rep., 1941)
Jesse James at Bay (Rep., 1941)

Red River Valley (Rep., 1941)
The Man from Cheyenne (Rep., 1942)
South of Santa Fe (Rep., 1942)
Sunset on the Desert (Rep., 1942)
Romance on the Range (Rep., 1942)
Sons of the Pioneers (Rep., 1942)
Sunset Serenade (Rep., 1942)
Heart of the Golden West (Rep., 1942)
Ridin' Down the Canyon (Rep., 1942)
Idaho (Rep., 1943)
King of the Cowboys (Rep., 1943)
Song of Texas (Rep., 1943)
Silver Spurs (Rep., 1943)
Man from Music Mountain (Rep., 1943)
Hands Across the Border (Rep., 1943)
Cowboy and the Senorita (Rep., 1944)
The Yellow Rose of Texas (Rep., 1944)
Song of Nevada (Rep., 1944)
San Fernando Valley (Rep., 1944)
Lights of Old Santa Fe (Rep., 1944)
Utah (Rep., 1945)
Bells of Rosarita (Rep., 1945)
Man from Oklahoma (Rep., 1945)
Sunset in El Dorado (Rep., 1945)
Don't Fence Me In (Rep., 1945)
Along the Navajo Trail (Rep., 1945)
Song of Arizona (Rep., 1946)
Rainbow over Texas (Rep., 1946)
My Pal Trigger (Rep., 1946)
Under Nevada Skies (Rep., 1946)
Roll on Texas Moon (Rep., 1946)
Home in Oklahoma (Rep., 1946)
Out California Way (Rep., 1946)
Helldorado (Rep., 1946)
Apache Rose (Rep., 1947)
Bells of San Angelo (Rep., 1947)

Springtime in the Sierras (Rep., 1947)
On the Old Spanish Trail (Rep., 1947)
The Gay Ranchero (Rep., 1948)
Under California Skies (Rep., 1948)
Eyes of Texas (Rep., 1948)
Melody Time (RKO, 1948)
Night Time in Nevada (Rep., 1948)
Grand Canyon Trail (Rep., 1948)
The Far Frontier (Rep., 1948)
Susanna Pass (Rep., 1949)
Down Dakota Way (Rep., 1949)
The Golden Stallion (Rep., 1949)
Bells of Coronado (Rep., 1950)
Twilight in the Sierras (Rep., 1950)

Trigger Jr. (Rep., 1950)
Sunset in the West (Rep., 1950)
North of the Great Divide (Rep., 1950)
Trail of Robin Hood (Rep., 1950)
Spoilers of the Plains (Rep., 1951)
Heart of the Rockies (Rep., 1951)
In Old Amarillo (Rep., 1951)
South of Caliente (Rep., 1951)
Pals of the Golden West (Rep., 1951)
Son of Paleface (Par., 1952)
Alias Jesse James (UA., 1959)
Mackintosh and T.J. (Pennland
    Productions, 1976)

Donald "Red" Barry, in action pose.

Donald "Red" Barry

(James Cagney of the plains)

Born: January 11, 1912, Houston Tex.
Married: Peggy Stewart (1944); divorced
  (1953); child: Michael; remarried:
  Betty Kalb (1963); children: Kristine,
  Deborah

A SCREEN NAME tag can often help promote a show-business career. Such was the case with Donald Barry, one of the best of the B-Western actors. Because of his early screen portrayal of Red Ryder, the actor was often billed as Don "Red" Barry, despite the fact he did not have red hair.

Born Donald Barry DeAcosta, he was educated in the Houston school system, excelled as an athlete in high school, and was elected to the Texas All-Stars in 1929 upon graduating from Texas School of Mines. After graduation he went to Los Angeles where he was employed as an advertising agent. There he became interested in acting through summer-stock work. In 1933, because of his youthful looks, he was chosen to portray a high school student in Cecil B. DeMille's *This Day and Age.* After this feature he made some two-reeler entries and then toured in a road company of *Tobacco Road.*

Returning to Hollywood in 1936, he became a bit player, often having only a walk-on in a film. However, the year 1939 saw him in two impressive screen roles: the way-station operator in *Only Angels Have Wings* (Columbia) and the young fugitive in *Wyoming Outlaw,* one of Republic's "Three Mesquiteers" series.

It was in 1940 that Don was cast in the lead in *The Adventures of Red Ryder,* a serial based on the comic-book character. He then graduated to his own starring unit of Westerns at Republic, and from 1942 to 1945 was one of the top ten Western stars in the *Motion Picture Herald* poll.

Unlike many of his sagebrush comrades, Don often appeared in modern-dress melodramas such as *Remember Pearl Harbor* (1942), *The Purple Heart* (1944), and *The Chicago Kid* (1945).

Despite his popularity, Don yearned for more demanding roles, and in 1949 began a two-year association with Robert L. Lippert's low-budget releasing company where he often produced his own features (many non-Westerns). By 1951 he had left features for television and did not return to

105

the field until 1954, when he directed and starred in the privately financed *Jesse James' Women*. The production, however, was not successful. Barry was forced to return to supporting parts in A-pictures and guesting spots on TV.

In the late fifties he became a regular on the "Sugarfoot" teleseries starring Will Hutchins. In 1960 he also joined the cast of ABC-TV's "Surfside Six" as a police detective. When Jack Webb returned to television in 1966 with "Dragnet" and various other public service-oriented programs, Barry became one of the featured performers on these shows. One of his performances on Webb's "Adam-12" series was considered for an Emmy Award.

During the sixties Don appeared in Westerns produced by A. C. Lyles for Paramount. In 1964 he had a starring role in *Iron Angel*. In 1965 he starred in *Convict Stage*, which he wrote himself. This was his last starring role to date. He has, however, remained constantly active by taking supporting roles in films.

Whenever he was not working as a freelance actor in the sixties, Barry taught at Mickey Rooney's acting school. Later in the decade, he was, at one point, the only screen personality to entertain U.S. troops stationed in Vietnam.

In 1970 Barry announced he was planning to return to the B-Western

In Ghost Valley Raiders *(1940) with LeRoy Mason.*

106

At home
with wife
Peggy Stewart.

field as the producer-star of a series of small-budget oaters, the first to be *The Kid from Sundance*. The actor asked his fans for "loans" to help finance the production, but to date no such films have been made. His old films, though, continue to be shown throughout the country and in 1970 one TV station, KWHY-TV in Los Angeles, reported that Barry ranked second only to John Wayne in audience popularity.

Even though, like Bob Steele, Barry is small of stature, he nevertheless has been rated as one of the foremost ladies' men in Hollywood. Thrice married, he made headlines in 1955 when he and costar Susan Hayward of *I'll Cry Tomorrow* were found together one morning at his home by his girlfriend of the moment, starlet Jill Jarmyn. He would later say of redheaded Susan: "If a man is lucky enough to know a woman like Susan Hayward, he is lucky indeed. She's one of the finest ladies I've ever known." In his lengthy Hollywood tenure, Barry also dated such beauties as Joan Crawford, Linda Darnell, and Ann Sheridan.

Still popular, Barry is a frequent guest star at Western film-buff conventions. A very religious man, he tries to appear in family-type entertainment. Action and good acting were his main contributions to the Western genre, and he apparently longs for the return of the days when he made energetic sagebrush yarns at Republic Pictures.

Western Film Credits

Saga of Death Valley (Rep., 1939)
Days of Jesse James (Rep., 1939)
Wyoming Outlaw (Rep., 1939)
The Adventures of Red Ryder (serial) (Rep., 1940)
Ghost Valley Raiders (Rep., 1940)
One Man's Law (Rep., 1940)
Texas Terrors (Rep., 1940)
The Tulsa Kid (Rep., 1940)
Frontier Vengeance (Rep., 1940)
Wyoming Wildcat (Rep., 1941)
Phantom Cowboy (Rep., 1941)
Two-Gun Sheriff (Rep., 1941)
Desert Bandit (Rep., 1941)
Kansas Cyclone (Rep., 1941)
Death Valley Outlaws (Rep., 1941)
Apache Kid (Rep., 1941)
A Missouri Outlaw (Rep., 1941)
Arizona Terror (Rep., 1942)
Stagecoach Express (Rep., 1942)
Jesse James, Jr. (Rep., 1942)
Cyclone Kid (Rep., 1942)
Sombrero Kid (Rep., 1942)
Outlaws of Pine Ridge (Rep., 1942)
Sundown Kid (Rep., 1942)
Dead Man's Gulch (Rep., 1943)
Carson City Cyclone (Rep., 1943)
Days of Old Cheyenne (Rep., 1943)
Fugitive from Sonora (Rep., 1943)
Black Hills Express (Rep., 1943)
Man from the Rio Grande (Rep., 1943)
California Joe (Rep., 1943)
Canyon City (Rep., 1944)
Outlaws of Santa Fe (Rep., 1944)
Bells of Rosarita (Rep., 1945)
Out California Way (Rep., 1946)
The Plainsman and the Lady (Rep., 1946)
Square Dance Jubilee (Lip., 1949)
The Dalton Gang (Lip., 1949)

Red Desert (Lip., 1949)
Gunfire (Lip., 1950)
Train to Tombstone (Lip., 1950)
I Shot Billy the Kid (Lip., 1950)
Border Rangers (Lip., 1950)
Jesse James' Women (UA, 1954)
Untamed Heiress (Rep., 1954)
The Twinkle in God's Eye (Rep., 1955)
Seven Men from Now (WB, 1956)
Gun Duel at Durango (UA, 1957)
Born Reckless (WB, 1959)
Warlock (20th, 1959)
Walk Like a Dragon (Par., 1960)
Buffalo Gun (Independent, 1962)
Law of the Lawless (Par., 1964)
War Party (20th, 1965)
Convict Stage (20th, 1965)
Fort Courageous (20th, 1965)
Town Tamer (Par., 1965)
Apache Uprising (Par., 1966)
Alvarez Kelly (Col., 1966)
Red Tomahawk (Par., 1967)
Hostile Guns (Par., 1967)
Fort Utah (Par., 1967)
Shakiest Gun in the West (Univ., 1968)
Shalako (Cinerama, 1968)
Bandolero! (20th, 1968)
Cockeyed Cowboys of Calico County (Univ., 1969)
Dirty Dingus Magee (MGM, 1970)
Rio Lobo (NGP, 1970)
One More Train to Rob (Univ., 1971)
The Gatling Gun (Gold Key, 1972)
Junior Bonner (Cinerama, 1972)
Showdown (Univ., 1973)
Boss Nigger (Dimension, 1975)
Blazing Stewardesses (Independent-International, 1975)

Larry "Buster" Crabbe with comic actor Al "Fuzzy" St. John (left).

Larry "Buster" Crabbe

(Space heroics to oaters)

Born: February 7, 1908, Oakland, Calif.
Married: Virginia Held (1933);
   children: Cullen, Caren

CLARENCE LINDEN CRABBE set out to become a great swimming champion. He also made movies for money, wanted to be a director, and today wishes he could have appeared in at least one top-flight production. Yet in his nearly one hundred film appearances he became popular enough for his fans of today still to call him the King of Action and the King of the Sound Serial. His Flash Gordon and Buck Rogers films are constantly being viewed in movie and television revivals. In addition, now seventy-one, he continues to be one of the nation's best swimmers.

When he was two years old, California-born Clarence and his family moved to Hawaii, where he spent his boyhood. There he became a top-flight swimmer. In 1928 he swam for the U.S. team at the Olympics in Amsterdam and won third place in the 400- and 1,500-meter events. That year he enrolled at the University of Southern California, set on a law career.

Times were rough, however, and Crabbe found it difficult to work his way through college. To make ends meet, he worked in movies, appearing in MGM's *Good News* (1930) in a bit part. In order to retain his sports amateur standing, Larry did some stunting for no fee. In the 1932 Olympic games, Crabbe won the 400-meter event by breaking Johnny Weissmuller's world record of 4:52 by four seconds. He later broke his own record by swimming the event in 4:38.

It was at Paramount that Crabbe won a film contract. The studio cast him as the athletic Tarzan-like lead in *King of the Jungle* (1933). In the role of Kaspa the Lion Man he was billed as Buster Crabbe. Paramount sent him to the Pasadena Playhouse for acting experience, but took the opportunity to loan him to Sol Lesser for the shoddy twelve-chapter serial *Tarzan the Fearless* (1933).

In the early thirties Paramount produced a Zane Grey-derived series of low-budget Westerns and Buster was placed in them (often remakes of silent versions of Grey's perennial favorites, using stock footage from the earlier editions). Occasionally he landed juvenile leads, as in *You're Telling Me* (1934), a W. C. Fields comedy. Generally, however, he was cast in

111

In Sheriff of Sage Valley *(1942) with Maxine Leslie, Curley Dresden, and Lynton Brent.*

sagebrush and college football capers. Finally the studio placed him in *Lady, Be Careful* (1936), and his performance as a cocky marine brought him good notices. The studio promised him better parts, but none materialized. In 1936, however, he was listed tenth in a poll of the year's top moneymaking Western stars.

It was also in 1936 that Buster's big break occurred. Universal borrowed him for the lead in the serial *Flash Gordon*. It became an immediate success and spawned two additional serials with Buster as the mighty foe of evil Emperor Ming (Charles Middleton) of Mongo. His home studio, strangely, did not capitalize on his growing fame and continued to sidetrack Crabbe into thankless supporting roles in B-gangster films. On the other hand, Universal wisely kept him active in further serial leads, including *Red Barry* (1938) and *Buck Rogers* (1939). Ironically, his Paramount contract was allowed to lapse in 1939.

It was at the newly formed Producers Releasing Corporation (PRC) that Buster's reputation as a staunch Western lead was firmly established. He took over the lead role from departing Bob Steele in the Billy the Kid series, approaching the part with an extremely wholesome characterization (much like the later Audie Murphy, but without the latter's cold-eyed appeal). Buster was supported by silent-era comedy star Al "Fuzzy" St. John. Later, when parents complained about their children identifying too much with an outlaw, the Crabbe character name was changed to Billy Carson. Between 1941 and 1946 Crabbe (with his pet mount Falcon) and St. John made thirty-six of those low-grade PRC Westerns. Occasionally Buster would appear in a nonsagebrush entry, such as *Nabonga* (1944).

After leaving PRC, Buster teamed with Tarzan Johnny Weissmuller for a couple of actioners, *Swamp Fire* (1946) and *Captive Girl* (1950), and he won good notices as the Indian Magua in *The Last of the Redmen* (1947), and as the villain clown in *Caged Fury* (1948). The still agile Buster also returned to the serial field, starring in three chapter plays for Columbia.

In the early fifties Buster had his own exercise-health TV program in New York. Later, for WOR-TV, he hosted a program which screened his PRC oaters. This job led to still another video outing, "Buster Crabbe's Silver Saddle Wild West Show." With his son "Cuffy" he costarred with Fuzzy Knight from 1955 to 1957 in the popular action series "Captain Gallant of the Foreign Legion." During this time he also developed a swimming-pool company bearing his name and became active in a children's camp in upper New York State.

In 1956 Crabbe began his last series of Westerns, ending with *Gunfighters of Abilene* (1960). By now, thanks to his *Flash Gordon* and *Buck Rogers* entries, he had become a camp figure to a new generation.

Crabbe always enjoyed his villainous screen portrayals more than his heroic roles and got a good opportunity to chew the scenery in *The Bounty Killer* (1965). An early seventies film, *The Comeback Trail*, has yet to be released, and he did a bit in *Swim Team* (1979).

In the mid-sixties he entered the recording field when he reprised his Flash Gordon character on an LP album. He at that time also joined a New York stock firm as a broker and appeared occasionally on TV talk shows (Johnny Carson, Merv Griffin, Mike Douglas, etc.). In the seventies he revitalized his swimming career and now often takes part in the Amateur Athletic Union's National Masters Swimming championships.

Although the movies were good to Buster, he still regrets that he did not become a top-name star. "Even though I say it myself, I was a lot better actor than a lot of people give me credit for. I didn't have the training, of course. But I feel if I had really been given the proper chance I could have become a really good top-rate actor. I didn't make it like a Gable or a Boyer. But I often wonder what would have happened to my screen career had things been a little bit different."

Western Film Credits

Man of the Forest (Par., 1933)
To the Last Man (Par., 1933)
The Thundering Herd (Par., 1933)

Wanderer of the Wasteland (Par., 1935)
Nevada (Par., 1935)

Drift Fence (Par., 1936)
Desert Gold (Par., 1936)
The Arizona Raiders (Par., 1936)
Arizona Mahoney (Par., 1936)
Forlorn River (Par., 1937)
Sophie Lang Goes West (Par., 1937)
Colorado Sunset (Rep., 1939)
Billy the Kid Wanted (PRC, 1941)
Billy the Kid's Roundup (PRC, 1941)
Billy the Kid Trapped (PRC, 1941)
Billy the Kid's Smoking Guns (PRC, 1942)
Billy the Kid's Law and Order (PRC, 1942)
Mysterious Rider (PRC, 1942)
Sheriff of Sage Valley (PRC, 1942)
The Kid Rides Again (PRC, 1943)
Fugitive of the Plains (PRC, 1943)
Western Cyclone (PRC, 1943)
The Renegade (PRC, 1943)
Cattle Stampede (PRC, 1943)
Blazing Frontier (PRC, 1943)
Devil Riders (PRC, 1943)
The Drifter (PRC, 1943)
Frontier Outlaws (PRC, 1944)
Thundering Gunslingers (PRC, 1944)
Valley of Vengeance (PRC, 1944)

Fuzzy Settles Down (PRC, 1944)
Rustler's Hideout (PRC, 1944)
Wild Horse Phantom (PRC, 1944)
Oath of Vengeance (PRC, 1944)
His Brother's Ghost (PRC, 1945)
Shadows of Death (PRC, 1945)
Gangster's Den (PRC, 1945)
Stagecoach Outlaws (PRC, 1945)
Border Badmen (PRC, 1945)
Fighting Bill Carson (PRC, 1945)
Prairie Rustlers (PRC, 1945)
Lightning Raiders (PRC, 1945)
Ghosts of Hidden Valley (PRC, 1946)
Gentlemen with Guns (PRC, 1946)
Prairie Badmen (PRC, 1946)
Terrors on Horseback (PRC, 1946)
Overland Raiders (PRC, 1946)
Outlaw of the Plains (PRC, 1946)
The Last of the Redmen (Col., 1947)
Gun Brothers (UA, 1956)
The Lawless Eighties (Rep., 1957)
Badman's Territory (WB, 1958)
Gunfighters of Abilene (UA, 1960)
The Bounty Killer (Emb., 1965)
Arizona Raiders (Col., 1965)
The Comeback Trail (unreleased) (1971)

Sunset "Kit" Carson, in 1974.

Sunset "Kit" Carson

(Tallest young star in the saddle)

Born: November 12, 1927, Plainview, Tex.
Married

THERE'S A COWBOY superstar who can still boast that he sits taller in the saddle than John Wayne ever did—and he can prove it. He's six foot six Sunset "Kit" Carson, who is now fifty-one and was a Western matinee idol between 1945 and 1950, but who, like many other saddleburners of that era, faded out with the advent of television.

Today, though, Sunset's on the comeback trail, ridin' hard. He started his screen comeback in 1971 by making *Outlaw Grizzly*, for Screen Gems. Warner Brothers was so impressed with his acting it signed him to a nine-year contract. In 1976 Sunset completed a major Western picture, *The Marshal of Windy Hollow*, which he both directed and starred in. The film was shot on location near Windy Hollow, Kentucky.

During April 1976, Sunset took Tim McCoy's place in the Wild West show part of Tommy Scott's Country Music Caravan, while the elder former Western superstar was recuperating from a slipped disc. McCoy was starring in Scott's show, riding and cracking his bullwhip and reminiscing over his old movie days, when the accident happened. Sunset immediately filled in.

Sunset does fancy handgun draws and fan-shots, as well as fancy rifle shooting, to the delight of his many fans, young and old. He also plugs his newest film with clips at each performance. "Once my fans come to see me again," says Sunset, "they'll know ol' Sunset is on th' comeback trail—in a *big* way!"

Sunset first tasted fame as a young boy, having competed in over forty rodeos by the time he was twelve years old. Although he was big and tall for his age, a little fibbing "was necessary for me to get a man's work," says Sunset. But when it came to riding, roping, bronc riding, and bull-dogging, no fibbing was necessary.

Sunset won every known riding contest a teenager could enter: bronc busting, bulldogging, calf roping, and trick riding. He also became a crack shot with a rifle and a six-gun. In fact, he was such an excellent all-round performer the late Tom Mix contracted him to trick-ride in his Wild West circus.

"Actually," says Sunset, "I thought there was no other cowboy star

117

In Santa Fe
Saddlemates
(1945).

In 1946.

greater than ol' Ken Maynard, God rest his soul, and I secretly kinda patterned my whole life as a performer after him."

After spending some time as a feature attraction with Tom Mix's circus, recalls Sunset, "I kinda got itchy feet, like ol' Ken said he used t' get, and I decided t' go t' South America. I'd heard all about them gauchos down there, th' world-famous 'cowboys,' and I wanted t' see just how good they was compared t' me." The time was 1941-42, when Sunset was only fourteen.

"I learned a lot from them gauchos on th' pampas of South America, and I learned t' throw th' bolo expertly.

"About then, war clouds was gatherin' and things got a little uneasy in Argentina, where I finally wound up, so I abruptly ended my visit in South America and hightailed it back t' th' States.

"I arrived by boat in Los Angeles and looked up ol' Tom Mix—only t' find he'd been killed in an auto accident out in Arizona. But another old friend of Tom's, my idol Ken Maynard, was livin' in Hollywood so I looked him up.

"Ol' Ken and I spent many hours palaverin' about rodeos and Wild West shows we'd been in, and he was truly interested in all I had t' tell him about th' gauchos of South America and what truly fine cowboys they were.

"Ol' Ken wanted t' know what my plans were, so I told him I kinda had a hankerin' t' be a big cowboy star, just like he was. He tried hard t' advise me against it, warning me about th' long hours and hard work and th' pitfalls along th' road in becomin' a big-name cowboy movie star. But none of what he said could sway me away. I was determined. So Ken pulled some influential strings and got me a screen test at Republic."

Sunset's screen test was approved by the powers that be at Republic, and he was sent to the Pasadena Playhouse to receive tutoring as an actor. "It was kinda like takin' th' long route around th' mountain t' get what I wanted," admits Sunset, "but it finally paid off in a big way for me."

His brief experience of being tutored for acting won him the role as "Texas" in the Sol Lesser production of *Stage Door Canteen* (1943). Republic officials were so impressed with him they began to give him starring parts.

Sunset's career was launched by Republic in the middle 1940s. He went on to star in twenty pictures, all Westerns. His career was interrupted briefly for a year or so of service in the U.S. Army, but he was young enough when discharged at nineteen to vault back into the saddle again for Republic.

Sunset's lie about his age at the outset eventually proved a focal point of argument, along with fairer pay standards, at the studio when an actors' union was organized (now the Screen Actors Guild). Sunset had told the studio he was twenty-one years old at the outset, but the army's discharge records differed. His youth occasioned many arguments by studio execu-

119

Sunset shows friend Tommy Scott how to trick shoot.

tives, arguments finally resolved, but not to Sunset's liking so far as remuneration was concerned. This, followed by a serious automobile accident, cost Sunset his career as a cowboy superstar.

Leaving behind a record of being rated number eight among the nation's top ten favorite cowboy stars in 1950, Sunset joined Clyde Beatty's circus as a trick rider for several seasons. He also did personal appearances on numerous TV talk shows, and was the only cowboy star since Tom Mix to play the Steel Pier in Atlantic City.

Sunset completed a personal worldwide tour and had five command performances to his credit by performing for the king and queen of Siam. While on the island of Matsu to perform for General Yeh, the island was under fire from the mainland and Sunset received a special citation for bravery.

In Tokyo he did a series of charity shows for typhoon victims. His sharpshooting act with rifle and pistol, supplemented with trick riding, was the most spectacular ever witnessed by Far East showgoing enthusiasts. His fan club there still numbers well over twenty million youngsters. He is referred to as the "cowboy ambassador of goodwill" because he has never refused to perform for any deserving charity.

From Asia he traveled to nearly every country in Europe. He spent three years performing abroad, appearing in shows in Spain, Egypt, India, Cambodia, South Vietnam, Hawaii, Alaska, Nova Scotia, and Mexico. He has also performed in every state in the continental U.S.

In 1970 he hit it big again. He was introduced to actress Shelley Winters and landed the aforementioned film contract with Warner Bros. And now Sunset's busy planning another picture, which will be a Western filmed in Kentucky or Arkansas.

Perhaps Sunset's comeback is best remarked by cartoonist Mario DeMarco, who in the 1950s did Sunset's life history in a comic-book series: "I first met this tall, good-looking cowboy star in Hollywood in 1945, when he was busy turning out B-Western action oaters for Republic Studios. Standing six feet six inches tall, he was the tallest Western star that ever rode a horse across the silver screen. And like his height and popularity suggest: everything that Sunset "Kit" Carson did was done in a *big* way."

Sunset's always eager to receive mail from his many fans and encourages them to write to him in Middletown, Kentucky.

Western Film Credits

Call of the Rockies (Rep., 1944)
Bordertown Trail (Rep., 1944)
Code of the Prairie (Rep., 1944)
Firebrands of Arizona (Rep., 1944)
Sheriff of Cimarron (Rep., 1945)
Bells of Rosarita (Rep., 1945)
Santa Fe Saddlemates (Rep., 1945)
Oregon Trail (Rep., 1945)
Bandits of the Badlands (Rep., 1945)
Rough Riders of Cheyenne (Rep., 1945)
The Cherokee Flash (Rep., 1945)

Days of Buffalo Bill (Rep., 1946)
Alias Billy the Kid (Rep., 1946)
The El Paso Kid (Rep., 1946)
Red River Renegades (Rep., 1946)
Fighting Mustang (Astor, 1948)
Sunset Carson Rides Again (Astor, 1948)
The Deadline (Astor, 1948)
The Battling Marshal (Astor, 1949)
Rio Grande (Astor, 1949)
Outlaw Grizzly (Screen Gems, 1971)
Marshal of Windy Hollow (WB, 1976)

Lash LaRue, ready for action.

Alfred "Lash" LaRue

("Bogey" with a whip)

Born: March 5, 1921, Chicago, Ill.
Married: Eloise Mulhall (1946);
   divorced (1947)

ALFRED "LASH" LaRUE, whose bullwhip and six-gun punished many a bad guy in Western films during the 1947-56 era, is today an evangelist in Florida "whipping" drunks and derelicts into shape for the Lord.

The former Cheyenne Kid, who looked a lot like Humphrey Bogart but unfortunately could not act like Bogey, has indeed put many miles on his boots since that day in Miami years ago when he thought he had reached the end of his trail. Arrested for vagrancy, with only thirty-five cents in his jeans, he says he asked the arresting policeman to shoot him and "get my ordeal over with."

But the officer was an understanding, friendly cop and put Lash in touch with Mission Power Headquarters and Home of the Apostles. Here Lash began a new career of helping drunks and derelicts become God-fearing souls.

The mission, founded by evangelist John "3:16" Cook, works with drifters, drunks, and derelicts in the city of St. Petersburg. Cook takes his middle tag from chapter *three,* verse *sixteen* of the Gospel of St. John: "For God so loved the world, that He gave His only begotten Son, that whosoever believeth in Him should not perish, but have everlasting life."

One project of the mission, which is a favorite of LaRue's, is the "Hollywood Western Revue for the Lord." The show features tricky whip cracking and gun handling—all still capably performed by LaRue—old Lash LaRue movies, and a smattering of oldtime religion.

"I got myself sidetracked in the world of tough competition back in the early fifties and somehow got myself lost," admits LaRue. "I was in a situation that was bad for me and my many fans, so I ran out on the business."

LaRue actually got into a fiery discussion with his studio about higher pay per film and was fired.

"I was low, mighty low," LaRue continued, "and tried to find the solution in drink. But I soon learned there is no solution to troubles in a bottle, that the latter in fact is bottomless and like a whirlpool keeps sucking you down into its alcoholic vortex.

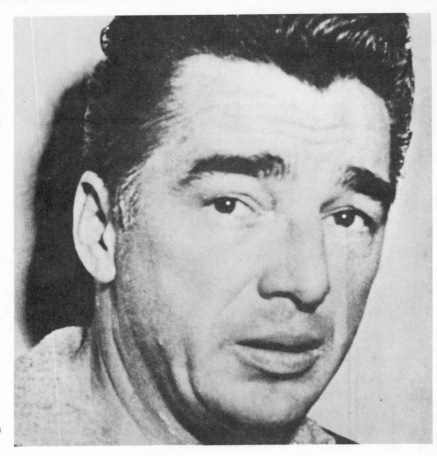

As he looked during his heyday as a Western star between 1947-56.

In Ghost Town Renegades *(1947) with Al St. John and Steve Clark.*

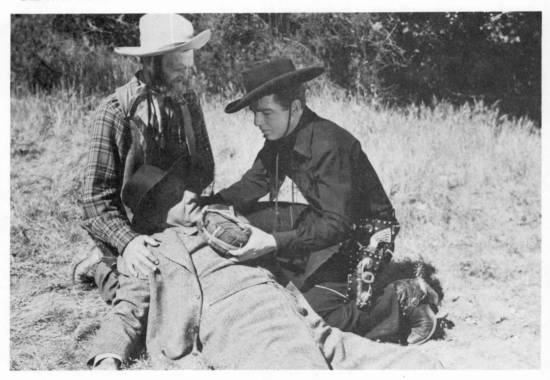

124

As he appears today in the real-life role of evangelist in St. Petersburg, Florida.

"I was in a situation that had to be remedied, but fast. I didn't make a bargain with the Lord, but I did dedicate my life, what's left of it, to Him as His personal servant. Since I did this, my whole sense of values and way of thinking have changed completely. I'm like a new man—*a man reborn!*"

Lash first became filmdom's King of the Bullwhip in 1946. He came to Hollywood with his Bogart looks and speech, took a screen test, and landed a contract. However, after a few bit roles (equivalent to today's spot TV commercials) it was evident LaRue could by no means hold a candle to Bogart's acting abilities, but since there was a shortage of leading men for Westerns because of the war, he was groomed for Western stardom.

"The whip idea was a gimmick thought up by publicity men," LaRue admits, adding, "but I fooled them all and became very proficient at it. So good, in fact, that they tagged the name 'Lash' onto me and wrote scripts for me to star in. They starred me in the beginning as the Cheyenne Kid, later changing it to Lash LaRue."

125

LaRue frequently won the girl in his **PRC** films and rode off into the sunset dozens of times before leaving Hollywood permanently in 1961. Lash LaRue comic books sold twelve million copies in 1952, so Lash capitalized on his fame for a while by taking his whip act across the country in one carnival, rodeo, or state fair after another, with a few personal appearances in theaters thrown in.

"Things began going drastically downhill for me from that time on," says LaRue. "I finally wound up in Nevada, managing—or trying to—a restaurant in Reno."

Then evangelist Bob Woodward came to town.

"I wasn't too taken with preaching at the time," says LaRue, "but I went to see Woodward out of sheer curiosity. I'd heard about a couple other evangelists—Billy Graham and Oral Roberts—who were making the rounds, saving and healing lost souls, so I wondered if Woodward could do the same. And during his sermon, he mentioned something that stuck with me. He said he'd once been a bank president in Chicago. I was born in Chicago, and I figured anyone who once ran a big bank should know plenty about the world, so I paid more attention to what he was saying. The Lord's Spirit moved inside me then, but not quite hard enough."

LaRue continued to drink and gamble and got into debt. Heavy debt. It took him years of working long hours to repay his debtors. Then he began wandering and finally wound up in Miami, where the kind police officer found him.

LaRue was accepted by Cook to help out at the mission because Cook said that he and LaRue were about as down and out as people could get, and now that they had been saved they were better able to know and to deal with the many complex problems of the people they were helping.

"We were both married," says LaRue, "and in each case the woman took us to the cleaners. But now we have brand new lives—serving Him."

There is only one very clashing contrast between the two men. Lash still wears black Western outfits, whereas Cook prefers mod attire. Regardless, both are now serving the very same purpose.

Western Film Credits

Song of Old Wyoming (PRC, 1945)
The Caravan Trail (PRC, 1946)
Wild West (PRC, 1946)
Border Feud (PRC, 1947)
Cheyenne Takes Over (Eagle Lion, 1947)
Return of the Lash (Eagle Lion, 1947)
The Fighting Vigilantes (Eagle Lion, 1947)
Ghost Town Renegades (PRC, 1947)
Law of the Lash (PRC, 1947)
Pioneer Justice (PRC, 1947)
Stage to Mesa City (Eagle Lion, 1947)

Dead Man's Gold (SG, 1948)
Frontier Revenge (SG, 1948)
Mark of the Lash (SG, 1949)
Outlaw Country (SG, 1949)
Son of Bad Man (SG, 1949)
Son of Billy the Kid (SG, 1949)
Dalton's Women (Howco, 1950)
King of the Bullwhip (SG, 1950)
The Thundering Trail (SG, 1951)
Vanishing Outpost (SG, 1951)
Black Lash (Realart, 1952)
Frontier Phantom (Realart, 1952)

Rex Allen, in Hills of Oklahoma *(1950), with Trevor Bardette.*

Rex Allen

(The Arizona Cowboy)

Born: September 10, 1923, Willcox, Ariz.
Married: Bonnie Smith (1945);
   children: Rex, Curt, Mark, Bonita

AN "IDIOT IN a white hat" is the way Rex Allen today candidly recalls himself as a singing cowboy superstar of the movies.

Allen, now fifty-five and a successful music publisher, took over at the movie matinees when Roy Rogers and Gene Autry turned to television. Looking back on "those good old days," the silver-haired executive explained how he "got into the cowboy business" in the first place.

"I was pretty hot on radio doing a barn-dance program, and suddenly everything just fell into place. It was time for Roy Rogers and Gene Autry to leave movies and go into television. And it seemed what the country needed for the silver screen was another singing cowboy with a young, fresh face.

"So the studio [Republic] began looking for another idiot in a white hat. I went directly from the radio station to the movie set for *The Arizona Cowboy* (1950). And if you want to know what kind of a job I did as a non-trained actor, go see it sometime. It was awful."

Awful or not, the movie was a smash hit at the box office, and Allen ever after was known as the Arizona Cowboy. Coincidentally he hails from that state though today he lives in Los Angeles.

Rex and his wife Bonnie have four children. One of them, Rex Jr., is following in his dad's footsteps as a popular country and Western singer.

After his first film success, Rex Sr. went on to make thirty forgettable second features, like *The Old Overland Trail* (1953) and *The Phantom Stallion* (1954).

In the late fifties Rex followed Gene and Roy into TV, starring in seventy-eight segments of a series titled "Frontier Doctor" (CBS-TV).

"There's been a lot of talk about resuming production for additional B-grade Westerns," says Allen, "but I personally think that's a joke. It would cost too much to begin with—probably around $300,000 a picture by today's prices. We used to do a picture for about $60,000.

"Besides, who's going to star in B-Westerns today? Not me! Today, if I made it through one fight sequence, they'd have to take me to the hospital to revive me," said Allen, smiling.

Besides, publishing music, appearing at rodeos, making the occasional dog-food commercial and hosting a Walt Disney TV feature are far too lucrative to coax Allen back into the saddle again.

"You get paid a lot more for commercials and voice-over narrations," he says shrewdly. "And you don't have to feel idiotic wearing a white sombrero either."

Western Film Credits

The Arizona Cowboy (Rep., 1950)
Hills of Oklahoma (Rep., 1950)
Under Mexicali Stars (Rep., 1950)
Redwood Forest Trail (Rep., 1950)
Silver City Bonanza (Rep., 1951)
Thunder in God's Country (Rep., 1951)
Rodeo King and the Senorita (Rep., 1951)
Utah Wagon Train (Rep., 1951)
Old Oklahoma Plains (Rep., 1952)

The Last Musketeer (Rep., 1952)
Border Saddlemates (Rep., 1952)
Colorado Sundown (Rep., 1952)
South Pacific Trail (Rep., 1952)
Red River Shore (Rep., 1953)
Down Laredo Way (Rep., 1953)
Iron Mountain Trail (Rep., 1953)
Shadows of Tombstone (Rep., 1953)
Old Overland Trail (Rep., 1953)
Phantom Stallion (Rep., 1954)

Noah Beery, Jr., in The Texas Rangers *(1951).*

Noah Beery, Jr.

(Ol' Pidge to his friends)

Born: August 10, 1913, New York, N.Y.
Married: Maxine Jones (1940); divorced
   (1966); children: Maxine, Bucklind,
   Melissa; remarried: Lisa (1969)

AS A PERFORMER, Noah Beery of NBC-TV's "Rockford Files," who dropped "Jr." from his name some years back, is much like his famous movie-star uncle, Wallace Beery. He has the same sheepish "Aw shucks" smile, and even indoors he seems to be kicking at a nonexistent clod.

As a man, however, he is more like his father, the late Noah Beery, Sr., villain of villains in scores of motion pictures. Although an actor most of his life, Noah Jr. was never a big star, but he has become a top supporting star. His lifestyle is as unlike Hollywood's as a lifestyle can be.

When the San Fernando Valley became too urbanized for his taste twenty-three years ago, he moved his family some one hundred-odd miles away, to a ranch across the Mojave Desert and the Tehachapi range. The Clear Creek-B Ranch, two winding, bumpy miles from the highway, lies on what was long ago the main road from Bakersfield to Mojave. The house was then a gas station and motel; on rocks beside the road can still be seen, dimly, painted signs reading FLATS FIXED—25¢.

Noah Beery of necessity may have rented a place at Malibu Beach for the duration of "The Rockford Files" but the ranch is home. The walls of the entrance hall are covered with still photos of old films: Uncle Wally's, Noah Sr.'s, and Noah Jr.'s. On the floors throughout the house are Navajo rugs that Noah Sr. brought back from Arizona when he made the 1926 version of *Beau Geste,* and at the end of the hall is the saddle Uncle Wally rode in *Viva Villa!* In the living room are Noah's precious Charles Russell paintings and sculptures of the Old West, plus some bronze sculptures of his own, for the actor is also a sculptor whose works sell well in Western art galleries.

But in the high country Noah is a rancher. He gets into a battered jeep and drives off to feed the cows and calves. Some one hundred head of them come mooing when he shouts, "Whooo-ee!" He throws them bundles of hay he stores in the barn that was a dance hall when his homestead was a roadside way station.

Back in the environs of Hollywood, though, he is ever the competent, dependable actor. His "Rockford Files" colleague and TV "son" James

Garner says, "Ol' Pidge is a truly honest to goodness pro. He's so easy to work with, always prepared, always knows his lines." ("Pidge" was bestowed on Noah by Josie Cohan, sister of the immortal George M., not long after Noah's birth in New York, where his father was appearing on the stage.)

Noah never thought of anything except being an actor. "I was kinda born in the business, y' might say, and I couldn't have gotten outta it if I'd wanted to." And after almost a lifetime, he still wouldn't have it any other way. "No matter what anybody says, acting is a real fun game. Heck, even when it's lousy, it's fun!"

These sentiments apply, however, only to his professional life; his preoccupation with acting goes only as far as the soundstage door. His personal life remains completely separate, limited to family, "ranch friends," and the ranch itself. "I have many wonderful acquaintances in this business," says Noah, "but not being on the party circuit, I just see them all on the job." His daughter, Maxine, agrees. "Daddy loves show business, but he never got caught up in it. He simply prefers to count his cattle and watch over his sheep." His son, Bucklind, who is carrying the Beery acting tradition into the third generation, says, "We didn't ever hang around Hollywood much. We always lived on a ranch and had a lot of horses."

Noah Beery chose his lifestyle after seeing the old Hollywood first-hand. Or perhaps it is more correct to say that his father chose the lifestyle his son would follow.

When Pidge was a small boy, the family lived in Hollywood proper, in a big house at the head of Vine Street. Their friends were the other motion picture pioneers. "Old Hollywood was like one big happy family," says Noah. He went to school with Douglas Fairbanks, Jr., and Jesse Lasky, Jr., and Lon Chaney, Jr., at, of all places, the Hollywood School for Girls. And his father hired a man to take him places and see that no harm befell him.

Then, in the 1920s, Noah Sr. moved the family to the San Fernando Valley. "At first it was just a weekend place, but we liked it so well we moved there for good," says Noah. "Nobody from show business lived there then. It was all real country—with dirt roads and lotsa room."

Today, thinking back on life in old Hollywood, Noah says, "Heck, you just couldn't live there and believe all that stuff. You grow up and see all that, and you know there's gotta be something better. I'll take livin' in the country, on my ranch, *any* day!"

And live in the country he did through most of the years of his growing up. Childhood appearances in a few movies, like *The Mark of Zorro* (1920) and *Penrod and Sam* (1928), were more larks than anything else. But once he finished North Hollywood High School, Noah embarked upon an acting career.

At first he was cast in serials—cowboy, aviation, and jungle epics—

In an action scene from The Daltons Ride Again *(1945), with Lon Chaney, Jr., and Kent Taylor.*

many of which were made at Universal Studios, where "The Rockford Files" is shot. "I feel as if I'd been born here," Noah says. "It seemed as if they'd always make the aviation pictures, where you had to wear a leather coat and helmet, in the hot summer, and in the winter they'd make the jungle pictures, where you ran around in a breechcloth." In his earliest efforts he was the hero; it was not until *Tailspin Tommy* (1934) that he became the hero's friend, a role he found more to his liking. "You didn't have to be handsome and brave," he says, with his Uncle Wally's smile.

Many of the hundred-odd movies he has made are long—and best—forgotten: *Some Blondes Are Dangerous* (1937), *Bad Lands* (1939), *Flight at Midnight* (1939), *Calaboose* (1943), *The Cat Creeps* (1946). But some of the films in which he appeared are notable: *Of Mice and Men* (1939), *Sergeant York* (1941), *Red River* (1948), *Inherit the Wind* (1960). Of them all, *Red River* (starring John Wayne and Montgomery Clift) is his favorite. "I love the West," Noah emphasizes, "and working in *Red River* was like living it, like really being on that cattle drive. Heck, I could've stayed on that picture forever."

More recently he has appeared in two films: *Little Fauss and Big Halsy* (with Robert Redford, 1970) and *Walking Tall* (with Joe Don Baker, 1973).

Noah Beery, Jr., wants to clear up an old misunderstanding. He is the son of Noah Beery, Sr., (bottom left), not Wallace Beery, his uncle (top left).

For the past twenty-five years Noah has worked primarily in TV, as a guest star on many programs and as a regular in "Circus Boy," "Hondo," "Riverboat," and "Doc Elliot." Another actor played the role of Garner's father in "The Rockford Files" pilot film. "We thought of Noah Beery but he was doing 'Doc Elliot,'" says Meta Rosenberg, the program's executive producer. "By the time the series was sold he was available. We didn't choose him because of the physical resemblance to Jim Garner, although that is certainly there. We picked him because of his warmth, plus his unpretentiousness and the way he fits in. What he has most of all is warmth."

The warmth and unpretentiousness are as evident offscreen as on. Beery's relationship to the three grown children of his first marriage—twenty-five years to the daughter of the late cowboy superstar Buck Jones before their divorce in 1966—is close. Nine years ago he married Lisa, who has two teenage children who call him Pop. At the ranch, while Noah attends to the cows, horses, and mules, Lisa takes care of the sheep and goats, which troop after her when she calls them by name.

"There's a great rivalry between us," Noah says, recalling ancient Western feuds between cattlemen and sheepmen. But the only time any feeling becomes noticeable is when he lets his mules into the front yard to graze. Then Lisa will say, quietly but firmly, "Honey, you get your animals out of here before they eat my plants."

Every spring Noah goes on a weekend trek out of Santa Barbara with an exclusive group of mounted riders known as Rancheros Vistadores—socially prominent men, business tycoons, government officials, civic leaders, and a few actors of impeccable respectability. Most of them ride horses as blooded and impressive as themselves. But not Pidge. He rides a mule.

If he was given a chance to portray a superstar, say Wallace Beery, in a picture, would he accept the part?

Noah grins, wipes his nose in W.B. fashion, and says, "I'd love to do a portrayal of Uncle Wally. He in truth was an uncle, you know. Not my father, but an uncle. Yes, I would love to portray Wally, should such a role ever be offered to me."

How does he compare today's breed of cowboy star with himself?

"That's kind of a hard question for me to answer," says Noah, scratching his head. "I'm kind of both breed of cat myself, in lotsa ways, you know. Old breed and new. And I truly haven't studied the difference. I do know one thing, though. The old breed of cowboy star was a lot tougher and gutsier than today's star is. Course, most of the old ones was real cowboys and circus stars at one time too, and this all helped them as film stars.

"But today's cowboy star never has the chance or the rugged real-life experiences on the range the old stars had, so they naturally are softer when it comes to the he-man action stuff. I know for a fact I'm a lot softer today than I used to be, and can't take the bumps and spills I used to take at one time. I wasn't from a cowboy background either, but I roughed it enough on location sets with my folks to harden me up for all the minor roles I got in films. That's the best way I know of answering your question."

Who was his favorite Western star?

"Buck Jones, without question. My next best would be Duke Wayne. Had Buck not been killed saving people from that fire in Boston in 1942, he might've gone on to become one of the biggest Western stars Hollywood ever produced."

Western Film Credits

The Mark of Zorro (UA, 1920)

Heroes of the West (serial) (Univ., 1932)

Fighting with Kit Carson (serial) (Mas., 1933)

Five Bad Men (Sunset, 1933)

El Diablo Rides (Sunset, 1933)

Devil's Canyon (Sunset, 1933)

Rustler's Roundup (Univ., 1933)

The Trail Beyond (Mon., 1934)

Stormy (Univ., 1935)

The Mighty Treve (Univ., 1937)

Forbidden Valley (Univ., 1938)

Bad Lands (RKO, 1939)

The Light of Western Stars (Par., 1940)

The Carson City Kid (Rep., 1940)

Twenty-Mule Team (MGM, 1940)

Riders of Death Valley (serial) (Univ., 1941)

Dudes Are Pretty People (UA, 1942)

Overland Mail (serial) (Univ., 1942)

Calaboose (UA, 1943)

Prairie Chickens (UA, 1943)

Pardon My Gun (Col., 1943)

Frontier Badmen (Univ., 1943)

The Daltons Ride Again (Univ., 1945)

Under Western Skies (Univ., 1945)

Indian Agent (RKO, 1948)

Red River (UA, 1948)

The Doolins of Oklahoma (Col., 1949)

The Savage Horde (Rep., 1950)

Two Flags West (20th, 1950)

Davy Crockett, Indian Scout (UA, 1950)

The Cimarron Kid (UI, 1951)

The Last Outpost (Par., 1951)

The Texas Rangers (Col., 1951)

Wagons West (Mon., 1952)

The Story of Will Rogers (WB, 1952)

War Arrow (Univ., 1953)

Wings of the Hawk (Univ., 1953)

The Yellow Tomahawk (UA, 1954)

The Black Dakotas (Col., 1954)

White Feather (20th, 1955)

Jubal (Col., 1956)

The Fastest Gun Alive (MGM, 1956)

Decision at Sundown (Col., 1957)

Escort West (UA, 1959)

Guns of the Timberland (WB, 1960)

Seven Faces of Dr. Lao (MGM, 1964)

Incident at Phantom Hill (Univ., 1966)

Journey to Shiloh (Univ., 1968)

Heaven with a Gun (MGM, 1969)

The Cockeyed Cowboys of Calico County (Univ., 1970)

The Spikes Gang (UA, 1974)

Ben Johnson in Chisum *(1970).*

Ben Johnson

(From cowpoke to actor)

Born: October 8, 1922, Pawhuska, Okla.
Married: Carol Lynn (1940)

BEN JOHNSON HAS undoubtedly been in as many major Western films as big John Wayne since 1940, but always as a stuntman par excellence or a supporting actor, or both; never as a star of the film himself.

In *Fort Apache* he was Henry Fonda's double, and in *Horse Soldiers* he doubled for William Holden. He was a featured actor in *She Wore a Yellow Ribbon, Rio Lobo, Cheyenne Autumn,* and scores of other top Western films.

In 1972 his big moment finally arrived. He was nominated and won the Academy Award for Best Supporting Actor in the top box-office film, *The Last Picture Show.*

"Now I know how Duke Wayne felt after he made all them big pictures and finally won an Oscar for his role in *True Grit,* which in my own personal estimation was a put-down from the many good roles he'd already portrayed in films in years past. In my estimation th' award Duke won shoulda been his umpteenth Oscar instead of his first. But, that's Hollywood for ya. Ya never know exactly just who's gonna be watchin' ya act and when. And when they nominate ya for an Oscar and give it to ya, man—you're one surprised and flustered fella!"

Billionaire Howard Hughes ("and this here is a *true* story," says Johnson) coaxed seventeen-year-old cowpoke Ben Johnson to leave his father's ranch near Pawhuska, Oklahoma, in 1939 for an acting career in Hollywood and started him off on that career.

Ben was working for $1 a day on his father's ranch when Hughes visited his place searching for horses for a film he was producing, *The Outlaw.* The movie starred Jack Buetel and Jane Russell; Jack was Billy the Kid and Jane his love interest.

After Hughes had purchased several good mounts from Ben's father, he convinced the elder Johnson that his son should go along for the duration of the shooting of the film as top wrangler.

Ben recalls his first week's salary from Hughes ($175.00) and says, "With pay like that, they couldn't have run me off with a stick!"

"When th' train pulled into th' station in Hollywood," continued Ben, "I jumped down and started puttin' on a pretty good show, feelin' a lot more important because of th' good money they was payin' me than an ol' Oklahoma cowpoke ever had th' right to.

"I was yellin' instructions ta everyone, tellin' them what ta do with th' hosses. Th' feller there ta pick them up had brought his daughter Carol along with him. She saw me carryin' on like I was Hughes himself er somethin' and asked her daddy—loud enough so I would be sure and hear her—'Who does that big, lanky *jerk* think *he* is?'

"Well, believe this or not, but that's th' gal I married, and we've been together ever since."

Ben served under Hughes, who owned his own studio at the time, for three years, eventually working his way from wrangler to stuntman and extra on the screen.

Ben's big break finally came ten years after he came to Hollywood. He was Henry Fonda's double in *Fort Apache* (1948). He performed all the dangerous stunts called for in the role played by Fonda, luckily never once getting badly injured. An accident happened on the set when an old wagon went out of control behind a team of runaway horses and flipped over and trapped several men beneath it. Johnson sped to the scene on horseback and had pulled the last man from danger before help arrived. Within twenty-four hours John Ford rewarded his heroic act with a $5,000-a-week acting contract.

"I know danged well ol' Duke Wayne put John Ford up to givin' me that big contract," insists Ben, "because we got ta be good friends on th' set. I also got ta be a good friend of George O'Brien, one real fine actor. It's a shame he had ta stay in th' navy so long an' gave up his actin' career ta be an officer. He was one fine gent, and taught me plenty about actin'."

Asked if John Wayne also taught him a lot about acting, Ben smiled and said, "He taught me one helluva lot, but not right then. He was still comin' up th' ladder from his success in *Stagecoach* when *Fort Apache* was made. But later on, in all of th' films I was in with Duke, he showed me everything and taught me plenty. I doubt I'd ever won that Oscar if it hadn't been for Duke Wayne, John Ford, George O'Brien, and a lotta others who liked me."

For the next twenty years Ben acted in numerous films, mostly Westerns. Many people knew his face, but few knew his name.

A supporting role in Sam Peckinpah's *The Wild Bunch* in the late 1960s led to the role of Sam the Lion in Peter Bogdanovich's *The Last Picture Show* for which Ben won his Oscar.

But the former Oklahoma cowboy remains a cowboy at heart. He owns a 5,000-acre spread just outside Pawhuska, near the ranch his father used to own, to which he escapes from West Coast smog whenever he isn't making a picture. Here he raises horses, fishes, hunts, and plain old relaxes.

"Know what?" Ben said. "I know sure's hell that one mornin' I'm gonna wake up and they're gonna say 'Ben *who*?' and it'll all be over. Th' offers will stop comin' in ta me and so will all that there nice money.

As Sheriff "Mean John" Simpson in Kid Blue *(1973).*

"That's why I've got other interests, like my ranch and all in Oklahoma. That way I don't hafta hang around Hollywood all th' time and wonder where my next part is comin' from. I've seen too many scared, lonely people doin' that and it ain't for me.

"Hell, we're all scared, and we all get that lonely feelin' when we find out that we're not wanted. And that's when I get outta town and get busy on my ranch."

Ben and wife Carol have a modestly small home on an acre of land in California's San Fernando Valley. On the property is a small corral, a swimming pool, a few orange trees, and a beautiful view of the mountains.

"Our Hollywood home is kinda like a camp for th' wife and me when I'm here makin' pictures," said Ben. "Most of th' time we're in Oklahoma, our real home, on my ranch."

Asked about sex and profanity in films today, Ben says, "Hell, I'm old-fashioned. I can understand cussin' now and then, but ta have a guy in a film beller out them dirty words for all th' world ta hear—it ain't right. I personally think whoever spoke th' words or put them in th' script is pretty weak.

"Mind you, I'm no angel, by far. But I do most of my cussin' *off* th' screen, not on. I think movies should be made for *whole* families ta enjoy, not just th' older members of th' family. I think we've kinda lost respect for ourselves and we've gotta get ta winnin' it back."

What does he think about violence in movies and TV?

"Shoot, I think violence is a part of our history, a part of all of us, if you want my personal opinion. Our nation, especially th' West, was founded by violent men and not Milquetoasts behind desks or weak sisters for mothers. Women in them old days—they was mean and rough-talkin' old gals. Movies used ta show them that way, but not any more. Today, old pioneer gals comin' West are pruned and prissied up ta look like I don't know what as compared ta th' real old gals. Same for the men. Today, except for Duke Wayne, they're all dudes, or drugstore cowboys, not for real at all."

What kind of role would he like to star in?

"Y'know what? I wouldn't mind a' tall if they was ta star me in a series role as th' wagonmaster of a wagon train. Sort of like th' role Ward Bond played in th' 'Wagon Train' series on TV—Major Seth Adams. I kinda dig that type of role. I could contribute a lot to th' character and head a series that would keep a steady paycheck comin' in every week. Meanwhile, I'll go on makin' pictures and, who can tell, maybe even win myself another Oscar.

"I may be considered square or conceited and the like for carryin' on like this, but that's okay with me. I got broad enough shoulders to take it, and then some. . . ."

Does he feel "left out" of Howard Hughes' final will?

"Oh, hell no. I never asked for nothin' from Mr. Hughes, an' therefore don't expect nothin'. Mr. Hughes always treated me okay, so I got no complaints. He was a fine man, despite all th' controversy about him."

Western Film Credits

The Outlaw (RKO, 1943)
Red River (UA, 1948)
Three Godfathers (MGM, 1948)
She Wore a Yellow Ribbon (RKO, 1949)
Wagonmaster (RKO, 1950)
Rio Grande (Rep., 1950)
Fort Defiance (UA, 1951)
Wild Stallion (Mon., 1952)
Shane (Par., 1953)
Hondo (WB, 1953)
Rebel in Town (UA, 1956)
The Tin Star (Par., 1957)
War Drums (UA, 1957)
Slim Carter (Univ, 1957)
Fort Bowie (UA, 1958)
Warlock (20th, 1959)
Ten Who Dared (BV, 1960)
One-Eyed Jacks (Par., 1961)
How the West Was Won (MGM, 1962)

Ride the High Country (MGM, 1962)
Cheyenne Autumn (WB, 1964)
Major Dundee (Col., 1965)
The Rare Breed (Univ., 1965)
El Dorado (Par., 1967)
The War Wagon (Univ., 1967)
Hang 'Em High (UA, 1968)
Will Penny (Par., 1968)
The Wild Bunch (WB, 1969)
The Undefeated (20th, 1969)
Chisum (WB, 1970)
Rio Lobo (NGP, 1970)
Junior Bonner (Cinerama, 1972)
The Train Robbers (WB, 1973)
Kid Blue (20th, 1973)
Bite the Bullet (Col., 1975)
Rooster Cogburn (Univ., 1975)
The Shootist (Par., 1976)

PART TWO

New Breed of Cowboy TV-Movie Star, 1950-79

Enter the New Breed

AS THE FORTIES drew to a close, the B-Western well found itself running dry. Too many external forces were threatening the continuance of the little action gems that many of today's Americans grew up with. Costs over the years had risen spectacularly. In the thirties, for example, a Western film could be made for well under the $50,000 mark, and this included big-name stars and slam-bang action. In the forties the cost of an identical film had doubled, and the wages paid actors for the same kind of oldtime action left studios feeling cheated. To this add the fact that World War II had begun and many of B-Westerns' young stars were volunteering for or being drafted into the armed forces. New faces were sorely needed, but studios were forced to make do with the older faces until the end of the war.

In addition, television, the bugaboo to virtually every motion picture studio, was then beginning to make itself known. Hollywood continued to play down the new menace harassing its industry, but when the war ended its efforts were in vain. TV rose majestically to take its rightful place in filmdom history, and making Westerns was an integral part of its plans.

Gene Autry and William Boyd bought up the rights to all of their films and sold them to TV. The wise move made both men millionaires—Boyd from reruns of his Hopalong Cassidy series, and Autry from his own films plus his own television production company that released films through Columbia Studios.

A brand new era of B-Westerns was begun on television. And though production costs were high, they were not nearly so high as the costs assessed film companies to make B-Westerns with old stars trying to look like young heroes for the youth of America.

As the bugaboo "sound" in the early thirties dethroned stars like Tom Mix, Art Acord, Bill Cody, etc., so TV became the enemy in the late forties and toppled such big-name cowboy movie stars as Johnny Mack Brown, Bob Steele, Tim McCoy, Ken Maynard, Charles Starrett, etc., from filmdom.

The television Western stars who eventually replaced the old Western movie stars, except, of course, John Wayne, are found in this section. They are still active and very popular.

James Arness as Marshal Matt Dillon in "Gunsmoke" TV series.

James Arness

(Alias Matt Dillon)

Born: October 22, 1921, near Minneapolis,
   Minn.
Married

"GUNSMOKE" BEGAN IN the fall of 1955 as a thirty-minute Western series. It became an hour program in 1962, because of its widespread popularity, and continued until 1975, when it went off the air after nineteen successive years. No other television series can boast such success.

James Arness, who portrayed Matt Dillon, U.S. marshal, was cast as lead in the series for two reasons: his good friend John Wayne had turned it down—"Hell, give th' role t' Jim, 'cause I don't wanna be tied down t' no damned TV series!"—and Jim himself was deserving of the role. By 1959 Jim had become a polished actor with tremendous potential. He had starred in way-out horror thrillers like *The Thing* (1951) and *Them!* (1954) and with Wayne in a series of pictures, some Westerns and some CIA-type adventures. Thanks to the Duke he had learned the fundamentals of what it takes to become a good actor. His performance with Wayne in *Big Jim McLain* (1952), plus Duke's persuasion of certain CBS-TV producers, got Jim his big chance in the role of Matt Dillon in "Gunsmoke."

"Ironically, I wasn't too pleased with the deal at the time," confessed Jim in 1974, "even though my good buddy Duke Wayne went to bat for me. I thought starring in a Western series on TV would take up too much of my time and ruin my chances for a career in motion pictures. So I took the role of Matt Dillon in 'Gunsmoke' with a great many misgivings. However, once I got into the swing of things and learned what a great supporting cast I had in Dennis Weaver, Milburn Stone, Ken Curtis, and Glenn Strange, I knew I had it made. And I was correct too. We lasted nineteen years. We're ending 'Gunsmoke' now and going on to other outlets in television and movies. I'll continue to star in Westerns, if possible, because I'm identified with them now and have a large following of fans. I doubt I would retain such a good following of fans, however, if I switched to private-eye series, or the like. (He's "Zeb Macahan" now in the popular ABC-TV series "How the West Was Won.")

"I don't know about the rest of the cast. I imagine Milburn will retire and Ken will shrug off his Festus character and go into something else. I've seen Amanda [Amanda Blake, who played Kitty for thirteen of the

With Buck Taylor, Milburn Stone, and Ken Curtis in "Gunsmoke."

With Amanda Blake and Milburn Stone in "Gunsmoke."

With Patti Cohoon and Clay O'Brien in a segment of "Gunsmoke."

nineteen years of 'Gunsmoke'] in several movies made for TV and she's pretty good as an actress. She'll go a long way, I'm sure, and I wish her every success.

"What made 'Gunsmoke' such a long-lasting success? I think I can sum it up in one word: dedication. Each of us that retained tenure of length on 'Gunsmoke' was dedicated to doing the best job he could as a Western star. Dennis pulled away from us first and put Chester to rest; Burt Reynolds also pulled away, and we had to hire another blacksmith. But the rest of us remained dedicated to doing our thing, as Western stars, and that is why we lasted so long.

"I attribute this antiviolence thing as the reason our show had to end; otherwise, we might've lasted another two or three seasons. But the ban imposed on violence, even when it was essential to our script, is what ruined things. If I can't portray Matt Dillon like millions of fans expect me to, why portray him? What good is old Matt if he can't fire his six-gun? What good is it to portray the taming of a frontier town without using guns? See what I mean? It's plain ridiculous. And it's better to quit while you're ahead than destroy all that you've tried to build in characters over nineteen years."

How does Jim Arness see Westerns today as compared with the B-Western oaters of past years?

"Well, it kinda depends on what you mean by B-Westerns. If you mean the prewar kind like Tom Mix, Buck Jones, Ken Maynard, Hoot Gibson, Tim McCoy, and so on, used to make—there's no comparison to them. They were done on location at minimum expense, whereas ours are done on soundstages and outdoors at great expense. But if you mean the comparison of ours today with the *post*war kind, which starred Johnny Mack Brown, Charles Starrett, Bob Steele, Gene Autry, Roy Rogers, and so on, I'd rate them about equal. Except for the overhead, of course, and ours is twice as much today as theirs was in postwar days.

"I guess I'm kinda like my good friend Duke Wayne. I respect *all* Western filmmaking and TV series, yesterday and today, because it's an art that's darned hard to duplicate today. And it's a good training ground, sort of, for about every dramatic star on TV shows today."

Born on a farm near Minneapolis as James Aurness, Jim and his younger brother Peter (Peter Graves of the now defunct "Mission Impossible") grew up together and loved the outdoors. When not attending school, they enjoyed fishing, hunting, swimming, and taking long hikes through the woods that surrounded their father's farm.

In high school Jim excelled at baseball and football, and Peter was an outstanding swimmer. Both boys graduated from high school as A-students. Peter went on to college and Jim joined the army just after World War II broke out.

Jim was badly wounded in the left leg at Anzio Beach in 1943, and spent long pain-filled months recuperating and learning to walk again.

New-breed star.

He was awarded the Purple Heart, plus a few other decorations modesty prevents his mentioning. "I call my old PH the Medal for Stupidity," says Jim, "because I forgot to duck when I was supposed to."

During sequence filming of "Gunsmoke, when Jim was tired his left leg would bother him and he would limp visibly. But he tried not to let his bad leg interrupt the shooting schedule. He even did his own stunting when he felt up to it.

Jim has a yacht and loves to sail when he has the time. Like Buddy Ebsen, another good friend, Jim is an experienced seaman.

Recently remarried, Jim refuses to mention his family since the tragic death of his daughter.

Western Film-TV Credits

Wagonmaster (RKO, 1950)
Wyoming Mail (Univ., 1950)
Cavalry Scout (Mon., 1951)
Hellgate (Lip., 1952)
Horizons West (Univ., 1952)
Lone Hand (Univ., 1953)
Hondo (WB, 1953)
Many Rivers to Cross (MGM, 1955)

The First Traveling Saleslady (RKO, 1956)
Gun the Man Down (UA, 1956)

"Gunsmoke" (CBS-TV, 1955-1975)
The Macahans (TV pilot, 1976)
"The Macahans"/"How the West Was Won" (series) (ABC-TV, 1977-79)

Dennis Weaver as Marshal Sam McCloud.

Dennis Weaver

(Chester changes to McCloud)

Born: June 4, 1924, Joplin, Mo.
Married: Geraldine Stowell (1945);
 children: Rick, Robby, Rusty

NO FAITHFUL FAN of "Gunsmoke" will ever forget the stiff-legged character Chester Goode, who for nine years dogged his employer with "Mr. Dillon! You know what, Mr. Dillon?" But, alas, he grew tired of the role of the cripple and decided to show his histrionic versatility by striking out on his own.

Dennis Weaver is now a superstar. He appeared regularly for seven seasons as Marshal Sam McCloud in the title role of the now canceled NBC-TV series. He frequently has a starring role in ABC-TV's "Movie of the Week," and has made numerous other appearances as well.

For an actor of Dennis' talents, that's not really so surprising, except for one fact—he is one of the few actors ever to leave a second-banana series berth and wind up as a constantly-in-demand leading man. Dennis, admittedly, had the courage of his wife Gerry's convictions. She was convinced that as an actor he had grown as much as he could after nine years of playing Chester on "Gunsmoke."

He had earned an Emmy Award as Marshal Dillon's gimpy-legged sidekick. He had given the character of Chester a dimension way beyond the conception of its creators. In short, the role of Chester had become a classic. Additionally, Dennis had a rare thing going for him, or for any actor—financial security. He sought new fields and found them. One was the lead in his own series, "Kentucky Jones," for NBC-TV (1964-65), playing a veterinarian who adopts a Chinese orphan.

Soon after "Kentucky Jones" bombed out, Dennis began reading movie scripts submitted by producers who were very much aware of his varied talents as an actor. Dennis was fascinated with a script which called for him to play a heavy in a Western entitled *Duel at Diablo.* The picture was a fast-moving super-Western with classical overtones and a suspense story, scripted by Marvin H. Alpert from his novel *Apache Uprising.*

For the first time in his screen career, Dennis found himself wearing a black hat (a role in complete contrast to the drawling, law-abiding Chester he played on "Gunsmoke") and proved his versatility as an actor.

Another facet of Dennis' talent was tapped in 1966 by 20th Century-Fox Pictures and Jerry Lewis when he was chosen to play an astronaut circa 1994 who lands on the moon in the Lewis comedy *Way . . . Way Out*. Both Jerry and producer Malcolm Stuart remembered the masterful humor Dennis injected into the role of Chester, which was the key to the success and popularity of the unique Western character.

In talking about Chester and his years in the successful "Gunsmoke" series, Dennis is honest and straightforward in his analysis of his career.

"I wanted to grow as an actor, to create, to expand," he says, "and quitting 'Gunsmoke' was the biggest decision I had to make in my life. In addition, I just couldn't see fit to make only one solitary character my entire life's work as an actor. Oh, from the standpoint of money, it couldn't be beat. Chester remuneration grew beyond my expectations, in fact is still coming in every month from residuals. But money is a drag if you allow it to become an end instead of a means. So I discussed how I felt with Gerry, and we decided I'd have to make a clean break with Chester and 'Gunsmoke' if I was ever going to fully accomplish what I wanted as an actor."

The industry was not entirely unaware of the scope of Dennis' talents, for in 1960 he appeared on a televised Emmy Awards show and stepped out of his Chester character to give an audience-electrifying performance by seriously rendering a parody of "Hamlet." According to Academy executives, "It was like Barrymore reading from the telephone book."

Dennis returned to CBS for the 1967-69 seasons as the star of a new TV series, "Gentle Ben," in which he played the role of a game warden and the father of a seven-year-old boy (Clint Howard) who had a 700-pound bear as a pet.

When "Gentle Ben" went off the air after two seasons, Dennis left for Europe (Italy and Spain) to costar with James Garner in the Western *A Man Called Sledge* (1971), produced by Dino DeLaurentiis for Columbia Pictures release. Following the completion of the film, Dennis did several guest appearances on popular TV shows of that time.

He did a cameo in *The Great Man's Whiskers*, a Universal NBC-TV world-premiere movie, in which he realized an actor's dream—that of portraying one of America's greatest presidents, Lincoln. He then starred in another world-premiere movie, *McCloud*, from which his series was a spinoff.

Dennis feels he came full circle with McCloud and found the ideal character to portray. He in fact goes so far as to make this personal analysis of Sam McCloud:

"I had a real deep feeling for old Sam. He was a rural character in a complex metropolitan situation and, therefore, a classic underdog. The fish is out of water, so to speak. In this setting something interesting

158

As Chester on "Gunsmoke."

happened to him week after week. He was also simplistic in a way—but tough. Plenty tough. He had a bite and a dry sense of humor and he always saw things through fresh eyes because—he cared. Yes, I had an affinity for old Sam. He's a character I really lived with."

A work-a-holic, Weaver wasted no time bemoaning the cancellation of "McCloud," after seven successful years. "Although it's interesting to note the show was the sixth most popular in the country the week it was cancelled," he recalls wonderingly. Dennis has just completed one of the busiest periods of his professional career totaling an incredible twenty-three hours of programming over all three major television networks during the 1978-79 season.

Starring in a very different kind of love story, *Intimate Strangers*, a two-hour movie for ABC-TV, Dennis gave an intensely moving portrayal of a man whose frustrations lead to violent rages against those he loves most. The film was one of the network's highest rated movies-for-TV. In quick succession, he starred in a two-hour special, "Police Story—The Price Is Wrong"; "Centennial—The Longhorns," a two-hour portion of the twenty-five hour adaptation of James Michener's bestseller; and *Ishi—The Last of His Tribe*, a three-hour movie about the last North American "wild" Indian—all for NBC-TV. He also starred in ABC-TV's six-hour mini-series "Pearl" and *The Islander*, a two-hour movie for CBS-TV, both of which were filmed entirely on location in Hawaii. In addition he was a guest on "A Country Christmas," a CBS-TV special. His most recent project was *Get Patty Hearst*, a three-hour movie for ABC-TV, in which he portrayed Charles Bates, head of the San Francisco FBI bureau, in charge of the case.

One would think that this would be more than enough to satisfy the creative need in almost anyone—but not so for Dennis Weaver. Also on the Weaver drawing board is a two-hour movie special, *Tonk*, which he has created and written himself and in which he will star.

He has concluded an agreement with Universal Television, his own Gerry Productions, and ABC-TV to star in a new series debuting in the fall of 1979. Titled "Stone," the series will premiere with a special two-hour episode and will be followed thereafter with one-hour episodes. The initial show has been completed and production is in progress on the first four hour-long segments.

He has done several "Movie of the Week" films for ABC-TV. He received great acclaim for his role of a returned marine veteran, who had been listed as missing in action, in *The Forgotten Man*. *Duel* was so well received that Universal Pictures added some scenes and released it as a theatrical feature in the European market. Other pictures Dennis has starred in for ABC-TV are *The Rolling Man* and *Female Artillery*.

Dennis Weaver, born with that name, was a top-flight athlete during his high school and college days and divided his time almost equally between dramatic studies and sports. His favorite movie stars were Ken

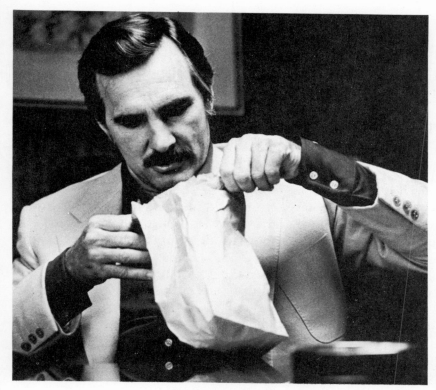

Lunch comes out of a brown paper bag. It's vegetarian and he brought it along from home to his Los Angeles office when he was president of the Screen Actors Guild.

In Female Artillery *(1972). Ida Lupino is lower left.*

161

Maynard and Buck Jones. "They both were rugged, individualistic performers, and I liked that," says Dennis.

While attending schools in Joplin, Dennis set many records in football and in track and field; some remain unbroken to this day. He was hailed as one of the Midwest's top-notch athletes.

Dennis spent a year at Joplin Junior College before interrupting his education to join the U.S. Naval Reserve. Discharged as an ensign after twenty-seven months in the Navy Air Force, during which time he set a speed and agility test record as a member of the navy's track and field team, Dennis resumed his education by enrolling at the University of Oklahoma. It was the first time in seven years the university had a man who could qualify for the decathlon, and Dennis led his squad to national championships and to first-place honors in all competition with other midwestern universities.

In 1948 the young athlete represented the university at the New Jersey tryouts for the Olympic games, and of thirty-six entrants placed sixth in the nation.

In addition to his many athletic endeavors and scholastic pursuits at Oklahoma, Dennis somehow managed to participate in many of the school's dramatic presentations. And this interest soon won him the title of the university's Most Versatile Man.

Versatility seems to be the key word in Dennis' private and professional life. He loves the theater and often appears in various roles whenever he can find the time from his TV production schedule.

Dennis, like many top-flight Hollywood stars—Marlon Brando, Paul Newman, Joanne Woodward—was accepted into New York's famous Actors' Studio soon after his graduation from the University of Oklahoma. In the spring of 1951 he made his Broadway debut and then toured nationally with Shirley Booth and Sidney Blackmer in William Inge's prize-winning *Come Back, Little Sheba*. He also played Stanley Kowalski (the role that shot Brando to stardom) in the Circle Theatre production of *A Streetcar Named Desire*, with Shelley Winters, at the Circle Theatre in Hollywood.

It was while he was at the Actors' Studio that he first met Miss Winters, who praised him so highly to her studio, Universal-International, that he was signed to a contract by the company.

However, the few years he spent at Universal were unhappy ones for Dennis. The studio was assigning its best roles to actors like Rock Hudson, Tony Curtis, and Jeff Chandler, and there weren't enough to go around. Dennis was relegated to small roles in almost every Western the company produced—and there were a lot of them. He finally refused to be typed as a strictly Western actor and secured his release from the contract.

During 1954-55 he appeared in four major films: *Dragnet*, *The Bridges at Toko-Ri*, *Ten Wanted Men*, and *Seven Angry Men*. He was then offered the part of Chester in the pilot film for the TV series "Gunsmoke," and the rest is history.

Meanwhile, Dennis organized the Dennis Weaver Actors' Workshop, which he personally directed for several years and which ranked with schools and classes maintained by Anthony Quinn, Jeffrey Hayden, and Richard Boone. The workshop was in fact the *only* Hollywood actors' school that presented plays to the public. His workshop production of *Quadrivium* at the Hollywood Repertory Theatre ran one entire summer and was forced to close only because various members of the cast had other commitments to fulfill.

Dennis also coproduced the workshop's revival of the play *Machinal*, which was presented at the Center Theatre, and which, incidentally, originally brought Clark Gable to Hollywood. It played to capacity audiences for eight weeks.

As an actor, Dennis gained acclaim for his starring role in a "Playhouse 90" presentation, "Dungeon." In fact, public reaction was so laudatory the show was rerun a second time the same season. Dennis also surprised his "Gunsmoke" fans with a brilliant dramatic performance in "Burst of Fire" on the "Climax" show. Orson Welles knew his reputation as a fine actor so well he hired him for an important role in the film *Touch of Evil* without ever having met or interviewed Dennis.

By nature, Dennis is not one to stay inactive long. He and wife Gerry devote much of their time to community activities and to charitable groups and organizations in their community of Calabasas, California. They were named Family of the Year by the citizenry there because of their "outstanding moral, social, and civic leadership."

Dennis married the former Geraldine Stowell, whom he met while in college, on October 20, 1945. They have three sons: Richard Dennis (Rick), Rob, and Rustin. Home is a beautiful and spacious abode that Dennis partly built himself in the San Fernando Valley area.

Yes, Dennis has come a long way since Chester.

Western Film-TV Credits

The Raiders (UI, 1952)
The Lawless Breed (UI, 1952)
Horizons West (UI, 1952)
The Redhead from Wyoming (UI, 1952)
Law and Order (UI, 1953)
Column South (UI, 1953)
The Man from the Alamo (UI, 1953)
The Nebraskan (Col., 1953)
War Arrow (UI, 1953)
Seven Angry Men (AA, 1955)
Chief Crazy Horse (Univ., 1955)
Ten Wanted Men (Col., 1955)

Duel at Diablo (UA, 1966)
A Man Called Sledge (Col., 1971)

"Gunsmoke" (CBS-TV, 1955-63)
McCloud (pilot) (NBC-TV, 1970)
"McCloud" (series) (NBC-TV, 1971-78)
Female Artillery (TV film) (ABC-TV, 1972)
Centennial (segment) (NBC-TV, 1978-79)
Ishi—The Last of His Tribe (NBC-TV, 1978)

Richard Boone, in one of his favorite poses as the crusty old curmudgeon "Hec Ramsey."

Richard Boone
(Paladin-Ramsey's looking for a saddle)

Born: June 18, 1916, Los Angeles, Calif.
Married: Claire McAloon (1951); child: Peter

FIFTEEN YEARS AGO, after one spectacular television success and one ambitious failure, Richard Boone sailed away to Hawaii on a boat full of money. Far from the bustle and smog of Hollywood, Boone fished and sailed and became a partner in a saloon on the Kona Coast, debated about running for governor of Hawaii, watched his son Peter grow into manhood, showered much affection on his lovely wife Claire, and occasionally played some juicy part in a film that took his fancy.

He already had the honor of being the first actor to become a major star through the medium of television, and later, along with James Arness, led the new breed of cowboy star into action on virtually every prime-time TV show in America.

Now, fifteen years later, at a mellowing sixty-two, after another ambitious failure of a TV Western ("Hec Ramsey"), Boone is again in Hawaii to hibernate, lick his wounds, and lament the causes of his recent failure.

"I swore and be damned that when I hung up my Paladin rig and went to Hawaii I'd never—ever—return to the strenuous life of being on a TV series Western again. Yet, I mellowed, and when my good friend Jack Webb offered me the shot of Hec Ramsey, I grabbed it. It should, by all signs, have been a booming success—except for one factor: violence. To me violence played an integral part in taming the West and I wanted violence in scripts where it was called for. But we ran afoul of antiviolent Milquetoasts who put so many damned restraints on what we could and could not include in scripts I couldn't live with it and do a good job and told them so in no uncertain language. Jack sided with me too, but even though he produced the show there were powers higher than he—advertisers—and they won in the end.

"The scripts we'd laboriously planned ahead for old Hec meant nothing with the new restraints and cuttings to them, and so our series died a quick death, befitting that of a typical Western shootout scene. Oh, we've got thousands of letters from loyal fans who loved old Hec and what I was trying to build into him, and who bitterly complained about our show being canceled. But how the hell do you sit down and patiently try to write each fan a letter explaining what truly happened? It's impossible.

"I've since talked to my good buddy Jim Arness and learned his longest-running series on TV met the same inevitable fate mine did. Big-money advertisers would simply not sponsor any or all segments of our shows with violence in them. In other words, you'd have both Hec and Matt Dillon trying to be Western-type Columbos talking their way in and out of battles but never drawing a gun. I dunno. So help me, sometimes I think the whole country's going effeminate—conned into it by antiviolence Milquetoasts, be they viewers, producers, or advertisers!"

Boone and Jack Webb met and became close friends in 1950, when they were doing the marine epic *The Halls of Montezuma*, which starred Richard Widmark and the late Jeffrey Hunter, among others. Dick's performance was of such quality Twentieth Century-Fox signed him to a long-term contract which later led to his role as Paladin in "Have Gun, Will Travel."

"I learned one very definite thing when I left the Paladin role," Boone says, "that Americans don't easily forget the image one of their favorite actors on the tube leaves with them. No matter what I tried to do or where I went, I was always Paladin to people, here and abroad, and I couldn't shake it.

"I set up my own repertory company and called it 'The Richard Boone Show,' but it didn't work out. In fact, that idea and the latest Hec Ramsey deals are about the only two that haven't panned out right for me. It's too bad. I had a lot of talented actors and actresses in my company and latest series, real talent that might have eventually gotten somewhere had the shows been successful. But, well, that's show biz . . . to be corny."

The project that officially brought Dick Boone back from his earlier triumph, and his first Hawaii hibernation, was a ninety-minute made-for-TV movie, *In Broad Daylight*. Supporting Dick were John Marley, Stella Stevens, and Suzanne Pleshette. The script was by Harry Cohen, and the director was the talented young Englishman Robert Day, who has since become one of the best directors in Tinseltown. The movie was a big success and garnered good ratings. It paved the way for Jack Webb to offer Dick the role of Hec Ramsey.

"Old Jack didn't know it then," Dick recalls in a raspy, chuckling manner, "but I'd heard about the new show he'd been planning and that he wanted me to star in it. So when he offered me the role of Hec Ramsey, I grabbed it so fast it surprised him. Afterward I told him the truth and we had a good laugh, and he called me a few choice friendly names I can't repeat for print."

But Dick Boone isn't always crusty, salty-tongued, and pranksterish. He displays touching tenderness at all times toward Claire, his wife of twenty-seven years, and son Peter, a music major graduate from Stanford University—the same institution from which Dick himself was expelled for having offended Mrs. Herbert Hoover with a student prank (he had deposited a catsup-smeared dummy in the street in front of his dormitory, just as the ex-president's wife drove by in her car).

When in the States Dick makes his permanent home in St. Augustine, Florida, so he can teach acting the way *he* thinks it should be taught, minus antiviolence pressures. And his students, at nearby Flagler College, revere him. He also is revered by numerous fellow actors in Hollywood, who inevitably compare him with another noted curmudgeon, George C. Scott. One such admirer is Harry Morgan, who portrayed the barber-doctor on "Hec Ramsey" and was Jack Webb's partner in "Dragnet," 1969-70. "Dick," says Harry, "like George Scott, has a spongelike brain for acting. His instincts and techniques are perfect. He retains everything, then squeezes his knowledge onto students and friends alike. Only Dick and George, among all American actors today, can dominate the screen with such power. Dick can do it, morning after morning, no matter how enormous has been his night before, imbibing and carousing."

Dick Boone's knowledge is encyclopedic about music—country and western, classical, jazz, rock—as well as art, ballet, politics, and anthropology.

About his early years Dick says, "When Mrs. Hoover got me booted out of Stanford, I said to hell with it and went to work as a roughneck in the oil fields near Long Beach. Then I took my oil-field money and settled down in Carmel, up the coast, to study art and to paint for a couple of years. This got me involved in scene design for summer theater, which in turn got me involved in acting.

"Then along came Pearl Harbor and the war. I joined the navy and served as an aerial gunner aboard SBDs and Avengers, on three different carriers, until four years later when the war ended. I practiced my writing during free time on the carriers and did several articles which were published in magazines. This put the zip in my ego and my desire to live out the war and become a writer, an artist, or an actor—or, maybe, all three.

"After I was honorably discharged from the navy, I put in for my GI benefits and studied drama at the Neighborhood Playhouse in New York. Then before I came to Hollywood I did three plays on Broadway. One of them was *Macbeth* which starred Michael Redgrave. And, I got myself fired. Reason: I didn't like Redgrave very much. I guess that alone contributed to my getting booted out."

Concerning his middle career years, Dick says, "I made all the to-hell-with-you money I'll ever need out of 'Have Gun, Will Travel,' on the tube. The role of Paladin was great and suited me fine. The series is still being rerun in various parts of the world and in this country and I still receive regular royalty checks. I moved to Hawaii with my family and stayed there until Peter was grown and in college. The rest is history."

Dick Boone needs a saddle to sit in again, in a series run *his* way and free from the pressures of anti-violence mongers. If John Wayne had to

167

wait until he was 62 to win an Oscar for his Rooster Cogburn in *True Grit,*
Dick Boone's opportunity may still be ahead.

Western Film-TV Credits

Way of a Gaucho (20th, 1952)
Return of the Texan (20th, 1952)
City of Badmen (20th, 1953)
The Siege at Red River (20th, 1954)
The Raid (20th, 1954)
Ten Wanted Men (Col., 1955)
Robbers' Roost (UA, 1955)
Star in the Dust (Univ., 1956)
The Tall T (Col., 1957)
The Alamo (UA, 1960)
A Thunder of Drums (MGM, 1961)

Rio Conchos (20th, 1964)
Hombre (20th, 1967)
Madron (Four Star-Excelsior, 1970)
Big Jake (NGP, 1971)
Against a Crooked Sky (Doty-Dayton, 1975)
The Shootist (Par., 1976)

"Have Gun, Will Travel" (NBC-TV, 1956-63)
"Hec Ramsey" (NBC-TV, 1972-74)

Lorne Greene, as Ben Cartright in "Bonanza."

Lorne Greene

(A better Ben Cartright than a Griff)

Born: February 12, 1915, Ottawa, Ont.,
  Canada
Married: Nancy Deale (1961); child: Gillian

AFTER SPENDING FOURTEEN years as Ben Cartright on the popular
TV series "Bonanza," which made Lorne Greene and his fellow actors—
Michael Landon, Dan Blocker and Pernell Roberts—famous here and in
eighty countries abroad, most of Lorne's close friends expected him
finally to treat himself and his family to a prolonged holiday of relaxation
before plunging into any new endeavor.

But they were disappointed. Much as he enjoys travel and relaxation,
acting is even more of a joy to Lorne. After only thirty days off from
"Bonanza," Lorne signed for the starring role in the series "Griff" on
ABC-TV. He played a private detective returned from retirement in the
short-lived series and, typical of Lorne, gave it all he had, but it wasn't
enough. He couldn't change from Ben Cartright to Griff so rapidly, at least
not in the viewers' eyes, and the series was canceled. Lorne made a charac-
teristically straightforward statement:

"I will not offer any copout explanations of why the show failed. I
gave Griff all I had, but it obviously was not enough. The show just didn't
work out and that says it all. Period."

In contrast with the statements of other stars who have been faced
with similar situations and who complained about lack of network support, bad time slots, or poor scripts, Lorne's statement was refreshing for
its honesty.

In 1974 Lorne returned to Universal Studios for a costarring role with
George Kennedy and Charlton Heston in the blockbuster *Earthquake*. He
followed that with two TV movies for Universal. In 1978-79 he starred as
"Adamo" in ABC-TV's "Battlestar Galactica," a sci-fi series far removed
from the old Ponderosa days.

Lorne had a most distinguished career long before "Bonanza" was
ever conceived. His parents, Daniel and Dora Greene, were themselves
interested in the theater and Lorne was early inclined in that direction. He
enrolled at Queen's University intending to become a chemical engineer,
but he soon realized that his bent for the theater was not to be denied. He
became active in the Drama Guild and by the time he graduated from college had played in and directed many productions.

The fruit of these efforts was a fellowship to New York's famous Neighborhood Playhouse (Dennis Weaver also attended this actors' school) where he studied with Sanford Meisner and Martha Graham. Two years later he returned to Canada. Since there was no professional theater there, he got a job as program supervisor with an advertising agency. His salary was a pitiful $10 a week, which Lorne vividly remembers to this day. The cost of living was considerably more than that, so he became active in radio and eventually became chief announcer for the Canadian Broadcasting Corporation and chief news broadcaster for the network. He also did many "Voice of America" broadcasts beamed into Nazi-occupied nations, in cooperation with the National Broadcasting Company in the United States.

After service in World War II—a flying officer in the RCAF—Lorne returned to Canadian radio, became a cofounder of the Jupiter Theatre in Toronto, and established the Academy of Radio Arts, a highly successful school where students chose to call him Dean Greene.

At one point, Lorne was not only serving as director of the academy, but he was also performing on radio in fifteen regular shows a week, lecturing at the university, and producing for theater and radio—a full life indeed.

Lorne explains it this way: "I became aware at an early age of the fact that while the body has its limitations the mind never reaches its full potential, so I was determined to use as much of me as possible for as long as I was alive. I don't know now that I by any means have reached the ultimate use of my potential—nor do I ever expect to know—but I certainly keep right on trying.

"I know that if there is any trick at all to living a reasonably happy life, that's it. I keep seeking things both in my acting and my everyday life that will stretch what abilities I have. I have observed over the years that most people who get on in years and still seem to remain youthful do exactly that.

"I work from twelve to thirteen hours a day on the set, arriving there at 7:15 every morning. I come home for dinner and, since my wife and I both like to talk, we will discuss things or read at least until midnight or later. Then I'm up again at six in the morning. Fortunately I don't seem to need more sleep than four or five hours."

Lorne came to Hollywood from Canada via New York. He had gone to New York to market a special stopwatch he had developed for use in radio and TV. In New York City he ran into producer Fletcher Markle, who offered him the role of Big Brother in Studio One's version of *1984*. He went on to do a variety of top television shows, then starred in three Broadway plays, *The Prescott Proposals*, *Speaking of Murder*, and *Edwin Booth*. He also had time to star in plays presented by the Stratford Shakespeare Festival in Canada.

By this time his versatile career had come to the attention of various

motion picture producers, and he went to Hollywood for major roles in a series of films, starting with *The Silver Chalice* (1954). After his years of experience in California, Lorne has some very refreshing thoughts about Hollywood, which he affectionately calls "the hand that feeds me."

"When I hear someone in our business complaining about Hollywood," says Lorne, "someone who looks down, perhaps, on what he's doing, I'm both amazed and annoyed. As the writer Donald Ogden Stewart said many years ago: 'No one puts a gun to your head and forces you to accept all this money and the swimming pool and the fine car and big home.' And, brother—that's a *fact*.

"If you accept a job here in Hollywood—in fact, if you accept any kind of job anywhere and accept the money for doing it—you ought to have the good grace to do the very best you can and try to respect the work you are doing. To do less, I feel, is to demean yourself.

"If you feel you have a major talent that is being wasted in Hollywood (or in whatever field you're working), you need only go off and do your thing and adjust your living standards to your own deepest needs. And no one can make that decision for you—no more than anyone can decide for you that you have to earn a nice, fat paycheck."

Surely no one can accuse Lorne Greene of not putting his talent to

173

work in as many ways as he can. He has guest-starred on a wide range of variety shows; narrated numerous TV specials; appeared in feature films; made personal appearances at fairs, rodeos, and supper clubs; and covered such special events as nationally televised holiday parades.

In another direction, Lorne attained the number one spot on the best-seller charts of the music trade papers. His single "Ringo" went over a million sales, earning him a gold record, and his album "Welcome to the Ponderosa" was another long-time major chart entry.

In yet another direction, he narrated "Peter and the Wolf" for RCA Victor, and, as though to offer contrast, he went to Nashville to record several contemporary numbers, including "Daddy, I'm Proud to Be Your Son," "I Love a Rainbow," and "The First Word."

As though such diversification were not enough, Lorne received the rare honor of being asked to serve as master of ceremonies at the Royal Command Performance when Queen Elizabeth visited Canada a few years ago. Certainly no pleasure, but a distinction nonetheless, was his invitation to preside over the hour-long nationally televised memorial tribute to President John F. Kennedy following his assassination.

To round out this manifestly taxing schedule, Lorne is in constant demand as a guest speaker at all manner of functions. He has served as master of ceremonies or principal speaker, or both, at countless civic and charitable functions. His generosity has been acknowledged by innumerable awards, including the Brotherhood Award from the National Conference of Christians and Jews; Man of the Year Award for spearheading Canada's Bonds for Israel drive; and, in 1970, the King David Award for the U.S. Bonds for Israel campaign. Not least are Greene's numerous special awards, among them the Heart Award (Variety Club of America) and the John Swett Award (California Teachers Association), plus the Most Popular TV Star (*Radio-TV Mirror*) and Best Performance by an Actor (Foreign Press Association) awards.

Lorne and his charming wife Nancy live in a sprawling, comfortable home in Bel Air. They have a daughter, Gillian Dania. He also has twins, Charles and Linda, by a former marriage.

Lorne derives special pleasure from his stable of race horses, twenty at this writing. He and his partner Lee McLaughlin have their own stables, Greene-Lee in Chatsworth, California, a recent acquisition. The Greene racing colors are purple and gold and among his favorite horses are Nancy's Protest, named with tongue-in-cheek after his wife, and Little Gillian, after his daughter.

Lorne's exercise regimen includes tennis, walking, and swimming. His extensive reading habits embrace current events, novels, and nonfiction. He is also a formidable bridge player whose prowess was hailed by no less an authority than Omar Sharif, himself an international bridge master. Sharif says Lorne is one of the best bridge players in show business. It seems a fitting description of a man who thus far has made his life a grand slam.

Western Film-TV Credits

The Hard Man (Col., 1957)
The Last of the Fast Guns (Univ., 1958)
Waco (sang title song) (Par., 1966)
Nevada Smith (MGM-TV, 1975)

"Bonanza" (NBC-TV, 1959-73)
Lorne Greene's American West (narrator) (NBC-TV, 1975)
Lewis and Clark Expedition (NBC-TV, 1976)

Glenn Ford, with Angie Dickinson in The Last Challenge *(1967).*

Glenn Ford

(From blue serge to blue jeans)

Born: October 12, 1916, Quebec, Canada
Married: Eleanor Powell (1943); divorced
  (1959); remarried: Kathryn Hays (1966);
  divorced (1968)

SOME PEOPLE THINK that the now defunct "Cade's County" was Glenn Ford's first television series. But that's not exactly correct.

As far back as 1958, when Glenn was named Number One Box Office Star, it seemed as if he were also the star of a late-night tube program called "The Late Show." His endless string of rawhide-and-redskin classics—A, B, and C Westerns—were galloping across television screens night after night.

But other people (TV bigwigs, namely) were slower to appreciate this sagebrush magnetism of Glenn's—CBS-TV president Robert Wood and the network's director of programming Fred Silverman being two prime examples. Their original TV plans for Glenn carried him far from the fragrance of a corral into an urban setting, where he was to be a policeman who ran a sort of halfway house for teenagers in trouble. This half-hour series was set to begin shooting when inspiration struck the network's executive offices.

Try to imagine, if possible, the historic moment when Silverman and Wood decided to relax from a tough day of screening by going to the Glenn Ford Film Festival playing in New York City at the time. Try to envision the awestruck moment when Silverman, with amazement in his voice, said, "You know, Bob, Glenn Ford might just be damned good in a Western series." And with the canniness characteristic of network bigshots, as soon as they got back to their offices from the movie theater, they dug out a property they had had for several years but were unable to cast: "Cade's County." Exit the cop-owns-halfway-house series.

Glenn admits he couldn't have been happier than to be back in his cowboy boots—"Hell, I *love* to make Westerns!" But when he asked for a salary adjustment of twice the original price, "Cade's County" almost ended sooner than it did. But Glenn did get his new asking price and the series got under way.

"The main reason I believe the show went under," says Glenn, "is the feature movie competition in prime-time Sunday hours. I know, it sounds like a copout, but I believe it's true nevertheless. Our show's rat-

177

ings shot up the minute it didn't have to compete with a big-budget movie."

According to a survey taken after the show ended, Glenn was only partly correct. "Cade" went under not only because of competitive prime-time, big-budget movie scheduling but also because the scripts were badly plotted, or the plots were hackneyed and the attempts to upgrade them were clumsily done. In addition, the premise of the show was cops-and-robbers, despite the Western setting, and this made the show seem in the viewer's opinion like just another detective show.

What is fascinating is how Wood and Silverman had the role of Cade tailored to fit their choice of star.

Executive producer David Gerber and head writer Cliff Gould studied Glenn's best Westerns: *The Sheepman, The Fastest Gun Alive, 3:10 to Yuma, Cowboy,* and *Cimarron.* From these films they developed a "Ford profile," a composite of traits which they wrote into the "Cade" series. The traits constitute a basic primer of the strong-silent stereotype going back through Gary Cooper at least to Tom Mix and William S. Hart.

Each trait was then broken down:

> *Cimarron:* A gentleman . . . not afraid that his manhood might be challenged by showing that quality. Extremely physical [Glenn cracked a vertebra in his back filming this one] . . . does his own stunting.
> *The Sheepman:* Very dry sense of humor . . . often delivering lines of a serious nature with a twinkle in his eyes. Not by nature violent, yet is capable of greeting impending violence with hard-nosed bluntness. Beneath the ruggedly casual exterior, the easygoing grin, a bone-cold cool regulates hair-trigger reflexes. A maverick who'll bend the rules to get a job done.
> *Cowboy:* More comfortable around other men. Terse, soft-spoken . . . a man with great sensitivity and quiet strength.
> *The Fastest Gun Alive:* Doesn't draw his gun unless he is going to shoot and when he does shoot—he hits the target dead center. Does not believe that there is bravery in gun play of any kind.
> *3:10 to Yuma:* Ford's speeches are consistently short and to the point. Suspect he gives half his dialogue to other players. He's one helluva good listener.

This cowboy profile of Glenn is not dissimilar to his own. He still keeps a small stable in San Fernando Valley. His fascination with horse-flesh began in his youth as a stablehand on Will Rogers' ranch. The famed humorist taught Glenn trick riding and cowboy stunts. Glenn recalls it vividly: "Will Rogers used to wear his hat with a turned-down front brim, and I admired him so much he used to give me all his old hats. They were too big for me, but I lined the inner sweatbands with newspaper, folded, and then the hats fit fine. I still wear hats similar to that today. I think it kinda suits my Westerner personality."

He made his first Western, *Texas,* in 1941, and his costar was William Holden. They're still good friends.

"The Western is a man's world, and I love it," says Glenn. "If I could do whatever I wanted to do for the rest of my life, I wouldn't do anything but Westerns.

"The Western, in my opinion, is very straightforward and uncomplicated. Simple stories about big emotions. That's one reason they appeal to people in foreign nations so much. My Western pictures are still very popular in countries like Japan, Italy, France, and Germany. You literally don't have to speak English to understand the story.

"Take a good, classic John Ford Western film—you can understand the whole story without having to hear one line of dialogue. Ford—no relation—was so graphic that he told the story with his camera, his attitudes. The real drama is played out on the faces of the people. John Ford, along with Hank Hathaway and George Marshall and a few others, learned long ago that talkies have a tendency to talk too much. They thus have the ability to make a lean picture, a picture devoid of all that extraneous fat.

"I don't think a good director should get nervous when there's a little bit of silence. Some think there's nothing going on if you don't talk all the time, but I disagree. To sum it all up in a couple of hackneyed phrases: silence is golden; action speaks louder than words."

Was he angry when "Cade's County" was canceled?

"Well, no, not exactly. I'd be a damn liar if I said I wasn't real disappointed, because I was, but I wasn't mad, at least not at the time. But then I sit back and watch the tube on Sundays and see a series that's as kooky as hell continue year after year, and I begin to get a little mad, thinking about how they killed a good show like mine for a junky one like this."

Does he plan to star in another Western series soon?

"Who knows? I seriously doubt it, a series that is, until they, the producers and writers and directors, *know* which way they want to go. I'll consider starring in another series only if it depicts the West as it should be, not all farced up like some shows I've seen recently."

Which shows was he talking about?

"That, friend, is a trade secret. One thing I'll never do is pan another actor, no matter how bad he is. I might pan his show by insinuations, but never him. And never the show by title."

Has he ever starred in a Western with John Wayne? [This interview preceded Wayne's death in 1979.]

"You know what, by God, that's a good question—one nobody's asked me before. No, I can truthfully say that I haven't, but can just as truthfully say that I'd love to. I know Duke very well and like him as a friend and respect him as an actor. But somehow we just haven't gotten together in a film or series yet. But I'd love to. I think it would be a rewarding experience for me, for us both, and maybe our viewers as well. I think, now that you've asked me, that both Duke and I could contribute heavily to the art of Western filmmaking if we starred in a film or a series together."

Meaning on an equal basis, not one starred over the other, and if the remuneration was right?

"The remuneration, namely, and if Duke and I and the writers could work out a fifty-fifty appearance deal."

Did he prefer any Western he made to others?

"As a matter of fact, yes. I had more darned fun makin' *The Rounders*, with Hank Fonda, than a lot of my other films. Critics panned the picture and said it was horrible, and they even withdrew it from the theaters and put it on late-night TV, but I had more fun making it with Hank than many of the others, all of which were moneymakers on the home and foreign markets."

Glenn was born in Quebec, Canada, in 1916. When he was twelve, his parents moved to Los Angeles because his father accepted a job with a firm based there. Glenn was educated mostly in Los Angeles public schools and also has some college credits. He was married twice and divorced. His grown son Peter, whom he loves deeply, also starred in the defunct "Cade" series.

"Pete will be a great actor one of these days," says Glenn proudly. "All he needs is a little more experience, camera exposure, and he'll be on his way up."

Does Peter love to make Westerns like his father?

"Well, no, not exactly. Pete *likes* to make Westerns, yes, but he doesn't *love* to. And right there is a big difference. No, I think Pete'll probably follow my path into dramatic acting, but because he wants to and not because a producer *makes* him act drama or else, like in my own case. Yep, Pete has the world ahead of him in this business, and I hope he shoots right up to the top soon. In fact," Glenn musingly adds, "so does he."

When did he (Glenn) decide to become an actor?

"I started out as a stage manager for a production of *Golden Boy*, and every night I had to run across the stage yelling, 'It's sensational! It's a knockout!' In those days the stage manager also had to understudy all the male characters in the play, so I ended up acting a lot. But I never thought it was a job. I thought it was like *stealing* money. But I got tired of seeing actors come in, put on their makeup, say three lines, and collect $75, while I was working from dawn to dusk getting $25. That's when I decided to pretend I was an actor too."

Why was he cast in so many dramatic roles when he loved playing Western roles so much?

"That's another good question. In those days, the late thirties and early forties, a bunch of new dramatic actors were starting to rise while the B-Western actors were pretty well fixed. They had Ken Maynard, Buck

Jones, Bob Steele, Tim McCoy, et cetera, to do any type of Western they had in mind. But they didn't have enough dramatic actors to fulfill the roles upcoming—or so I was informed. Thus I was cast in both types of films, Westerns and dramas, and it was decided I had great potential for the latter, so they concentrated on making me a big star.

"The war started and spoiled everything for them. Most of the dramatic leading men—like Tyrone Power, Alan Ladd and John Payne—left to serve their country. That produced big gaps to fill in the drama departments of the studios. I might have become a very big star indeed, but the draft got hotter so I enlisted in the Marine Corps. I spent most of the war in Hawaii doing personal appearance duties, unlike Ty Power and others who actually got into combat.

"After the war I returned to Hollywood and got work right away in adventure and detective films. Then a few comedies, a love film or two, and then—TV posed its threat and nearly wrecked the motion picture industry. I was lucky. I got with a company and transitioned into TV films, and made most of my Westerns. And that's it."

In his private life Glenn was once the picture of swinging bachelorhood, hitting the gossip columns regularly with Hope Lange, Linda Christian, Connie Stevens, Judy Garland, and Debbie Reynolds, among others, before and after his marriages to Eleanor Powell (1943-59) and Kathryn Hays (1966-68).

But recently his life has been as hidden from the public eye as a Trappist monk's. "Believe me, I have a very active social life," he insists, defensively, "and I'm not a recluse, or a morbid, brooding old man. I'm just damn sick and tired of being married-by-magazine to every girl I happen to date. For the last year, as an example, every fan magazine practically has been printing that the biggest romance going in Hollywood is between me and Doris Day. Hell, man, I've never even *met* the woman!"

He explains his social life this way: "Let me give you a metaphor. If you walk down the streets in residential Paris, you find everything is quiet, forbidding, with shuttered windows. Well, I have a flat there on the Rue Canada which opens onto a marvelous garden and offers me a wonderful social life when I'm in France. I greatly admire that respect the French have for privacy, and I try to keep the shuttered door closed on my personal life.

"Will I ever get married again? Who can tell? I'd be a fool to say I'd never consider marriage again, but I'd be a bigger fool to get enmeshed in another marriage that didn't work out. Hell, man, trying to afford women who've divorced you is damned expensive, you'd better believe. So any future plans in that line will have to be long considered and well thought out first."

Was it true he once was almost shanghaied into the French Foreign Legion?

"Crazy, but true," he confesses. "One night I was in Marseilles, doing a film. I was going through the end of a very unsatisfactory love affair with a singer [unnamed] who at that time was singing with the Paris Opera. I'd had about five brandies, sitting in a bar with another actor [unnamed], and I announced: 'I'm going to forget this woman, Hollywood, the world, and join the French Foreign Legion.'

"Next thing I knew, my actor friend had me in a taxi and down to legion headquarters, where I was being examined by a one-eyed recruiting sergeant. I woke up the next morning in a room with fifty other guys and discovered, believe it or not, that we were being shipped out to the Sahara that very day. I yelled like mad and got my producer, the French consul, and the Theatre Libre to swear that 135 Frenchmen would be out of work if I were shipped out to the desert. After a lot of hassle, they took back my little blanket and let me out."

It is a bit hard to reconcile this bon vivant lifestyle with the simplicity of Glenn's life as a home owner. By his own count he grows 157 varieties of fruits and vegetables on his property in Beverly Hills. "I'll go through phases of not eating meat for a month," says Glenn, "but I'm not what you'd call a real vegetarian nut."

Born an Episcopalian, he attends churches of all faiths and considers himself a "profoundly religious man." He remains deeply attached to his mother, who lives nearby. "I abhor the negative attitudes of many young people in this country regarding their parents," he says with conviction. "If you like your mother, you're accused of momism. Well, I love my mother a great deal and will always be grateful that she had faith in me when I was young. Without her unrelenting faith, I'd never have made it. I'd have fallen flat years ago."

Glenn is a captain in the U.S. Naval Reserve (he decided he liked the navy better than he did the Marine Corps), and spent time in 1967 with the marines in Vietnam. "I maintain my rank," he says, "because I've met some of the finest men I've ever known in my life, some of my dearest friends, in the service. And—I don't quite know how to say this—it's such a departure from the life and the people you meet in Hollywood. The service is a tremendous leveler, a sobering influence, keeping you in contact with the American people. But on a people—not a fan—level, if you see what I mean.

"The traditional American values, the folklore of the common man are important to me. I never forget my roots. When I drive to the studio, I go by a corner where I used to sell newspapers, and a shop where I used to wash windows every Saturday. And I most especially never want to forget that my *real* name is Gwyllyn."

Western Film-TV Credits

Texas (Col., 1941)
Go West Young Lady (Col., 1941)
The Desperadoes (Col., 1943)
The Man from Colorado (Col., 1948)
Lust for Gold (Col., 1949)
The Redhead and the Cowboy (Par., 1951)
The Secret of Convict Lake (20th, 1951)
The Man from the Alamo (Univ., 1953)
The Violent Men (Col., 1955)
The Americano (RKO, 1955)
The Fastest Gun Alive (MGM, 1956)
3:10 to Yuma (Col., 1957)

The Sheepman (MGM, 1958)
Cowboy (Col., 1958)
Cimarron (MGM, 1961)
Advance to the Rear (MGM, 1964)
The Rounders (MGM, 1965)
The Last Challenge (MGM, 1967)
A Time for Killing (Col., 1967)
Day of the Evil Gun (MGM, 1968)
Heaven with a Gun (MGM, 1969)
Smith! (BV, 1969)
Santee (Crown, 1973)

"Cade's County" (series) (ABC-TV, 1972-74)

Dale Robertson, Western star.

Dale Robertson

(Shades of Ken Maynard)

Born: July 14, 1923, Harrah, Okla.
Married: Lu Ann; divorced (1977);
  remarried: Lulu Mae Harding (1977);
  children: Rochelle, Rebel

IT IS THE consensus of top NBC-TV network executives that actor Dale Robertson is a dead-ringer for cowboy superstar Ken Maynard. Dale was host-star on the long-running TV series "Death Valley Days."

"Just watching Dale ride a horse, or watching him go into action in a Western, reminds me of the late Ken Maynard in every way, shape, and form," says Henry Hathaway, a top Hollywood director, and a host of his colleagues agree with him.

How does Dale feel about this?

"I consider it a real honor," says Dale, "to be thought of in so complimentary a manner in regards to the late Ken Maynard. Old Ken was my favorite Western actor ever since I can remember, as a kid and young man, and I can't imagine a better honor than to be thought of as looking and acting like him. Yessir, it's a real compliment!"

Did he ever meet Ken Maynard?

"Yeah, once before he died. Ken, unfortunately, had a consecutive series of bad-luck episodes in his later life, and it left him both ill and impoverished. I remember the time I went out to visit him, as if it was yesterday.

"I'd been around Hollywood a good long time before I learned from a conversation with a fellow actor that old Ken was still alive. I'd thought all along that he'd died long ago, after he dropped out of sight like he did not long after we got into World War II. But my friend assured me Ken was alive and told me how to get to the trailer camp he was staying at.

"I'd never met Ken Maynard person-to-person and, even though I was a star and all, it somehow tensed me up with the thought of gettin' to meet him. My friend, whom I'll not name, got the trailer camp's number and got Ken on the phone and let me talk to him. I told him who I was and all, and he right away started complimentin' me on my actin' in 'Wells Fargo,' 'Iron Horse,' and 'Death Valley Days,' like it all happened yesterday. I told him what a favorite he was of mine and that I wanted to visit him. He hesitated a bit, but agreed to our visit—providin' I didn't mind the clutter in his trailer too much.

185

"I didn't know what to expect, so when I got to the Lone Star Camp and located Ken's trailer, I was indeed kinda shocked. I had no idea at all that he was in such a bad way, financially and healthwise. But I acted like nothin' happened and knocked on his trailer door. When it opened, I got shock number two.

"The tall, liver-splotched, cigar-smokin', baldheaded old man who stood in the door lookin' at me was not exactly the Ken Maynard I'd admired as a cowboy star. Even his false-toothed smile changed his facial features, so he didn't look anything like the same man he used to. Only his voice, kinda high, fast, and nasal, sounded like the Ken of old days. But that was all.

"I did the best job of acting in my career, as I sat in Ken's outdated, cluttered trailer pretending nothing was wrong and chatting with him and listening to him as he got out old photos of himself and Tarzan, his Wonder Horse, and discussed his days as a star and how he never had considered himself anything but a good cowboy. He also told me about his youth and his days as a circus trick rider and rodeo performer, and how he'd come by Hollywood in the first place. He told me all of this in about the space of an hour, like he was never gonna get the chance to tell it to anyone again. I understand that you [this author] got the last interview with him—after my visit—before he died [part three of this book]. And I'm glad. I'm glad someone of the press learned Ken was alive and got his story, sad though it is . . . .

"Anyway, after Ken got through it was my turn to tell him about me. That lasted about another half-hour. Ken smoked two cigars during my visit. He offered me a drink, but I declined. I wanted one, but I knew his illness and wanted to make it easy on him. He never had a drop while I was there, but I'm sure he had a couple, like I did, after our visit ended and I left.

"I hinted that I would like to assist him financially, or any other way if I could, but Ken declined my offer like the grand old trouper he was: 'I didn't ask no one t' get me in this shape, and I'm not about t' ask anyone t' help me get outta it. But I shore do appreciate you askin'.

"I kinda felt that I'd embarrassed old Ken, and it touched me and showed. So he started reminiscing about then and smoothed everything over. But I still feel that Ken Maynard was the greatest cowboy star alive, and I'm only too proud to be honored by bein' thought of as his likeness."

Would he consider portraying the life of Ken Maynard if the opportunity ever arose?

"I'd be only too happy to," said Dale positively, adding, "depending upon the script, remuneration, and so on, of course."

Despite his natural Western modesty, Dale Robertson has been an outstanding motion picture-TV star for over twenty-five years. After a brilliant athletic career in his home state of Oklahoma, he moved to Hollywood and was quickly signed to a seven-year contract by 20th Century-Fox. He was almost immediately a box-office hit. In all, he starred in

The star out of Western garb.

forty-two films for Fox, among which were *Call Me Mister* (1951), *Golden Girl* (1951), *The Outcasts of Poker Flat* (1952), *The Farmer Takes a Wife* (1953), *City of Bad Men* (1953), and *The Gambler from Natchez* (1954). He also starred in twenty feature films for other producers.

The lithe (6′1″, 185 pounds) hazel-eyed actor, who now has a budding white streak coursing through his thick brown hair, was an energetic competitor in his youth and won twenty-two letters in high school and college sports. While attending Oklahoma Military College he spent his summer vacations working as a cowboy near Tulsa. This experience forged one of the finest riders starring in Westerns. He also excelled at boxing in college and won several trophies in the heavyweight division. He was equally gifted at football (left end) and fancied a career in professional football when he graduated. But World War II interrupted his dreams for the future and Dale gave three years to the army as an officer.

After the war Dale, who had studied drama in college and had participated in USO functions as an army officer, decided to become a motion picture actor. He set out for Hollywood with big hopes and ambition, and his handsome looks and personality won him a screen test at Fox Studios. Having passed the test with an "excellent" rating, he was signed to a long-term contract by Fox and sent to its acting school. Fox gave him small roles in several pictures. These proved so successful he was given some costarring roles in big-budget films. Once again successful, he was graduated to starring roles.

Dale then turned his talents toward television and soon landed a contract to star in the Western series "Wells Fargo." The series was a huge success, lasted six and a half years at the top of the Nielsen ratings, and established Dale as one of the top Western stars in the business. He then went on to star in the series "Iron Horse," which lasted only two seasons but succeeded in assuring a secure future for Dale.

Shifting his talents once again, Dale applied his efforts to every facet of motion picture making. He spent two years at the University of Southern California's College of Cinema, seven years with Elmo Williams studying motion picture editing, and an equal period of time studying motion picture music scoring with Lionel and Alfred Newman. Dale then spent two years each with Leon Shamroy and Paul Vogel learning the art of color and black-and-white cinematography. In addition, he has written numerous scripts for both feature and TV films and served as president of United Screen Arts, which financed and distributed motion pictures throughout the world.

Aside from his varied entertainment interests, Dale is extremely active in horse breeding and training. His Haymaker Farms in Yukon, Oklahoma, is today one of the outstanding quarter-horse centers in the world. Here Dale conducts the country's largest quarter-horse sale twice a year. Many fellow actors and good friends—among them James Brolin, Lorne Greene, James Cagney, Doc Severinsen, John Wayne, Clint Walker, the late Robert Taylor—have been on his sales list of clientele, not to mention numerous sports and professional figures.

A true outdoorsman, Dale is an active pilot, hunter, and fisherman. He was instrumental in developing the TV series "The American Sportsman," and has interests in "Wild Kingdom" as well. He often "stars" in "Sportsman" segments, filming and narrating his hunting expeditions all over the North American continent and in countries around the world.

Dale, his wife Lu, and daughter Rebel live on a ten-acre ranch in California; he also owns two big ranches in New Mexico and Oklahoma. His older daughter Rochelle is married now after attending school in Switzerland.

Dale starred in the feature motion picture *The Walking Major*, which was filmed in Japan. It was nominated the Best English Language Foreign Film by the Hollywood Foreign Press Association.

A country and western music enthusiast, Dale recorded for Artco Records in 1973 an album which has done well in sales. He won the Country and Western (CMA) golf tournament in Nashville in 1971, and was on the winning team of the Glen Campbell Los Angeles open golf tournament in 1972.

Dale is currently devoting his many talents to filming for TV a new series (neither named nor described yet by his agency) in which he will star. In addition, Dale is in constant demand for personal appearances at home, in England, and Australia; at state fairs, rodeos, and on television.

Unlike Ken Maynard, Dale has worked hard to secure his future for himself and his family and to maintain it. He is in fact a millionaire today, although he modestly avoids mentioning it. But much like Ken, he rides tall in the saddle and hell-bent for action.

Western Film-TV Credits

Fighting Man of the Plains (20th, 1949)

The Cariboo Trail (20th, 1950)

Two Flags West (20th, 1950)

Golden Girl (20th, 1951)

The Outcasts of Poker Flat (20th, 1952)

Return of the Texan (20th, 1952)

The Silver Whip (20th, 1953)

City of Bad Men (20th, 1953)

Devil's Canyon (RKO, 1953)

The Gambler from Natchez (20th, 1954)

Sitting Bull (UA, 1954)

Dakota Incident (Rep., 1956)

A Day of Fury (Univ., 1956)

Hell Canyon Outlaws (Rep., 1957)

Law of the Lawless (Par., 1964)

Blood on the Arrow (AA, 1964)

The Man from Button Willow (voice only) (United Screen Arts, 1965)

"Tales of Wells Fargo" (series) (NBC-TV, 1956-62)

Scalplock (Col.-TV, 1966)

"Iron Horse" (series) (NBC-TV, 1966-68)

"Death Valley Days" (series) (NBC-TV, 1965-70)

Clint Eastwood, with Jean Seberg and Lee Marvin in Paint Your Wagon *(1969).*

Clint Eastwood

(Rowdy Yates to Dirty Harry)

Born: May 31, 1930, San Francisco, Calif.
Married: Maggie Johnson (1953); separated
 (1979); children: Kyle, Allison

WHEN A WESTERN motion picture actor has been the world's number one box-office star for several years in a row, there are hazards to his emotional stability.

But not so with Clint Eastwood. If the emotional strain of being a top Western film-TV star is too much for him, Clint's versatility as an actor can ease the tension and pull him through. He can become Dirty Harry the police detective, venting his wrath and pent-up emotions by doing all his own stunts—those allowable under insurance provisions in his contract—and feel better.

As for being changed by being first at the box office, Clint hasn't changed one iota. He remains himself, a remote man, almost shy to those he doesn't know. He understands what is expected of him and handles himself with slow, deliberate care. There's nothing pretentious or flamboyant about him. As a superstar, he avoids making his private life grist for the Tinseltown rumor mills. Away from the cameras he's about as dull as a small-town Boy Scout.

Clint is an old-fashioned man, unsophisticated but very intelligent. He lives in a male world of beer drinking, motorcycles and cars, admiring women, and uncomplicated language, a world where he's often known as Slick. Most of Clint's friends today are the same people he met in the days when he was a hungry, struggling young actor.

"I'm sure enough about who I am," says Clint today. "I don't have to prove anything, and these are the people I liked when the going was rough. Why change? There are already too many people trying to get a piece of my action. But not my old friends, the good people I suffered with. They like me for what I am, for myself, the same as I like them. And to me—*that's true friendship.*" For emphasis he adds, "All the things I do are what I *like* to do, not what some damned fools *think* I should do."

Clint is also a complicated man, an amateur archaeologist, a jazz fan, a fine mechanic to his several speedy cars and motorcycles, and a health-food faddist. He loves carrots and papaya melons and deems the Japanese diet "some of *the* healthiest food going. All that raw fish . . . not greasy and low in fat."

Clint never eats cake, ice cream, junk foods, or frozen vegetables. He loves organically grown vegetables. For breakfast he likes grapefruit juice and white raisins. Lunch is usually a tunafish sandwich, avocado, alfalfa sprouts, and oatmeal cookies. And dinner is the same sort of light meal. He never overeats; very, very seldom has a shot of whiskey—usually a beer. He has never smoked a cigarette in his life, despite rumors to the contrary.

Every day he works out on a punching bag and with weights and when possible runs four miles on the beach. He is an excellent golfer and a good tennis player.

"I've always felt more comfortable outdoors," Clint admits. "I think I'd hate to work in an office. I think it would kill me not to be able to move around freely, do what I want."

Clint is a realist about his success and his phenomenal box-office appeal. He knows how capricious the business is.

"Hollywood is one helluva strange place," says Clint. "I think about everyone is looking for a formula. One year it's two guys on a bike, the next it's a girl dying of cancer, and they flood the market with poor imitations.

"For years after I got out of the army I bummed around the industry trying to get a job and it was always the same old story: my voice was too soft, my teeth needed capping, I was too tall, I squinted too much. All that constant tearing down of my ego was bound to eventually turn me into a better person or a complete bastard.

"And I know that right now, today, if I walked into a casting office and nobody recognized me as Clint Eastwood, star, I'd get the same old crap. Everything they said that was wrong with me is still there, but now I'm *Clint Eastwood*, and all the other guys who are too tall and squint too much and talk too softly are the guys cussing me. It's tough to figure out this town. Real tough.

"Hell, it could end for me just like that," he emphasizes by snapping his fingers. "But while I'm on top I'm damn sure going to make the most of it. I've learned one big lesson after all these years: *any* actor in pictures has to have something real *special*. That's what makes a star, that something real special, while a lot of damn good actors get passed by. The public knows they're good, but won't pay three bucks a ticket to see them. The public goes to see the stars. I didn't invent the rules. That's just the way it all is and I've cashed in on them."

Clint's spectacular rise to superstardom was capped in 1973 by his appointment—along with Rosalind Russell—by President Nixon to the National Council on the Arts for a six-year term to represent the motion picture industry. At the same time, those powerful forces within the industry, the National Association of Theatre Owners and the International Motion Picture Distributors, declared him International Film Star of 1972.

Clint has demonstrated rather conclusively that the star system,

As he appeared in a non-Western role in Magnum Force *(1973)*.

193

which was the mother's milk for Hollywood for so many years, is not dead by a long shot. At least not so in Clint's case. All over the world, according to surveys, people are going to Clint Eastwood movies—going, mind you, not because of the story, or the background, or the other performers, but because of *Clint Eastwood,* the star.

As for Universal Pictures, Clint at one time remarked,"They had me under contract once and then let me go. They'll pay dearly for that mistake!" It was after Clint was released from his contract with Universal years ago that things began to break right for him.

One day, out of work, and not particularly concerned about it (at this time he was being referred to as East-*who* in casting offices), he dropped in at CBS to visit a friend. While Clint was rapping with his friend, a man he had never met before stopped him in midconversation and asked, "Hey, Slim, you an actor?"

Clint, in the time-honored tradition of Western actors (and very Gary Cooperishly), replied, "Yup." He continued to say yup and added a nope or two for the next eight years. The man who had stopped him was Robert Sparks, executive television producer. Clint became Rowdy Yates, the number two drover under Gil Favor (portrayed by the late Eric Fleming), on the successful CBS-TV series "Rawhide," which made him a familiar face to U.S. tube audiences, if not a superstar.

It was during the seventh year of "Rawhide" that "East-*who*" sensed it all would soon be over and wandered to Italy to make the first of his "spaghetti Westerns"—which made him famous.

Ironically, Clint's stardom grew out of a throwback to the old American movie staple, the Western, and it was the Italian product, not Hollywood's, that made him an internationally known star. As in most cases involving big-screen charisma, the audience discovered him. He was not sold to the public over here by any high-powered, expensive publicity campaign, as in the old days.

They discovered Clint in *A Fistful of Dollars* (1964), which was made for peanuts by Sergio Leone in Spain, but which eventually wound up papering the box offices of the world with gold certificates. Clint received $15,000 for six weeks' work, a far cry from his $750,000 per film today, plus his usual "piece of the action."

The second most successful and exploitable film is the police detective story. Eastwood proved that with Warner Brothers' *Dirty Harry* (1971) and its sequels, *Magnum Force* (1973), and *The Enforcer* (1976). Like John Wayne, Clint deviates from making Westerns now and then to show his versatility as an actor, and to make huge profits, but like Wayne he prefers Westerns because they "relax" him and "let me be more like myself." After returning to American Westerns Clint's initial picture, *Hang 'Em High* (1968), went into profits ten weeks after release, the fastest payoff in United Artists' history. His spaghetti Westerns outdrew *Ben Hur* in

Italy. On its fourth release in England in less than eighteen months, *Hang 'Em High* shattered its own box-office records.

Six feet four inches tall, weighing a constant 198 pounds, Clint Eastwood is the complete movie star. His brown hair and green eyes set off well-arranged features, large fists, and the quiet demeanor of a strong and very secure man. And he, unlike many of his contemporaries, has led an exemplary life.

He was married in 1953 to Maggie Johnson, a pretty blonde model whom he had met on a blind date a few months before. (Their separation was announced in 1979.) They have two children: a son, Kyle Clinton, born May 19, 1968, and a daughter, Allison, born May 23, 1972.

In recent years Clint and Maggie Eastwood have virtually deserted their home in the San Fernando Valley community of Sherman Oaks for a residence near the Seventeen Mile Drive bordering Pebble Beach, on the beautiful Monterey peninsula near Clint's birthplace, San Francisco. There the star-director head of Malpaso Productions (*malpaso* means "bad pass" or "bad step" in Spanish) can live and relax as he pleases, usually in jeans and V-necked T-shirts. He still drives a Chevy pickup truck, but a Ferrari, and Norton and Triumph motorcycles are on hand when the urge moves him to travel faster.

Once a golf buff ("Hell, it took too damn much time to go around the course"), Clint now has become an avid and excellent tennis player, keeping pace with Maggie, who also wields a skillful racquet.

Susan Clark, who played opposite Clint in *Coogan's Bluff* (1968), likes to tell about a scene in which Clint had to pull off her boots.

"They were those tight, vinyl things," she recalls, musingly, "and he tugged and tugged but couldn't pull the boot off. So they filled the boot with talcum powder and filmed the scene again. Clint gave a hard tug. The boot came off all right—but Clint got his face full of powder along with it. Wow! He sure lost his cool that time. He stomped off the set enraged, and refused to work for the rest of the day. Wow! I'd never ever want to be the target for his temper."

Clint can also be the complete, no-nonsense actor. During the filming of *Hang 'Em High,* on location in Las Cruces, New Mexico, a scene called for Clint, the target of a lynching mob, to be dragged across the shallow Rio Grande behind the business end of a horse with a rope tied around his neck. A stuntman double was standing by to do this rather risky scene.

But Clint would have none of it. He insisted on playing the scene himself, without a double, much to the consternation of director Ted Post. Clint did the scene and received some good lumps for his trouble. When asked why he was so insistent on doing his own stunt, he said:

"So I could feel what it was really like and what my reaction would be to being dragged across a river on the end of a rope. Then I could play the scene which followed with conviction and feeling."

Producer Leonard Freeman, absent from the location site at the time, had a fit when he heard about it but didn't dare confront Clint and tell him *not* to do it again. "He was doing his thing," said Freeman.

Such derring-do is without doubt one of the main reasons for Clint's phenomenal success and popularity. He doesn't fake anything, his acting, his feelings, or his emotions.

"It's very nice to be a success," says Clint, "but people treat you in a different way. Maybe it isn't the way I want, but that's how it is.

"I don't need all that pretentiousness either. People are always asking me why we don't move to Bel Air. Hell, I'd go crazy in a big old pretentious house. But a nice secluded place with a lot of land around it, man, that's for me.

"I'd like to be able to always stay as I am, and be able to go anywhere I want to in jeans and a T-shirt."

"I know exactly what I can do and what I can't do," says Clint positively. "I've developed a sense of what is right for me. And what *is* right for me is what I'll do."

He doubtless will.

Western Film-TV Credits

The First Traveling Saleslady (RKO, 1956)

Star in the Dust (Univ., 1956)

Ambush at Cimarron Pass (20th, 1958)

A Fistful of Dollars (It., 1964)

For a Few Dollars More (It., 1965)

The Good, the Bad, and the Ugly (It., 1966)

Hang 'Em High (UA, 1968)

Coogan's Bluff (Univ., 1968)

Paint Your Wagon (Par., 1969)

Two Mules for Sister Sarah (Univ., 1970)

The Beguiled (Univ., 1971)

Joe Kidd (Univ., 1972)

High Plains Drifter (Univ., 1973)

The Outlaw—Josey Wales (WB, 1976)

"Rawhide" (CBS-TV, 1960-67)

Robert Fuller, Western star.

Robert Fuller

(Westerns are his "thing")

Born: July 5, 1937, Troy, N.Y.
Married: Patty Lyon; children: Robert,
  Christine

"SOMEONE ONCE TOLD me that if I was ever to amount to much as an actor I'd first have to decide what *kind* of an actor I wanted to be and then *dedicate* myself to being that kind of an actor."

These words were spoken recently by Robert Fuller, star of NBC-TV's "Emergency," which had a five-year run before being cancelled in 1977.

"Okay," Fuller continued, "after starring for several years as Jess Harper in 'Laramie,' I decided I wanted to be a Western actor and tried to dedicate myself to it. It worked swell as long as the 'Wagon Train' series held up [Fuller replaced Robert Horton in the series after Ward Bond died and Horton left], but when the series folded it didn't work so well at all.

"But I kept dedicated and kept on trying, come hell or high water, and damned near ruined my career. Oh, I know the oldtimers'll tell you that they made good money and a good living by dedicating themselves as Western actors in the old days, but I want to go on record now in telling them and anyone else that those old days are gone, and so is anybody so dedicated."

This is not to intimate that Bob Fuller thinks the Western movie is finished, because it isn't. In fact, as of this writing Bob and a close friend, John English, have formed a production company and plan soon to start shooting a script about one of the meanest outlaws in Old West history: John Wesley Hardin. Fact number two: Bob is going to star in the film as Hardin.

"Truthfully, I'd rather play a Western role than eat," says Fuller. "But these days it often works out that way—about the eating, that is. It took me a long time, but I finally learned a big lesson: always have a good-paying job and family security before dedicating yourself to playing a Western role. It pays off for you, whereas the other way, just being dedicated and holding out for a cowboy role, doesn't."

At one time Bob Fuller was a handsome young man who had everything going for him. He had arrived at a state of stardom by the usual avenues—theater usher, chorus boy, bit player, stuntman, and eventually leading man, first in "Laramie" and later in "Wagon Train." The beautiful part was that Bob had no pretensions about anything, least of all heavy acting, which made him just about perfect for a star in television.

To be sure, he had done a brief stint with drama coach Sanford Meisner at the Neighborhood Playhouse in New York City in the mid-fifties, but his heart wasn't really in it. He tried dancing, but in Troy, New York, where he was born and raised, dancing was thought sissified.

His idea of a good time was to split a fifth of bourbon with his hell-raising buddy Burt Reynolds, who shared Fuller's view that the world was a very physical place where manhood consisted of lifting heavier barbells than anybody else, mixing it up in more barroom brawls, or riding the bucking horse yourself, just to prove you could do it.

"I used to call him Marlon Jr.," says Bob, remembering Burt. "Made him absolutely furious."

Reynolds often said Bob was "wilder'n a March hare," and that when the studio wouldn't give him a door between dressing rooms, he "knocked the wall down!"

Bob had an admirably direct attitude toward his work, which may partly explain why he (and not the more flamboyant Reynolds) reached stardom first. He dedicated himself to being a Western star and readily found stardom in "Laramie" and "Wagon Train." He still feels today that his Jess Harper part will be the best he'll ever get.

"Truly," says Bob, "I'm a guy born about a hundred years too late. If I had my choice, I'd live in 1850. Either I'd be sheriff or the worst outlaw that ever lived. When I strap on a gun, I want to play the West like it really was. Whenever old Jess Harper shot 'em, they stayed dead. That way a guy who had a terrible day at the office can open a can of beer and really escape."

After the two Western series folded, Bob made his big mistake. He remained dedicated to Western roles. He was so adamant he began turning down other roles, thereby keeping the lid on the potential the studio saw in him as a dramatic actor.

Bob turned down "Run for Your Life," a TV series that made a big star of Ben Gazzara. "I couldn't identify with a guy who had only a year to live," insists Bob, "and I didn't think the audience would either."

He also refused the starring role in another series, "The Rat Patrol." "Hell, I'd have been fighting Germans in it and I couldn't run the risk of offending them. I'd just been named the top actor in Germany [for a film he made there called *Midsummer Night*]. I'd won five Ottos [an award like the Emmy] as best actor too, so, what the hell!"

He nixed the role opposite Glenn Ford in the film *The Rounders* because "I didn't want to do a *comedy* Western." Henry Fonda took the role and got raves.

In all, Bob says, he rejected a dozen series offers. The only role he really fancied was in "Bearcats," in which the "cowboys" rode around in vintage automobiles instead of on horses, and it was packaged for Rod

Taylor. "I thank my lucky stars I didn't get the part," says Bob. "The 'Bearcats' failed to last the season."

Meantime, Bob had painted himself into a corner. His fame, such as it was, resting on the insubstantial shoulders of Jess Harper, and his box office ice cold, he did what others in his predicament have done—made films abroad, in Germany and Israel.

Still, Bob stuck doggedly to "principles"; he knew what was "best" for him, and if he didn't, he refused to cry about it. "I starved a lot. But I managed to maintain my wife Patty and the children, my self-respect, and my personal integrity through some mighty lean years; for a while Patty, bless her, even sold saddles in a saddlery. I don't think wishing in this business makes it happen. It's good for a young actor to find that out—the hard way."

As a hell-raiser, Bob was now semiretired. He was content to leave the star behavior to his old sidekick Reynolds. The hungers that had driven him in the past no longer gnawed so insistently. "I haven't been in a real beef now in years," Bob observes. "What's more, I have no desire to."

Bob Fuller has become a family man. He dotes on his wife, former actress Patty Lyon—ten years his junior—and his two children, Robert, nine, and Christine, seven, who are being raised as Catholics by their mother. His home in the San Fernando Valley is a veritable temple of middle-class respectability.

How was it, living with the man who was voted "TV's most eligible bachelor" the same year they were married?

"Never a problem," says pert and pretty Patty. "I trust Bob implicitly. And he treats me like his most precious possession."

In an old-fashioned Western script such virtue would never go unrewarded. So follows life, at least in Bob's case. The first breakthrough came in 1969 when a friend suggested that Bob had the voice timbre for commercials. The first thing he knew he was spokesman for a variety of products and pulling down some $65,000 a year.

A year or so later Bob heard that producer Burt Topper was looking for a star of a low-budget motorcycle movie called *The Hard Ride* (1971). Like nearly everyone else in town, Topper had nearly forgotten that Bob existed. But after Bob reminded him, he quickly cast Bob in the role.

The film had at least two admirers: Bob, who thought it "superior" for the $113,000 it cost to produce; and Jack Webb, who on the basis of it decided that Bob was "the only guy in town" to play the role of Dr. Brackett in "Emergency."

When he discovered what Webb had in mind, Bob stuck doggedly to character. "No doctor series," he told his agent. "Nobody will buy me as any kind of doctor, young or old. I'd rather hold out for a Western."

He finally allowed himself to be coaxed into Webb's office, where the latter said: "I saw *The Hard Ride* and, Bob, you're one helluva actor!"

Bob says, grinning, "I puffed right up. I knew he had me, and *he* knew he had me."

So Bob had come full circle despite himself. "Emergency" lasted five seasons, commanding high Nielsen ratings each week.

Bob and his friend John English are deeply involved with their upcoming production of the John Wesley Hardin film. For despite success in the "Emergency" series, Bob Fuller is, down deep, dedicated to being a Western star. It might be the last Western film ever shot, but Bob doesn't think so. Meanwhile, he's practicing getting "mean as hell."

Other than that, he smiles warmly and says, "It's great to be back."

Western Film-TV Credits

Return of the Seven (UA, 1966)
Incident at Phantom Hill (Univ., 1966)
The Gatling Gun (Ellman, 1973)
Mustang Country (Univ., 1976)

"Laramie" (series) (NBC-TV, 1959-62)
"Wagon Train" (series) (NBC-TV, 1957-62, ABC-TV, 1962-65)

Jack Lord, as the star of the TV series "Stoney Burke."

Jack Lord

("Five-O's" Stoney Burke)

Born: January 5, 1921, New York, N.Y.
Married: Marie

JOHN J. P. RYAN, better known as Jack Lord, the rugged and tough cop McGarrett on "Hawaii Five-O," looks at least ten years younger than his fifty-eight years. The native New Yorker keeps himself in excellent shape beneath Hawaii's sun.

Jack, a former navy man during World War II, used the GI Bill after the war to study art. He became quite good at portrait and landscape paintings and sold many of his works at top prices in some of the nation's finest galleries.

Jack's older sister Marjorie, an actress, long has admired her brother, not only for his artistic ability but for his charisma and good looks as well. She encouraged him to try for a screen test in Hollywood and, she hoped, a career in films. He refused at first, but she was persistent and finally won him over. Jack took a test at Universal Studios and, true to his sister's belief, was signed to a contract.

He was not to become a star until Leonard Freeman recognized his acting savvy and good looks and cast him as the lead in a CBS-TV series, "Stoney Burke," in 1963. Jack had played a heavy opposite Gary Cooper and Glenn Ford in several Westerns, but as Stoney he now had his first big chance to show his stuff as the good-guy leading man.

Casey Tibbs, then the world's champion bronc rider, was brought in as adviser to Jack and showed him many tips and tricks that helped him in his characterization of Stoney. However, the sixties were glutted with TV Westerns, and unfortunately "Stoney Burke" was regarded as part of the glut and was canceled after one season.

But the name stuck to Lord like glue. Every time he was cast in another film or series his fans recognized him immediately as Stoney and not the character he was portraying. Lord was worried. He'd seen success come to many of his good friends in the business. He didn't want Lady Luck to pass him by, so he "gave hell" to every part he was given, whether small or big.

Leonard Freeman kept his eye on Jack Lord. He had once considered him for the lead in "The FBI," but decided to give it to Efrem Zimbalist, Jr., because of the latter's success in "77 Sunset Strip." But he did let Jack play a cop in a couple of segments and immediately decided he was right for the role of a dedicated kind of cop in a new series he was considering.

Thus Jack Lord became Steve McGarrett in "Five-O," and has soared to the pinnacle of success since. Now in his eleventh consecutive season as McGarrett, Lord is thinking about what he wants to do after the show ends and he again has free time to do what he pleases.

"I want to get the hell away from TV for a long time," Jack says firmly. "Why? Because this business of being tense all the time is a killer. Just when you think you've got the right slot [during prime time] and have it made, whammo! they switch you around and put a show like the old 'Mannix' in your spot and give you a slot opposite the competition's 'Movie of the Week,' which all means you have to be good, damn good, or they'll win with the movie and your show will be canceled.

"Up tight? Boy, am I ever! Look at me! I'm like a goddamned monk. And my poor wife Marie has been putting up with it for years. I told my partner, 'Lennie [Freeman], the show may be your natural child but it's my adopted one.' But I do love my job as McGarrett, whether I bitch about it or not, and wind up working about eighty-five hours a week to prove it."

Lord maintains a facade of calmness and reservedness, but let his Irish temper flare and—whammo! There's hell to pay. But he has tenderness too. Through all the years of being an actor, Jack, says Freeman, has shown numerous, sweet and touching expressions of it—always fresh and lovely, always unexpected. Many others echo Freeman.

But the side Jack shows to his coworkers is not always loving and tender. He tends to direct for his directors and light for his cameramen. Directors handle this in their various ways. "You have to treat him like Paul Scofield," says one, "otherwise he won't react to your direction."

"Jack Lord is undirectable," says another. "Since I'm a director, I find that unbearable."

Asked if he thinks himself a second Michael Landon on the set, Lord, with musing smile and calm voice, says, "I'm better than Michael Landon ever thought of being. Why? Because I've been in the business a lot longer than he has, and I'm a professional. A seasoned professional. I take everything on the set seriously, including my own acting, and I strive for perfection, even though I don't consider myself a complete perfectionist. Confusing? Maybe. But that's how I am, and nothing's going to change me."

He switches to talk about Hawaii. "I love that beautiful island. There's a sweetness, a gentleness, a naiveté, a goodness about the islands that is totally uncapturable. Example: when we're shooting, kids often come up with bags of potato chips for us, then run shyly away. No autographs, no hunkering for a tabloid 'exclusive' of some kind; just honest little kids showing their love for us the only way they know how to. It's beautiful.

"This show will be it for me, when it ends. I'll never leave Hawaii. They'll have to carry me out first. I love it here."

Freeman elucidated when asked about his protégé's portrayal of the cowboy Stoney Burke: "If Jack today could play the role of either Ken Maynard or Charles Starrett, he would be perfectly equipped for it. I, for one, think he's a natural in a cowboy rig; I'd like to see him reenact one of those old B-oaters as Ken or the Durango Kid. He'd be sensational. But Jack has a mind of his own, and I don't think Westerns are any part of it. He feels that Buffalo Bills are done on TV; that is to say, in plain language, that Westerns are finished on TV. I don't agree, but getting him to think my way is another matter. But I'd still like to see him reenact one of those old Saturday matinee idols. He'd be a natural!"

What does Jack Lord think of reenacting an old cowboy hero's part for a TV special?

"I'd have to think hard on that one," he said. "I'd have to hold a survey and study the current trends. If the survey showed Westerns were *in* again, could be. But I don't know. I'd have to think very hard on it."

Western Film-TV Credits

Man of the West (UA, 1958)
The Hangman (Par., 1959)
Walk Like a Dragon (Par., 1960)
The Ride to Hangman's Tree (Univ., 1967)

"Stoney Burke" (series) (ABC-TV, 1962-63)

James Garner, as Bret Maverick in the TV series "Maverick."

James Garner

(Maverick makes good as Rockford)

Born: April 7, 1928, Norman, Okla.
Married: Lois Clarke (1956);
  children: Kimberly, Greta

ONE SPRING MORNING in Munich, 2,000 student protesters clashed with the police. The young people were losing. Riot sticks swung, rocks flew on the Leopoldstrasse. Onto the scene walked James Baumgartner, better known to TV fans as James Garner ("Rockford Files," NBC-TV). He was en route to the airport but was now about to perform in his favorite offstage role. Garner calls the part "Crusader Rabbit rides—and runs—again."

Crusader Rabbit, says Jim, describes adequately his warrior habits. As Jim analyzes, the Rabbit possesses some strong rights-fighter qualities, but he's also most reluctant to suffer personal injury, so he relies upon cunning, deceit, and improvisation. In this West German instance, Jim began by yelling at the crowd: "Stop this! Move back! Stop now, you terrorists!"

He did this so loudly, and so uncertain was everyone which group he meant—the cops or the demonstrators—that a path was cleared for Jim toward a large police sergeant. Jim approached him with a broad, ingratiating smile. Whammo! The officer did not see the explosive right coming that decked him.

"The cop was down longer than Schmeling against Joe Louis," the six foot three and one-half inch Garner says today. "The kids needed help, so I stepped in. I put my entire 215 pounds in that punch too. You should have heard the cheers for Crusader Rabbit."

But true to his shrinking side, Jim kept right on walking (rapidly) down the strasse and melted into the crowd, where he was safe from arrest, or worse.

This same sly, conniving manner of mixing into trouble, yet escaping with a whole skin, has marked Garner's most successful acting turns—in the old "Maverick" series especially. As Bret he was always involved in trouble but always emerged smelling like the proverbial rose in the end. He used the same style in films too: *The Great Escape* (1963). *Cash McCall* (1960), *Support Your Local Sheriff* (1969), and *Nichols* (TV film, 1973).

Jim's friends believe his Rabbit style of life and films is not mere coincidence. They say that the offscreen Garner bears considerable resemblance to the characters he plays. As Bret Maverick, twenty years ago, he was a gun-fearing cardsharp and agitator who could squirm out of anything—to laughs.

At close quarters Garner squints from his eye corners at you—seemingly measuring your gullibility. Coworkers say that his antennae are always out, that he can overhear conversations over thirty feet away—and remember them long after.

To demonstrate that the lovable, crafty, subversive Jim of TV is much like the real Brentwood, California, taxpayer, Garner tells how he handled the Korean War problem in 1950. "The draft board okayed me," he relates, "and I had this football knee and I said, 'Hey, Doc, how about this crippled knee? It's real cottage cheese! No cartilage left in it. See it wobble? On top of that, I've got ulcers." But the official record shows that once in Korea Garner won sergeant's stripes and was a platoon leader who forged so far behind enemy lines that U.S. planes shot and wounded him, thinking him an enemy soldier. He was decorated by General MacArthur, no less.

Producer-writer Roy Huggins ("The Fugitive," "Alias Smith and Jones"), whose "Maverick" launched Jim's career, says, "The description of Jim is a bit inflated. Jim personally wouldn't cheat anybody. I do, however, agree that's he's wily, even slippery. He also has an unusual survival capacity. And he has a mind like a whip.

"Up to 1960 he was locked into a contract which paid him only $500 a week to start and a top of $1,250 for 'Maverick,' which had brought in over $8 million. He wanted out. It all ended in a big lawsuit against Warner Bros., which he figured to lose, but he outfoxed their lawyers and won his freedom. At one point he told the press, 'I thought I had some interest in this 'Maverick' gold mine—but all Warners gave me was the shaft. The smelly end, at that.'

"After that major victory," Huggins continued, "Jim went into movies, just a TV cowboy, at the time, against such talents as Julie Andrews, Shirley MacLaine, and Audrey Hepburn. He soon had them eating out of his hand, helping him to improve. Jim, you know, never flirts with his leading ladies. He sensed long ago that women stars hate that sort of presumption. Even when he broke one of Doris Day's ribs while overplaying a love scene, she forgave him!"

Dennis Weaver, one of Jim's cronies, points out that Garner survived a six-year string of films in which he still Okie-twanged his words and leaned largely upon nose wiggling, eye rolling, double taking, brow arching, and the larceny in his dimples. Weaver says, "I think his popularity comes from the cool, bemused, insolent competence he gets across, which is *real* Jim Garner. Nothing awes him. He has knocked around everywhere, known all the crooked games there are. He's a terrific poker player—bluff him in a game, you're the loser. Jimmy's been a deep-sea sailor, oil rigger, phone lineman, lifeguard, tree trimmer, tugboat hand, auto racer, and front-line soldier in Korea. I tell him, 'Jim, if you didn't own Cherokee Productions you'd be hustling in Las Vegas, on the *house* side of the table!' "

Cherokee is a Garner-owned corporation, a sturdy entry in the high-risk independent field. Against warnings not to go it alone, Jim formed the firm from the legal shambles of "Maverick." "Partially," Jim mentions, "because I found the heaviest producers were no smarter than I am—they only had more money."

After fifteen movie parts, he was in the $500,000 per role bracket and could well afford to gamble. Modestly capitalized, Cherokee grew and in 1969-71 reportedly grossed $1 million-plus with its slapstick pair *Support Your Local Sheriff* and *Support Your Local Gunfighter*, which enabled Garner to negotiate from strength for another network marketing of *Nichols,* a Cherokee creation.

Cherokee Productions stands alone in another respect. The firm's executive director is a woman, one of the few women in film history to hold such a high post. Meta Rosenberg is a svelte, cool, former literary agent. "Perhaps some were shocked when I was appointed boss," says Meta, "because there were several qualified male candidates. But I wasn't surprised. Jim's got pioneer in him, and none of those damn sex hangups of most producers in the business."

Of German ancestry with a Cherokee strain, Garner's a droll, happy man, married for twenty-two years to Lois Clarke, a Los Angeles-born girl who is slim and elegant. And he's a private man. He once bribed the neighborhood seller of a guide to stars' homes to omit him from the list. Other Garner traits—he puts on no airs and he bores easily. The latter may explain the roaming life he adopted, leaving hometown Norman, Oklahoma, at eighteen.

"I made the Mississippi tugboats, got drunk some, chased pretty women—but no married ones, that'll get you killed in Galveston or San Pedro—and left one merchant ship just before she sank in an Atlantic storm," he remembers.

How about it? Is Jim Garner really as Machiavellian away from work as he is on the job?

"Well," he replies, "before I escaped 'Maverick' and what I call 'Warners' Penitentiary'—and 'Maverick' was a bad show toward the end, and I was ashamed of it—I was offered $7,500 to go on Pat Boone's hour. But Warners wouldn't allow it. They owned me then. I never forgot what they did to me.

"Later, as an official of the Actors Guild, I found that actors were getting little or no pay for TV residuals. Ol' Jim shot his cuffs, made a few passes—and soon we had legislation that changed all of that, and about thirty-five Warners players collected a bundle."

Then he added, "We took care of the matter of WB contractees being forced to appear at rodeos, telethons, and peanut-pushing contests for free. Now the price went up to more than $500 per performer.

"I'm kinda like the oldtime fight promoter they called 'The Honest Brakeman.' Like him, I never stole a boxcar. But, yeah, I can be slick—when *pushed*."

Western Film-TV Credits

Shoot-Out at Medicine Bend (WB, 1957)
Duel at Diablo (UA, 1966)
Hour of the Gun (UA, 1967)
Support Your Local Sheriff (UA, 1969)
Support Your Local Gunfighter (UA, 1971)

A Man Called Sledge (Col., 1971)
Skin Game (WB, 1971)
One Little Indian (BV, 1973)
The Castaway Cowboy (BV, 1974)

"Maverick" (series) (ABC-TV, (1956-60)
Nichols (special) (ABC-TV, 1973)

Clayton Moore, as "The Lone Ranger" with his friend and sidekick "Tonto" (Jay Silverheels) on right.

Clayton Moore

(The Lone Ranger)

Born: September 14, 1914, Chicago, Ill.
Married: Sally Allen (1954); child: Dawn

THE HEAVY IRON door clangs shut. Behind it Jake Moran sullenly slumps onto the narrow cell cot. "Sheriff," he grumbles at the big man looking out the window, "who was that masked man?" The old lawman turns toward the outlaw and says, "Why, Moran, you dad-burned idiot! That's *the Lone Ranger!*"

Clayton Moore became the Lone Ranger when the popular masked rider of the radio waves was brought to television. Selected from hundreds of actors testing for the part, Moore filmed 221 half-hour episodes from 1949 to 1956.

Of course Clayton Moore was no stranger to the role of action hero. He starred in several serials for Republic Studios during the 1940s. In *Perils of Nyoka* (1942) Moore was involved with jungle girl Kay Aldridge who was searching for her lost father in Africa. They fought their way through the usual jungle perils, as well as wild Arabs and fanatics of a strange religious cult.

Other Republic serials in which Moore starred or costarred were *The Crimson Ghost* (1946), *Jesse James Rides Again* (1947), *The Adventures of Frank and Jesse James* (1948), and *G-Men Never Forget* (1948).

Clayton Moore was born and raised in Chicago. After high school graduation he got a job as a commercial photographer's model, and following that he joined a traveling circus, as part of a flying-trapeze act. For a while he was also a Powers model in New York. Then he headed for California with dreams of becoming a Western star.

His dreams materialized into screen roles, but instead of playing the hero he was the heavy in films with Gene Autry, Roy Rogers, and Charles Starrett.

In Republic's *Down Laredo Way* (1953), which also starred Rex Allen, Moore utilized his circus experience. He portrays a trapeze artist who is killed by Marjorie Lord, the villain in the film. Rex and his sidekick Slim Pickens set things straight for Moore's daughter at the end.

The Lone Ranger was created forty-five years ago by George W. Trendle. The program was written by Fran Striker and first broadcast over WXYZ in Detroit. Brace Beemer was the masked man in the forties and continued until the last live radio broadcast of the show in 1954.

215

Moore, nearly six feet tall and 190 pounds, auditioned for the Lone Ranger part on TV and won it. He looked great in the Ranger rig. He looked even better on the white stallion known as Silver to all fans. Jay Silverheels, a real Indian, won the part opposite Moore as Tonto.

Until recently Moore was still under the original contract which allowed him to appear only as the Lone Ranger. His mainstay was doing commercials for Dodge cars and trucks. He and former "Rifleman" Chuck Connors shared equal billing for Dodge. In 1979, a much publicized court order instructed Moore to make no more appearances as the Lone Ranger. Many of his loyal fans considered this an injustice. Nearing retirement age but still in top physical shape, Moore says of his tenure as the Lone Ranger:

"The Lone Ranger never killed anyone. He never shot to kill, always to wound. He stayed away from brutality but believed in fighting for that which is right. He never hit a man while he was down. He never swore or drank, and never kissed the heroine.

"One of the bit-players on our show was Jim Arness, who later made it big as Matt Dillon on 'Gunsmoke.' We paid him a mere $45 a day back then, but today he makes more like forty-five thou' a day. I hope his new show, 'How the West Was Won,' is a success like 'Gunsmoke' was."

What about Clayton Moore the man?

"My personal life is my own, thank you. But I think more and more of the Lone Ranger is rubbing off onto my personal life. I guess I should have been born back in the 1850s or 1860s. I love the woods and I love to fish. I would love to have taken a wagon train west, to the Great Divide.

"I used to live in Woodland Hills, California; last year we moved to Nevada, on Lake Tahoe. My wife's name is Sally, and we have a fourteen-year-old daughter named Dawn."

On TV Westerns Moore said:

"There are no heroes today on the screen or TV. The cowboy is sort of Americana, always has been, myth or not. The Lone Ranger programs always tried to deliver the message of the history of our country . . . and fair play.

"I've gone through generations of kids, but I'm ready to tackle the role again . . . if they are serious about filming a new Ranger series. From what I've heard, plans are in the mill. I'd love to play the role again before I get too old."

Western Film-TV Credits

Kit Carson (UA, 1940)

Along the Oregon Trail (Rep., 1947)

Jesse James Rides Again (serial) (Rep., 1947)

Adventures of Frank and Jesse James (serial) (Rep., 1948)

The Cowboy and the Indians (Col., 1949)

Riders of the Whistling Pines (Col., 1949)

The Ghost of Zorro (serial) (Rep., 1949)

Montana (WB, 1950)

Cyclone Fury (Col., 1951)

Buffalo Bill in Tomahawk Territory (UA, 1952)

Night Stage to Galveston (Col., 1952)

Montana Territory (Col., 1952)

Barbed Wire (Col., 1952)

Son of Geronimo (serial) (Col., 1952)

Hawk of Wild River (Col., 1952)

Kansas Pacific (AA, 1953)

Down Laredo Way (Rep., 1953)

Black Dakotas (Col., 1954)

Gunfighters of the Northwest (serial) (Col., 1954)

The Lone Ranger (WB, 1956)

The Lone Ranger and the Lost City of Gold (UA, 1958)

"The Lone Ranger" (series) (ABC-TV, 1949-56)

Gallery of Other New-Breed Stars

Rod Taylor and Dennis Cole tried their luck at making a Western TV series in "Bearcats" (CBS-TV, 1971). It fizzled out before the first season's shooting had ended.

George Peppard as Major John Harkness, commander of Fort Bravo in The Bravos, *a 1971 film made for television by Universal.*

Gregory Peck, with Thelma Ritter, Robert Preston, and Debbie Reynolds in How the West Was Won *(1963).*

Edd Byrnes strikes a Western hero's pose while making a "spaghetti Western" in Italy. He is best known for his portrayal of "Kookie" in the defunct TV series "77 Sunset Strip."

Dean Martin, with Raquel Welch in Bandolero! (1968).

Ben Murphy gained fame in "Alias Smith & Jones" (ABC-TV, 1971-73).

John McIntire and Jeanette Nolan (in real life Mrs. McIntire). He headed the cast of "Wagon Train" after Ward Bond died.

Clint Walker, better known to his many fans as Cheyenne Bodie, his role in "Cheyenne" (ABC-TV, 1956-1963).

Charles Bronson and Yul Brynner in the made-in-Spain Western Villa Rides *(1968).*

Steve McQueen, with Susan Oliver in a scene from the popular TV Western series "Wanted: Dead or Alive" (CBS-TV, 1958-61).

Fess Parker began his TV career in the role of Davy Crockett and went on to more fame in the title role of "Daniel Boone" (NBC-TV, 1964-1970).

Gene Barry gained prominence on TV for his portrayal of the title role in "Bat Masterson" (NBC-TV, 1957-1961).

Michael Landon is best known now as the star of "Little House on the Prairie" (NBC-TV, 1974-   ), but he first gained popularity as "Little Joe" Cartright in "Bonanza" (NBC-TV, 1959-73).

PART THREE

Ghost Riders in the Sky

A final tribute to the great
cowboy movie heroes who
have ridden into the sunset
for the last time

Last Roundup

LONG BEFORE THE advent of movies, the real Wild West had its heroes: Buffalo Bill Cody, Wild Bill Hickok, and Kit Carson. These real-life frontiersmen found their daring deeds aggrandized (as well as fictionalized) by such promotional tactics as the dime novel and the picture postcard. The man, even then, was inseparable from the myth.

Buffalo Bill was one who cashed in on his reputation with his own Wild West show (in which Ken Maynard was later to be a trick rider), and his skills were recorded for posterity by the earliest movie-makers.

The cowboy himself—the authentic working waddy—found the new movie industry a godsend, not only providing a new source of income but also preserving for him a way of life that was beginning to die out.

Hollywood, in turn, could hardly have existed without the cowboys. They moved stock equipment to locations, doubled for stars, handled livestock, and staged action sequences—not just for Westerns but for *all* movies. As Western movies increased in popularity, the lifestyle of the cowboy remained, for a time, alive; the original myths of the West were pushed into the background.

Youngsters playing cowboys and Indians in the 1900s vied for the honor of being Bill Hickok or Jesse James. In the teens and twenties they fought for the right to be William S. Hart or Fred Thomson, the cowboy actors who had portrayed those figures on the screen.

Wyatt Earp and Bat Masterson, both friends of Bill Hart, were still alive, but Hollywood regarded them more as colorless policemen than as glamorous frontiersmen. It wasn't until the talkies, and most especially the era of television, that they were established as myths—Hollywood-style.

As the movies became big business, the exploitation of stars increased, and it was never more obvious than with the Western star. Throughout the thirties, comic books and radio suggested to the youth of America that the Western star was as much a hero offscreen as on.

In the silent-film days Fox had very successfully publicized Tom Mix as a kind of soldier of fortune and Lone Ranger rolled into one. His admittedly exciting prescreen life was amplified by manufactured tales of his career as a Western lawman and by more adventures than Mix, or anyone else, could possibly experience in a lifetime.

But the strategy worked. The studios later tried repeating the process with Gene Autry, William Boyd, Charles Starrett, and other Western stars whose offscreen action was largely limited to making their bank deposits.

Kids playing cowboys and Indians in the 1930s tended to emulate the most publicized Western stars, or those whose films were filled with the most action. The best actors—or those who thought enough of their craft to work at achieving something worthwhile even within the limits of the B-film (particularly Tim McCoy and Buck Jones)—were often rather shabbily ignored by the street-corner "Westerners."

Kids today, however, play cowboys and Indians very little—in fact hardly at all. *Godzilla* and the like, along with the newest heroes of the Kung Fu movies, occupy them now. The Western, once shared by so many, is nearly a forgotten pleasure; only a few are being made in Hollywood and still fewer Western series remain on television.

Unlike those of yesteryear, youngsters today have no cowboy film heroes to idolize or identify with. Besides, today's youngster would be thought of by his comrades as a kook if he wanted to play cowboys and emulate such stars as James Arness, Clint Eastwood, and Robert Fuller, who themselves occasionally take other movie or TV roles just "to be different" or "as a refresher." Hence the need today to create heroes and myths out of our few remaining Western stars—if possible.

Far too many of our superstars of bygone days have mounted their hosses and taken that final ride. To them the following pages are dedicated as a final tribute for all of the wonderfully exciting Saturday afternoons they made us scream, yell, cry—and live the legends of the West again!

Colonel Tim McCoy in 1936.

Colonel Timothy J. McCoy

(Instilled the "Good Cowboy" image)

Born: April 10, 1891, Saginaw, Mich.
Married: Agnes Miller (1921); divorced
   (1931); children: two sons, one daughter;
   remarried: Inga Arvad (1945), died (1974);
   children: Ronald, Terry
Died: January 29, 1978

(Note: Colonel Timothy J. McCoy died shortly after this final interview was given. He is buried in Nogales, Arizona, near the house he built himself. The final interview is unchanged.)

WHEN MIKE TODD was casting *Around the World in 80 Days* he had only one man in mind for the officer commanding the U.S. Cavalry unit that arrives in time to rescue Phineas Fogg from an Indian attack. That man was Colonel Tim McCoy.

Todd's choice was a long-overdue tribute to the veteran soldier-actor, and Todd's personal gift to him for appearing was a set of miniatures of McCoy's thirteen campaign medals and decorations for heroism.

A year later, 1957, McCoy played a similiar part as the one-armed general in the Rod Steiger Western *Run of the Arrow*. Tim performed with the same air of authority he had displayed in all his Western pictures, but he wasn't offered another film part until 1965 when Alex Gordon called on him to appear as a circuit judge in *Requiem for a Gunfighter*, which starred Rod Cameron and had a slew of Western oldtimers in its cast, including such notables as Bob Steele and Johnny Mack Brown.

All considered, Hollywood could certainly have done better by Tim McCoy, one of its most famous oldtime, big box-office stars.

Tim first attained the rank of colonel, U.S. Army, in World War I and resumed it during World War II (he served as a reserve officer all through the years of his film career between the wars). When he returned home after World War II he found himself passé as a Western film idol, and like so many others he looked elsewhere for employment—circuses, Wild West shows, and television.

Although he had no ambition to be an actor, Tim had innate theatricalism. An articulate, well-spoken man, he performed with natural dignity, always very much the army officer. His personality and his appearance—immaculate, even to shined boots or shoes—set him apart from

231

more roughneck contemporaries like Buck Jones, Hoot Gibson, and Ken Maynard.

The Tim McCoy Westerns were for the most part detective stories *on the range,* but his image was always a distinct one: black shirt and trousers, wide-brimmed Stetson (white and black) worn at a jaunty angle, a large kerchief around his throat, and gloves. His pearl-handled pistol and his wide, worked-leather gunbelt with a large Mexican buckle were worn in all his films. He still wears this distinctive ensemble whenever he makes professional appearances today (with the Tommy Scott Country Caravan & Wild West Show, of which he is part owner, making 300 one-night stands a season), and he is immediately recognized by multitudes as their Saturday afternoon hero of three and four decades ago.

It does Hollywood producers little credit that Tim McCoy's value to the motion picture industry, if not as an actor then as an authority on the American West, was never fully appreciated or utilized.

McCoy is a lifetime student of Western history, and a sought-after expert on Indian sign languages. His knowledge was aptly demonstrated on his own television show, which he did from Hollywood in the early 1950s. The show varied in length—at one time it was ninety minutes, the first half-hour being a sort of illustrated lecture about the West (maps and still photographs) and the last portion being one of his old movies.

In 1951 the McCoy show won the Parent-Teacher Association award for television's most outstanding educational offering. It also won an Emmy for Tim, but no offer of work from a Hollywood studio as a consultant on Westerns, a position for which his learned background incomparably fitted him.

Tim, in fact, first began his film career as a consultant. In 1923 he was serving as adjutant general in Wyoming and in his free time pursuing his interest in Indian history and languages. His picture was often in newspapers and magazines of the West because of his research and discoveries. In an Arizona valley, for example, he located Wovoka, the ghost dance messiah of the Indians, and the photograph of the two of them has become famous. Furthermore, Tim was celebrated as one of the three soldiers who could use the sign languages of the Plains Indians. The two other experts were General Hugh L. Scott and Captain Philo Clark.

"I received a call from Hollywood," recalls Tim, "because they were going to make a picture called *The Covered Wagon* and they wanted 500 long-haired Indians from the Western states. They asked me if I would be interested in rounding up these Indians, which I did. I brought them to Hollywood in two special trains—Indians, squaws, papooses, tepees, dogs, everything. Because I was the only one who could converse with these Indians (sign language), who belonged to several tribes, Paramount, or Famous Players-Lasky as it was called in those days, asked me if I wouldn't get up a prologue of some sort and appear on the stage at

Grauman's Chinese Theatre in Hollywood with the showing of the picture. So I resigned my commission and did so.''

For such a prologue to *The Covered Wagon*, Tim selected Indians and others who had some historical importance. One of the latter was a red-haired white woman, Mrs. Broken Horn, who had been captured by Indians when a baby and couldn't speak a word of English. One of the Indians Tim picked had actually fought againt Custer.

The prologue was a success, and when *The Covered Wagon* was booked for London it was thought the best way to sell it there would be to use McCoy's prologue. Thus he appeared at the London Pavilion for almost a year.

When Tim returned to Hollywood after two widely publicized years of promoting *The Covered Wagon*, Irving Thalberg proposed starring him in a series of Westerns. Tim signed with MGM in 1926 and made a string of pictures for that studio in the ensuing three years.

Those silent films stressed authenticity in depicting Indians and Indian life. The first of the MGM Westerns was *War Paint*, made on location in Wyoming among the Arapaho and Shoshone Indians (Wyoming was McCoy's old stamping ground as a cowboy). One of Tim's leading ladies in those Westerns was a young Joan Crawford.

In 1930 Tim went to Universal to make that studio's first sound Western serial, *The Indians Are Coming*. The following year he did another serial, *Heroes of the Flames*, which was a paean to firefighting. These were the only two serials in which Tim starred.

He then was contracted by Columbia Pictures for four years. After making seventeen Westerns for Columbia, he was cast in other roles much more suited to the talents of such actors as Jack Holt and Richard Arlen—aviator, firefighter, newspaperman, racing driver, and policeman.

Columbia soon realized its mistake and put him back in the saddle again for an additional nine Westerns. And these films were excellent products of their kind. Each was made in two or three weeks, almost entirely on location.

Tim recalls that the extras in the films were all ex-cowboys. "They weren't drugstore cowboys and many of them were former rodeo champions." A few had escaped from the law in other states, but mostly they were cowpokes who had drifted into Hollywood when they found they could earn $7.50 a day in pictures as against $40.00 a month on the open range.

In 1935-36 Tim made ten Westerns for Puritan Pictures, and in these he tried to expand his acting technique. For the first time he decided to play a stock character, Lightnin' Bill Carson, whom he portrayed in several of the Puritan Westerns. And in some he also played character parts—a Mexican, a Chinese, a Gypsy, etc., in which guise the hero slipped into town to size up the local situation.

Tim sat astride his horse in a manner that has not been duplicated by any other Western film actor.

Tim continued until the early 1940s to make Westerns for lesser producers—Monogram, Victory, and PRC (Producers Releasing Corporation). He usually received $4,000 a picture, which today is the average star's salary for one day of television shooting for a series.

The quality of a Tim McCoy Western, like that of other Western stars' pictures, varied from film to film. The big problem, recalls Tim, was writers. "Very often, it was a case of a young writer from New York arriving and rewriting the last Western he'd seen. Thus, and regretfully, many Westerns became stereotyped. They looked as though they had been cut out with cookie cutters.

"The truth about the real West was twisted to conform to the writer's preconceptions, and when historical figures were used there was so much fiction they could have been anybody.

"However," Tim continues, "you always have to remember motion pictures are not made to serve as documentaries of history. Movies are for entertainment, but even so, I've always maintained, you can give audiences authenticity *with* the entertainment."

Inasmuch as Tim is a denizen of both the real West and the filmed one, he is often asked to compare the two. "The West depicted by films," he says, "is a living, breathing, American myth. Real cowboys were not fistfighters and usually avoided that sort of thing when possible. If they did engage in fisticuffs, it was over with quickly, not prolonged like today's John Wayne films. Why, if real cowboys ever fought so long, they'd drop in a few minutes of utter exhaustion!"

As for filmdom's hip-shooting and fast-draw, Tim has this to say: "The hip-shooting is the most exaggerated thing of all. How are you going to hit anything, or anyone, unless you are only five feet away? Any man who has ever handled firearms knows it takes all you can do to lay your sights, take a deep breath, exhale half of it, and slowly squeeze the trigger, if you're to hit anything with a pistol. However, audiences always love the long drawn-out fight scenes and gun duels . . . that's what they call 'box-office' selling points."

Tim's last Western films are of particular interest. In 1941 Monogram induced him to star with his friend Buck Jones in a series of Westerns that brought two of the finest of all Western stars together.

Jones (real name Charles Gebhart), whom Tim recalls as a very quiet, retiring man when not working and who is Tim's favorite film cowboy to this day, had started his film career in the late teens—when Fox hired him as a stunt double for Tom Mix. Jones had become a rodeo star and when Mix became difficult to deal with Fox began building up Jones.

Tim and Buck made eight well-written and well-produced, but rather slow-paced, Westerns. The series (*The Rough Riders*) came to an abrupt end when Tim was recalled to active duty with the army and Buck died in the Cocoanut Grove nightclub fire in Boston in 1942.

Tim pays him verbal tribute today: "He died trying to rescue people from the fire. He could have saved himself several times, but didn't. He kept going back into that inferno trying to save people, time after time, until the roof collapsed and killed him. But that daring to save people—that was typical of Buck. The films, the world, and I lost a real close friend in Buck Jones."

Tim's memory of his own heyday in films is warmly candid: "It was a lot of fun and darned remunerative. I liked the income and I loved the life. I certainly entertain no regrets whatever for having gone into films."

Tim McCoy grew up in Saginaw, Michigan. Here his father, who had been a soldier in his native Ireland, was chief of police. The elder McCoy instilled in his son a respect for military life and fostered his interest in the West.

"Those were the horse-and-buggy days, and the horses were brought from the West by real cowboys," explains Tim. "Whenever they came to town I used to visit their camps and listen to them. I got myself a horse and learned to rope and ride. After high school in Saginaw, I was sent to St. Ignatius College in Chicago, but my heart was 'way out West.'

"I quit college, bought myself a railroad ticket to Wyoming, where cattle still drifted on wide-open ranges, and landed in the town of Lander. I found work right away, on a ranch pitching hay, and became a cowboy.

"I worked in the Wind River country and it was there I first came into direct contact with the Indians—the Arapaho and Shoshone. It was my contacts with them, while rounding up stray cattle, that enabled me to learn their sign language. I learned it so well one of the Arapaho chiefs once said I 'must have been an Indian long ago.' "

Some years later the Arapaho adopted Tim into their tribe, and named him High Eagle.

By 1912 Tim was a hardened wrangler and something of a romantic. "I used to do a lot of dreaming on those long, lonely trail rides," he muses, "and I always imagined I would ride around the next bend and come across a beautiful young girl from England who was on a visit to her uncle."

It was this sort of romanticism that took him into an army career. "Teddy Roosevelt wanted to get into World War I," Tim says, "and decided to organize a cavalry division before America was actually in the war. I wrote to him and offered to recruit a squadron for him from Wyoming and Montana cowboys. He accepted and said I would be commissioned a captain.

"But we were denied permission to take any of those voluntary troops to Europe on the ground that World War I was not a 'Rough Riders' kind of war. I guess we really knew that trained troops, not someone waving his hat and shouting 'Follow me, boys!' were necessary. Teddy Roosevelt was a typical movie soldier. It's usually forgotten that when he led the charge up San Juan Hill he arrived with only thirty men."

Tim, however, did manage to get himself assigned to the U.S. field artillery. He later served with the 88th Infantry Division and was decorated several times for heroism. He didn't get back into the cavalry until the end of the war, at which time the army had only three mounted regiments.

With the resignation of a man who wishes he had been born earlier, Tim says: "The handwriting was on the wall for the cavalry. Mobility, tanks, trucks, and precision firepower did for it, and a commander was no longer a man who could lead a charge but a man who understood logistics, how to deploy resources and forces."

Tim liked military life and decided to make the army a career. He had been a marked success during World War I, and a series of swift field promotions had brought him to the rank of colonel before the age of thirty. Since he was interested in remaining in the West and in studying the actual sites, as well as the tactics, of old Indian campaigns, he accepted eagerly the post of adjutant general of Wyoming when it was offered.

Tim had the good fortune to meet and be liked by General Hugh Lenox Scott, who had served with the U.S. Cavalry, chiefly in the Dakotas and Oklahoma, during the years of the last Indian campaigns (1876-97). General Scott had become a specialist in the language and history of the Plains Indians and had been the army's chief of staff from 1914 to 1917. For a time Tim was Scott's aide and accompanied him on visits to some of the army's foremost Western posts: Forts Riley, Sill, Snelling, and, particularly, Washakie, the last being in Wyoming. After Scott retired from the army he was appointed head of the Board of Indian Commissioners and no doubt had a lot to do with Tim becoming adjutant general of Wyoming.

General Scott once said, "Tim McCoy knows more about the Indians than they indeed know about themselves." In appraising that compliment, one has to recall Tim's own aphorism: "The best way to find out an Indian's history is to tell it to him."

General Scott and Tim made a serious study of "Custer's last stand." Neither of them admired the flamboyant cavalry officer. They traced General Custer's route to the Little Big Horn and talked both to guides who had fought with Custer and to Indians who had fought against him. They concluded that Custer had made a grievous error and had he lived he would have been court-martialed. He ignored his orders, split his command in the face of a superior force, drove his troops to a point of fatigue, which made them unfit for combat—all because he was in trouble in Washington and needed a spectacular victory to vindicate himself with Grant and the War Department. The press, always on his side, played up his miserable, bloody defeat as a triumph of courage largely because it occurred nine days before July 4, 1876, the centennial of American independence.

These rare findings emerge partly because of Tim's discovery that five Arapaho Indians had been in the Sioux camp on the day Custer and his command fell. Tim discovered this during an Indian celebration in Lander, Wyoming, when he told some Arapaho chiefs that he and General Scott had just come from the Custer battleground.

With his partner Tommy Scott.

Advertisement.

As a performer in the Wild West Show of Tommy Scott's Western Caravan.

One of the old chiefs remarked that Water Man, an Indian seated near the fire, had been in that fight. "I talked to Water Man," says Tim, "and learned that another Arapaho, Left Hand, had also been in the Sioux camp."

Tim turned over to Colonel W. A. Graham the details he gleaned from Water Man and Left Hand for inclusion in Graham's *The Custer Myth*.

When Tim began making sizable amounts of money from his movies, he developed and enlarged the ranch he had acquired while working as a cowboy. Located fifty miles from Thermopolis, Wyoming, it became a working ranch of some five thousand acres. He sold it for a handsome profit upon his return from World War II.

Tim had asked for active duty in World War II after "I got my ears knocked down" in the election of 1942. Old guard Republicans had nominated him for U.S. senator from Wyoming. He lost the race and asked for active duty in the army. He served as an officer in liaison between ground and air tactical units. Again he distinguished himself under fire and received decorations for bravery and heroism. He was not wounded, luckily.

The ownership and development of his Wyoming ranch, prior to selling it, affected the image people in the movie industry had of him—and even the image audiences formed of him from his screen demeanors. "I always felt," says Tim, "that if my pals up around my ranch saw me on the screen trying to play a make-believe Westerner I'd have an awful lot of explaining to do." And whenever an interviewer would remark that he seemed a little too gentlemanly to play the part of a cowboy, Tim would reply: "You're thinking of Bret Harte's stories and the gold rush 49ers. People in the West aren't illiterates—they've been going to school for three or four generations."

Although he was a Western star, Tim mingled with the more sophisticated Hollywood actors. His closest friends were Ronald Colman, Warner Baxter, Gary Cooper, and Richard Barthelmess.

Tim has been married twice. His first marriage, during his years of stardom, produced two sons and a daughter and ended in divorce. In 1945 he married Inga Arvad, a Danish journalist he met when she asked to interview him upon his return from World War II. She had made something of a journalistic splash in Europe by her exclusive interviews before the war with Adolf Hitler and other high-ranking Nazis (she had known Goering's Swedish wife and had been one of the guests at Goering's wedding). After arriving in the United States she went to work for Cissie Patterson and at one time pinchhit for Sheilah Graham.

She also did a story about John F. Kennedy when he was a navy lieutenant in which she predicted he would have an important American future. She later had the story engraved on a plaque, which hangs today in the Nogales, Arizona, rancho-style home of the McCoys.

Their two sons, Ronald and Terry, are now grown. But they too are not without honors. Ronald won the American Legion National High School Oratorical Contest in 1966, and the same year was elected president of Boys' Nation. Terry followed his older brother by winning nearly identical honors for his efforts a year later. Both are grown and have families today.

"By now," Tim says with a laugh, "I should be sitting in an officers' mess having my whiskey brought to me by a batman."

But that is only his way of jesting. He is primarily the kind of man who must be busy to be happy, which is why he currently spends nine months of every year with the Tommy Scott show making 300 one-night stands in the U.S. and Canada. He still rides, shoots, does whip tricks, and, more important, tells stories—true ones—of the great American West.

"I'll never retire," says Tim firmly. "Doing what I do keeps me as young as I feel—about thirty-nine, like Jack Benny— and if I stopped I'd be my true age in a minute. I'd be dead."

Western Film Credits

The Covered Wagon (Par., 1923)
The Thundering Herd (Par., 1925)
War Paint (MGM, 1926)
Winners of the Wilderness (MGM, 1927)
California (MGM, 1927)
The Frontiersman (MGM, 1927)
Spoilers of the West (MGM, 1927)
Wyoming (MGM, 1928)
The Law of the Range (MGM, 1928)
Riders of the Dark (MGM, 1928)
Beyond the Sierras (MGM, 1928)
The Bush Ranger (MGM, 1928)
Morgan's Last Raid (MGM, 1929)
Sioux Blood (MGM, 1929)
The Overland Telegraph (MGM, 1929)
The Desert Rider (MGM, 1929)
The Indians Are Coming (serial) (Univ., 1930)
The One Way Trail (Col., 1931)
Shotgun Pass (Col., 1931)
The Fighting Marshal (Col., 1931)
The Fighting Fool (Col., 1932)
Texas Cyclone (Col., 1932)

Daring Danger (Col., 1932)
The Riding Tornado (Col., 1932)
Two-Fisted Law (Col., 1932)
Cornered (Col., 1932)
The Western Code (Col., 1932)
Fighting for Justice (Col., 1932)
End of the Trail (Col., 1932)
Man of Action (Col., 1933)
Silent Men (Col., 1933)
The Whirlwind (Col., 1933)
Rusty Rides Alone (Col., 1933)
Beyond the Law (Col., 1934)
The Prescott Kid (Col., 1934)
The Westerner (Col., 1934)
Square Shooter (Col., 1935)
Law Beyond the Range (Col., 1935)
The Revenge Rider (Col., 1935)
Fighting Shadows (Col., 1935)
Justice of the Range (Col., 1935)
Riding Wild (Col., 1935)
The Outlaw Deputy (Pur., 1935)
The Man from Guntown (Pur., 1935)
Bulldog Courage (Pur., 1935)
Roarin' Guns (Pur., 1936)
Border Caballero (Pur., 1936)

Lightnin' Bill Carson (Pur., 1936)
Aces and Eights (Pur., 1936)
The Lion's Den (Pur., 1936)
The Ghost Patrol (Pur., 1936)
The Traitor (Pur., 1936)
West of Rainbow's End (Mon., 1938)
Code of the Rangers (Mon., 1938)
Two-Gun Justice (Mon., 1938)
The Phantom Ranger (Mon., 1938)
Lightnin' Carson Rides Again (Vic., 1938)
Six-Gun Trail (Vic., 1938)
Code of the Cactus (Vic., 1939)
Texas Wildcats (Vic., 1939)
Outlaw's Paradise (Vic., 1939)
Trigger Fingers (Vic., 1939)
The Fighting Renegade (Vic., 1939)
Straight Shooter (Vic., 1939)
Texas Renegades (PRC, 1940)
Frontier Crusader (PRC, 1940)
Gun Code (PRC, 1940)
Arizona Gang Busters (PRC, 1940)
Riders of Black Mountain (PRC, 1940)
Outlaws of the Rio Grande (PRC, 1941)
The Texas Marshal (PRC, 1941)
Arizona Bound (Mon., 1941)
The Gunman from Bodie (Mon., 1941)
Forbidden Trails (Mon., 1941)
Below the Border (Mon., 1942)
Ghost Town Law (Mon., 1942)
Down Texas Way (Mon., 1942)
Riders of the West (Mon., 1942)
West of the Law (Mon., 1942)
Around the World in 80 Days (UA, 1956)
Run of the Arrow (UI, 1957)
Requiem for a Gunfighter (Embassy, 1965)

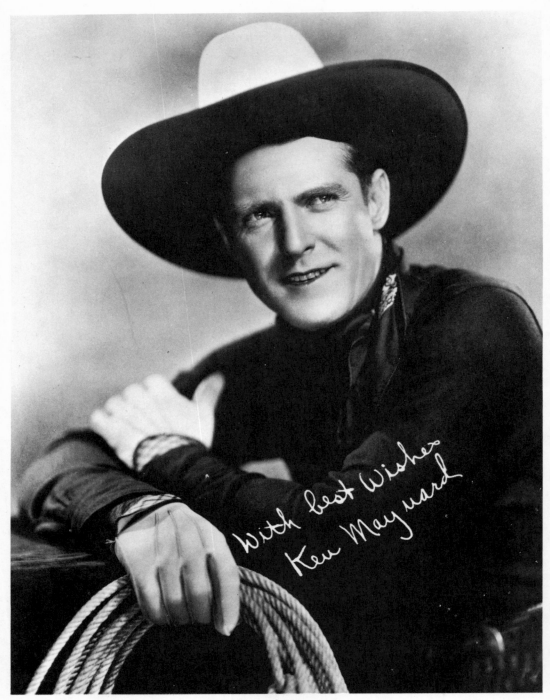

Ken Maynard, Western star.

Ken Maynard

("I'm just a plain old cowboy")

Born: July 27, 1895, Mission, Tex.
Married: Bertha Denham (1940)
Died: March 23, 1973

(Note: Ken Maynard died shortly after this final interview was given. He is buried in Paso Robles, California. The final interview is unchanged.)

BIG JOHN WAYNE's old films are getting plenty of viewer interest these days on TV. But few of Wayne's many fans realize that distant hard-riding scenes in his early films were all dubbed from footage of another great Western film star: Ken Maynard.

Back in the 1920s and 30s Ken Maynard was one of the top-ranking Western film stars in Hollywood, and John Wayne, a former University of Southern California All-American football star, was practically a screen unknown. Like Tom Mix, Tim McCoy, and Buck Jones, Ken Maynard was a cowboy in real life, as well as a champion rodeo bronc buster and a trick rider for the Barnum & Bailey Circus. He utilized all his know-how in achieving movie stardom.

For more than ten years he rode across the silver screen enthralling old and young Americans with his trick riding on Tarzan (his wonder horse) and his good-guy deeds against overwhelming odds. His name in filmdom was as popular in the 1920s, 30s, and early 40s as John Wayne's is today. And at one time he was rumored to be nearly a millionaire.

Then something happened—a secret which Ken carried to his grave. As a result, he began to drink heavily, and to spend his money lavishly, foolishly. He was even arrested several times—as late as 1956, in Texas—for drunkenness and disturbing the peace.

When Ken finally decided that the solution to whatever he was harboring was not in a bottle, he was almost broke. In the early 1940s he teamed up with Bob Steele and Hoot Gibson in a series of popular but shortlived "Trail Blazers" films.

Ken started drinking heavily again and practically faded from the circle of stardom after that, his name turning up only in connection with his aforementioned brushes with the law. His late brother Kermit always came to Ken's rescue with bail money until he died; then there was no one to stand up for Ken. He finally became a nearly forgotten man, living under impoverished conditions in a trailer camp in California's San Fernando Valley.

At the age of 77, shortly before his death, Ken was tall, erect, and alert, although telltale scars of tough, impoverished times lined his face. But he loved to talk about the "good old days" in Hollywood, as though it were yesterday instead of decades ago.

"It was old John Ringlin' and Tex Rickard," said Ken, "got hold of me one day and talked me into signin' up, and my very first time out I won th' title of World Champion Cowboy. I held that title from 1920, when I won $42,000, until I retired as a cowboy, undefeated, in 1922. That was th' year our show played Los Angeles and I asked a friend to take me out and show me th' movie studios since till then I'd just heard about them but had never seen them."

The trip to the film studios was a memorable one for Ken for it was during that visit that he was introduced to Lynn Reynolds, director for Tom Mix's pictures.

"Old Lynn looked me up and down, said I was okay, and before you know'd it I was makin' my first motion picture."

What Ken meant was that Lynn Reynolds urged him to take a screen test, which he did and passed with flying colors.

Ken's first films were silent and included such action titles as *The Demon Rider, The Grey Vulture, Fightin' Courage* (all released in 1924), and a host of others. Ken was signed by First National and made over fifteen films between 1926 and 1929. Then came the talkies.

"I had this kinda nasal-soundin' Texas voice, but it sounded real enough, so I made it into th' talkies," admits Ken.

His first real talking films appeared in 1930, when he did a series for Universal.

"I never did make no three hunnert-odd pictures like all them movie-magazine stories said I did," Ken confessed. "I'd say, to be tellin' th' truth, that it was more like a hunnert and fifty pictures I made altogether.

"People often asked me how much money I made as a cowboy movie star, and I just told them I didn't know 'cause I never did keep count. Dun and Bradstreet once said I was worth upwards of three million dollars, but I kinda think they was stretchin' things a bit, too.

"But in th' good ol' days I had th' whole danged Hollywood deal—th' big mansion, fancy limousine and driver, and I always told th' driver that whenever he took me somewhere to park on a side street, and whenever he took me home to stick on th' side streets until we got there. Why? 'Cause me settin' back there lettin' him drive me around was like showin' off too much, and I never wanted people to think anything like that about me.

"Confidentially, I never was a very good actor. Not in my own estimation. Why? 'Cause I was just a good ol' cowpoke, first, last, and always. Tell me, how can a real-life good cowboy act any way except himself? That's right. He cain't. And that's how I personally always felt about my actin' in them pictures. I always just tried to be myself, nobody else.

"Oh, I'm not sayin' I'd ever change a thing about them good-times

244

With Tarzan.

In Gun Justice *(1933) with Ed Brady.*

245

days, nosiree. Shucks, look at what all it done for me, look at what all I had!"

Where was he born?

"I was born in a little town in Texas, name of Mission, on July 27, 1895. My daddy owned a big spread near th' Matador Range country. I'm th' oldest of us five kids. Kermit, my youngest brother, who died recently, God rest his soul, was a movie star after I was. Maybe you remember him?

"Old Kermit played mostly in mountie pictures. He was a much better trick rider than me, and never even worked in a circus like I did."

Ken recalled having left home at the age of sixteen to join up with Buffalo Bill Cody's Wild West Show. He toured with it across the nation until the show finally folded, and then he signed on with Kit Carson's Wild West Show, then with the Pawnee Bill Show, and then with Hagenbeck and Wallace.

He had been with the Barnum & Bailey Circus six years as a stunt rider when he was talked into rodeo competition; he went on to capture the title of World Champion Cowboy. Then came the silver screen and fame and fortune.

"Last time I was officially in front of th' cameras was in th' fall of 1971, when I appeared as a special guest on 'Th' Merv Griffin Show.' Just prior to my appearin' on his show I'd taken a spill and had hurt my hip. So I didn't stay too long on Griffin's show as his guest cause my hip got to hurtin' and I had to get home and lay down awhile. But I really enjoyed bein' asked by Griffin to appear on his show, 'cause it was an oldtimer's thing and people I used to know like Gloria Swanson and Lilly Gish was there, plus a lotta others I used to know. Yesiree, it was a real nice friendly gatherin', and I'm sorry I couldn't stay too long on account of my sore hip."

Asked why he had faded from public view for so long a time after the "Trail Blazers" series ended, Ken mused: "Well, at first, I had to get ridda somethin' inside of me, somethin' personal, that bothered me a lot. Later, after I'd got over my troubles, it was too late to try for a film career comeback. Sooo, I just plumb forgot th' whole thing and did some jobs, here and there, some freelance writin' under another name [dime-novel Westerns, using the pseudonym Bliss Lomax], and finally used my retirement pay to live th' rest of my days out right here [in the trailer camp].

"Another writer from a magazine asked me not long ago what I wanted to be remembered as whenever I died. Shucks, that was easy. I right away told him I wanted to be remembered as a damned good cowpoke, nothin' more. That'd be plenty honor enough for me."

Asked what he thought about today's new breed of Western actor, on TV and in motion pictures, Ken shook his head and replied: "I can't rightly figure them out. A lot of them are pretty fair stunters, but lousy actors; but I don't want to set myself up as any judge, when I used to be a lousy actor myself. But I guess what's confusin' to me is how a lot of them make Westerns on TV and a name for themselves, then get tired and dissatisfied and want to do somethin' else. I think I heard them call it not wantin' to get stereotyped. Shucks, in my day we made Western actin' a *career*, not just a passin' fancy. Maybe that's what's wrong with these youngsters today, they can't decide what kinda career they want in films or TV so they take roles temporarily before movin' on. They get an audience followin' or what they call a Nielsen ratin', and then they change their minds and want to do different roles, like detectives, the likes. This confuses and disappoints a fan of theirs, whether they know that or not, and in th' end they usually end up losin' out anyway. This old stuff about young men changin' their minds . . . is for th' birds. They oughtta take their actin' more serious."

Asked if any of his old film pals ever wrote or came out to visit him, Ken sadly said, "Mostly, they've all been too busy for that. Old Hoot Gibson used to look me up whenever he came to town, and Bob Steele, Dale Robertson, and Gene Autry used to look me up every now and then, but they're about th' only ones. Th' rest, they either died off or were too busy tryin' to be big stars.

"Autry, in case you didn't know it, is a protégé of mine. His first screen role was in one of my pictures, *In Old Santa Fe,* where he sang and became so popular th' producer decided to star him in his own pictures. You know th' rest of th' story. . . . Ol' Gene became a big star and today he's a multimillionaire. I'm happy for him too. He was one fine young feller."

Asked what he thought about John Wayne films on TV these days, Ken said: "I really get a kick outta ol' Duke Wayne's pictures on TV today. I remember when I taught him a lotta th' tricks about ridin' and actin' he knows today; in fact, parts of my old silent pictures—th' hard-ridin' scenes with me on Tarzan—were used to 'patch up' some sequences in Duke's films, a little later on. That's when he didn't know how to ride very well, so they used shots of my films, taken at a distance, so you couldn't tell whether it was me or Duke on th' white horse, to 'patch up' his with.

"But I really enjoy watchin' his old films; it brings back a lotta good memories about my heyday as a star. But once you hang up your hat and spurs and six-guns, you sorta fade away and are soon forgotten. And . . . maybe it's all for th' best. I sure wouldn't want to cry my troubles to old friends anymore than I'd want them to come cryin' theirs to me. We're all too tough a breed of real cowboys for that kinda stuff."

Ken Maynard died shortly after this interview, his last. But he did not die as he had wished, as he thought a cowboy should—with his boots on.

Western Film Credits

$50,000 Reward (Davis Dist., 1925)   *The Demon Rider* (Davis Dist., 1925)
Fighting Courage (Davis Dist., 1925)   *The Haunted Range* (Davis Dist., 1925)

The North Star (AE, 1925)
The Grey Vulture (Davis Dist., 1926)
Senor Daredevil (FN, 1926)
Unknown Cavalier (FN, 1926)
The Overland Stage (FN, 1927)
Somewhere in Sonora (FN, 1927)
Land Beyond the Law (FN, 1927)
The Devil's Saddle (FN, 1927)
Gun Gospel (FN, 1927)
The Wagon Show (FN, 1928)
The Canyon of Adventure (FN, 1928)
Code of the Scarlet (FN, 1928)
The Upland Rider (FN, 1928)
The Glorious Trail (FN, 1928)
The Phantom City (FN, 1929)
Cheyenne (FN, 1929)
The Lawless Legion (FN, 1929)
California Mail (FN, 1929)
The Royal Rider (FN, 1929)
Wagon Master (Univ., 1929)
Senor Americano (Univ., 1930)
Lucky Larkin (Univ., 1930)
The Fighting Legion (Univ., 1930)
Mountain Justice (Univ., 1930)
Parade of the West (Univ., 1930)
Sons of the Saddle (Univ., 1930)
Song of the Caballero (Univ., 1930)
Fighting Thru (Tif., 1930)
The Two-Gun Man (Tif., 1931)
Alias the Bad Man (Tif., 1931)
Arizona Terror (Tif., 1931)
Range Law (Tif., 1931)
Branded Men (Tif., 1931)
Pocatello Kid (Tif., 1931)
Sunset Trail (Tif., 1932)
Whistlin' Dan (Tif., 1932)
Texas Gunfighter (Tif., 1932)
Hellfire Austin (Tif., 1932)
Between Fighting Men (WW, 1932)
Dynamite Ranch (WW, 1932)
Come On, Tarzan (WW, 1932)
Tombstone Canyon (WW, 1932)

Fargo Express (WW, 1932)
Drum Taps (WW, 1933)
The Lone Avenger (WW, 1933)
Phantom Thunderbolt (WW, 1933)
King of the Arena (Univ., 1933)
Fiddlin' Buckaroo (Univ., 1933)
The Strawberry Roan (Univ., 1933)
The Trail Drive (Univ., 1933)
Gun Justice (Univ., 1934)
Wheels of Destiny (Univ., 1934)
Honor of the Range (Univ., 1934)
Smoking Guns (Univ., 1934)
Mystery Mountain (serial) (Mas., 1934)
In Old Santa Fe (Mas., 1934)
Western Frontier (Col., 1935)
Heir to Trouble (Col., 1935)
Western Courage (Col., 1935)
Lawless Riders (Col., 1935)
The Cattle Thief (Col., 1936)
Heroes of the Range (Col., 1936)
Avenging Waters (Col., 1936)
The Fugitive Sheriff (Col., 1936)
Boots of Destiny (GN, 1937)
Trailin' Trouble (GN, 1937)
Whirlwind Horseman (GN, 1938)
Six-Shootin' Sheriff (GN, 1938)
Flaming Lead (Colony, 1939)
Death Rides the Range (Colony, 1939)
Phantom Rancher (Colony, 1939)
Lightning Strikes West (Colony, 1940)
Wild Horse Stampede (Mon., 1943)
The Law Rides Again (Mon., 1943)
Blazing Guns (Mon., 1943)
Death Valley Rangers (Mon., 1943)
Westward Bound (Mon., 1943)
Arizona Whirlwind (Mon., 1944)
White Stallion (also known as *Harmony Trail*) (Astor, 1944, released 1947)

Johnny Mack Brown, in Chip of the Flying U *(1939).*

Johnny Mack Brown

(Western hero deluxe)

Born: September 1, 1904, Dothan, Ala.
Married: Cornelina "Connie" Foster (1927);
  children: Jane, Lachlen, Cynthia, Sally
Died: November 14, 1974

(Note: Johnny Mack Brown died shortly after this final interview was given. He is buried in Hollywood. The final interview is unchanged.)

ALL-AMERICAN JOHNNY MACK BROWN was one of the greatest halfbacks ever to play for the University of Alabama's Crimson Tide. But when he graduated in 1927, he chose dramatic acting in Hollywood over playing professional football for any team of his pick.

Born to a farmer of modest means, young Johnny earned his keep at home from the time he was able to help his father harvest crops in the field. His earnings also helped defray his college costs.

Johnny was a good student in high school, with a B-average. He loved English and literature classes about as much as he loved athletics. He excelled in football, but also starred in basketball, baseball, and track, the last as a sprinter. With this combination of academic savvy and athletic prowess, he was, as his former high school coach, J. N. Hightower, said, "bound to be a big star player on the Alabama football team."

Upon graduation from 'Bama in 1927, Johnny was offered a contract by MGM. Officials there were very much aware of his prowess on the gridiron, but they had also scouted several plays in which he had acted in drama class and were mainly interested in developing the young halfback into a handsome leading man for stars like Greta Garbo, Mary Pickford, and Joan Crawford.

Johnny signed the contract, bade his parents and friends goodbye, and went to Hollywood. He was quartered at MGM and sent to its acting school for ninety days. A good deal of Johnny's natural shyness was overlooked when his screen test proved to Sam Goldwyn and others what they had known all along—Johnny Mack Brown was destined for stardom.

MGM tried him as one of the subleading men in *Our Dancing Daughters* and *The Fair Coed*, which starred Marion Davies. Johnny turned in excellent performances in both films and might have shot up to stardom had it not been for the nasty rumors about his torrid offstage love affair with Miss Davies. Johnny and Miss Davies vehemently denied the

In Ragtime Cowboy Joe *(1940) with Nell O'Day and Fuzzy Knight.*

In Six-Gun Mesa *(1950).*

Brown and sidekick Raymond Hatton get the drop on bad guy Dan White in Gunning for Justice *(1948).*

With Lyle Talbot in an early fifties film.

253

With Noah Beery, Jr., in Fighting with Kit Carson *(1933).*

persistent rumors, but by the time it was proven they were just good friends and innocent of any love affair, it was too late. The ill-begotten publicity injured Miss Davies, but ruined Johnny's chances of becoming a big romantic star.

Fortunately, his Hollywood career was rescued when his athletic ability and good looks came to the attention of director King Vidor who was looking for a star for *Billy the Kid* (1930). He offered Johnny his big break and set him on the road to becoming a major Western star.

In *Billy the Kid* Johnny turned in the best performance of his screen career. Not to say he wasn't good in all of his later films and serials; he was. But he gave the role of Billy so much, even to using the desperado's pistols for added realism, that it was deemed his best acting ever. William S. Hart worked on the film as technical advisor and contributed greatly to its feeling of authenticity.

Johnny then teamed with Leo Carrillo in *Lasca of the Rio Grande* (1931), which eventually led to his starring role in a serial, *Fighting with Kit Carson* (1933). Enhancing his already growing popularity still more were his hero roles in two Universal serials: *Wild West Days* (1937) and *Flaming Frontiers* (1938).

After World War II broke out and many of the leading Western stars enlisted or were drafted into service, Johnny (who was ready to serve his country but was never called upon), along with Charles Starrett and Roy Rogers, became a bread-and-butter star for nearly ten years. He starred in a score or more of B-Westerns.

Johnny semiretired from making films in the late fifties, returning only three more times—he was obese almost beyond recognition—for *The Bounty Hunter* (1965), *Requiem for a Gunfighter* (1965), and *Apache Uprising* (1966).

Thereafter, until his death, Johnny lived in permanent retirement. He refused any and all roles in films and, like Joel McCrea, withdrew his membership in the Screen Actors Guild as proof of his desire to remain retired.

Asked about any of his old films being rerun on TV, he said:

"I doubt that many films of mine are being rerun on TV these days; at least if there are any I haven't seen them. There was this terrible fire at the studio in the late forties, and nearly all of my old films went up in smoke. So even I have no copy of them, even if I did want to see myself in action again. Like anyone else watching TV, I too have to wait for Rod Cameron films shot in the forties, fifties, and sixties before I see myself again as an actor. But I do wish some of those old films were still available for rerunning on TV today, to fill in the gaps of Western filmmaking. Not just to sate my own ego and curiosity."

Who were Johnny Mack Brown's favorite Western actors in films and on TV?

"I'm sure Marion . . . er . . . John Wayne would have to stand out as my favorite all-around Western star in films, and Dick Boone my favorite as Hec Ramsey on TV. By my choice I naturally don't mean to put any of the rest of the stars down, because all of them were great fellows, actors, but you wanted my choice and I've given it."

Western Film Credits

The Bugle Call (MGM, 1927)

Montana Moon (MGM, 1930)

Billy the Kid (MGM, 1930)

The Great Meadow (MGM, 1931)

Lasca of the Rio Grande (Univ., 1931)

Vanishing Frontier (Par., 1932)

Fighting with Kit Carson (serial)
   (Mas., 1933)

Rustlers of Red Dog (serial) (Univ.,
   1935)

Branded a Coward (Sup., 1935)

Between Men (Sup., 1935)

Courageous Avenger (Sup., 1935)

Valley of the Lawless (Sup., 1936)

The Desert Phantom (Sup., 1936)

Rogue of the Range (Sup., 1936)

Everyman's Law (Sup., 1936)

The Crooked Trail (Sup., 1936)

Under Cover Man (Rep., 1936)

Lawless Land (Rep., 1936)

Bar Z Bad Men (Rep., 1937)

The Gambling Terror (Rep., 1937)

Trail of Vengeance (Rep., 1937)

Guns in the Dark (Rep., 1937)

A Lawman Is Born (Rep., 1937)

Wild West Days (serial) (Univ., 1937)

Boothill Brigade (Rep., 1937)

Born to the West (Par., 1937)

Wells Fargo (Par., 1937)

Flaming Frontiers (serial) (Univ.,
   1938)

The Oregon Trail (serial) (Univ.,
   1939)

Desperate Trails (Univ., 1939)

Oklahoma Frontier (Univ., 1939)

Chip of the Flying U (Univ., 1939)

West of Carson City (Univ., 1940)

Riders of Pasco Basin (Univ., 1940)

Bad Man from Red Butte (Univ., 1940)

Son of Roaring Dan (Univ., 1940)

Ragtime Cowboy Joe (Univ., 1940)

Law and Order (Univ., 1940)

Pony Post (Univ., 1940)

Boss of Bullion City (Univ., 1941)

Bury Me Not on the Lone Prairie
   (Univ., 1941)

Law of the Range (Univ., 1941)

Rawhide Rangers (Univ., 1941)

The Man from Montana (Univ., 1941)

The Masked Rider (Univ., 1941)

Arizona Cyclone (Univ., 1941)

Stagecoach Buckaroo (Univ., 1942)

Fighting Bill Fargo (Univ., 1942)

Ride 'Em Cowboy (Univ., 1942)

The Silver Bullet (Univ., 1942)

Boss of Hangtown Mesa (Univ.,
   1942)

Deep in the Heart of Texas (Univ.,
   1942)

Little Joe, the Wrangler (Univ., 1942)

The Old Chisholm Trail (Univ.,
   1942)

Tenting Tonight on the Old Camp
   Ground (Univ., 1943)

The Ghost Rider (Mon., 1943)

Cheyenne Roundup (Univ., 1943)

Raiders of San Joaquin (Univ., 1943)

The Stranger from Pecos (Mon., 1943)

The Lone Star Trail (Univ., 1943)

Six-Gun Gospel (Mon., 1943)

Outlaws of Stampede Pass (Mon.,
   1943)

The Texas Kid (Mon., 1943)

Raiders of the Border (Mon., 1944)

Partners of the Trail (Mon., 1944)

Law Men (Mon., 1944)

Range Law (Mon., 1944)

West of the Rio Grande (Mon., 1944)

Land of the Outlaws (Mon., 1944)

Law of the Valley (Mon., 1944)

Ghost Guns (Mon., 1944)

Navajo Trail (Mon., 1945)

Gun Smoke (Mon., 1945)

Stranger from Santa Fe (Mon., 1945)

Flame of the West (Mon., 1945)

The Lost Trail (Mon., 1945)

Frontier Feud (Mon., 1945)

Border Bandits (Mon., 1946)

Drifting Along (Mon., 1946)

The Haunted Mine (Mon., 1946)

Under Arizona Skies (Mon., 1946)

The Gentleman from Texas (Mon.,
   1946)

Shadows on the Range (Mon., 1946)

Trigger Fingers (Mon., 1946)
Silver Range (Mon., 1946)
Raiders of the South (Mon., 1947)
Valley of Fear (Mon., 1947)
Trailing Danger (Mon., 1947)
Land of the Lawless (Mon., 1947)
The Law Comes to Gunsight (Mon., 1947)
Code of the Saddle (Mon., 1947)
Flashing Guns (Mon., 1947)
Prairie Express (Mon., 1947)
Gun Talk (Mon., 1947)
Overland Trails (Mon., 1948)
Crossed Trails (Mon., 1948)
Frontier Agent (Mon., 1948)
Triggerman (Mon., 1948)
Back Trail (Mon., 1948)
The Fighting Ranger (Mon., 1948)
Sheriff of Medicine Bow (Mon., 1948)
Gunning for Justice (Mon., 1948)
Hidden Danger (Mon., 1948)
Law of the West (Mon., 1949)
Trail's End (Mon., 1949)
West of El Dorado (Mon., 1949)
Range Justice (Mon., 1949)
Stampede (AA, 1949)

Western Renegades (Mon., 1949)
Fence Riders (Mon., 1950)
West of Wyoming (Mon., 1950)
Over the Border (Mon., 1950)
Six-Gun Mesa (Mon., 1950)
Law of the Panhandle (Mon., 1950)
Outlaw Gold (Mon., 1950)
Short Grass (AA, 1950)
Colorado Ambush (Mon., 1951)
Man from Sonora (Mon., 1951)
Blazing Bullets (Mon., 1951)
Montana Desperado (Mon., 1951)
Oklahoma Justice (Mon., 1951)
Whistling Hills (Mon., 1951)
Texas Lawman (Mon, 1951)
Texas City (Mon., 1952)
Man from the Black Hills (Mon., 1952)
Dead Man's Trail (Mon., 1952)
Canyon Ambush (Mon., 1952)
The Marshal's Daughter (UA, 1953)
The Bounty Killer (Emb., 1965)
Requiem for a Gunfighter (Emb., 1965)
Apache Uprising (Par., 1966)

William S. Hart gives Johnny Mack Brown one of Billy the Kid's own guns on the set of Billy the Kid *(1930).*

William S. Hart

(First big cowboy star)

Born: December 6, 1870, Newburgh, N.Y.
Married: Winifred Westover (1921);
   divorced (1927); child: William, Jr.
Died: June 23, 1946

WILLIAM SURREY HART IS today the most impressive of all the early silent cowboy stars. Except for a prologue for the re-release of his famous *Tumbleweeds* (1925, 1939), he made no talking pictures. Yet his image remains imbedded in the minds of his fans, and his name is an important element in the history of the Western film.

Hart grew up in the Old West and loved Western lore and its people. To him the West was part of the American heritage that deserved to be preserved intact. He attempted to do just this in all of his films. Neither before nor after Bill Hart was as true a picture of the wild and woolly West portrayed oncamera as was done in his realistic films.

Above all else, Hart would not compromise his feelings towards his art or towards the land he loved. He was finally forced out of films in the early twenties because he would not indulge in the type of mythical streamlined Western made by Tom Mix, Buck Jones, Hoot Gibson, and George O'Brien. Today, Hart's films are still used as examples of the best of early Western filmmaking. They are testaments to the history and lore of the period.

Bill Hart was born in Newburgh, New York, the son of a vagabond-like miller who, with his family, later wandered around the Midwest. In this period, the twilight of the Indian nations, Hart grew to love and respect the Indians as well as the trail herders. It was from this roving youth that his deep affection for the Old West evolved. When illness befell his father, the family returned to New York where Bill Jr. took odd jobs.

At age nineteen, tall and stern, Bill took up theatrics with Daniel E. Bandmann's company of *Romeo and Juliet*. The young man soon developed into a fine Shakespearean actor. In later years publicists would assert that the performer's middle initial stood for the Bard.

In 1899 Hart won great acclaim for his stage role as Messala in *Ben Hur*. Several stage successes followed, many of which explored Western and pioneer motifs. Among the plays which converted him into a popular matinee idol were *The Squaw Man, Trail of the Lonesome Pine,* and *The*

Barrier. Throughout this period, one of his close friends was fellow actor Thomas H. Ince, with whom he roomed for a while.

During his stage years Hart was aghast at the inaccuracies found in Western films, especially in filmmakers' portrayals of the Indians. When Bill reached California in 1914 for a show tour, he met with Thomas H. Ince, then head of his own motion picture company in Santa Monica. Hart, impressed with the cowboys and Indians from the famed Miller Bros. 101 Ranch used in Ince's films, outlined his plans to his old friend for making authentic Western pictures.

Ince signed on Bill Hart at $75 per week. Under an assumed name he appeared as the bad guy in *His Hour of Manhood* and *Jim Cameron's Wife*, both two-reelers. Hart disliked his assignments and threatened to quit, but Ince persuaded the actor to remain.

In *On the Night Stage* (1915), third-billed Hart played road agent "Texas," the initial good-bad man he was to portray oncamera so often. With the release of a few other features, Bill was soon rivaling G. M. "Broncho Billy" Anderson and Harry Carey as a major Western film star.

Hart's salary was raised to $125 weekly and he began a series of starring two-reelers with *The Passing of Two-Gun Hicks*. In 1915 Triangle assumed control of the Mutual releases, and Hart's film output through 1917 was distributed through that source. It was for Triangle that Bill made his best early films, among them the classic *Hell's Hinges* (1916) and *The Return of Draw Eagan* (1916). In these pictures he presented the West not in flashy or idealized terms but as it truly was: harsh, austere, primeval, and fertile. His main characters were derived from actual people, Westerners he had seen and known in his youth. Most of Hart's features were morality plays encompassing the simple theme of good versus evil and right over wrong, and they emphasized the sanctity of womanhood and marriage. Hart starred his pinto horse "Fritz" in his pictures, and the animal became the screen's first horse star. During this period, Hart also made a few non-Westerns, to exercise his versatility as an all-around actor.

Later Hart moved over to Paramount Pictures. In 1919 he was invited to join Mary Pickford, Douglas Fairbanks, and D. W. Griffith in the formation of United Artists with Charles Chaplin, but he turned down the potentially lucrative offer—unwisely, as the future showed. At Paramount Bill began making longer feature films consistently depicting the Old West as it had been. Hart also enjoyed kidding the type of lighthearted films Douglas Fairbanks made, and his *Branding Broadway* (1918) was just such a lampoon.

Typical of Hart's Westerns was *The Toll Gate* (1920) in which he played a bad man who is reformed through a woman's devotion. At the finale, Hart leaves the heroine and dies as an outlaw. Perhaps it was this kind of unglamorous finale which eroded Hart's screen popularity. After all, theater audiences had the alternative of viewing Tom Mix's bright and breezy, action-packed productions, or the action-oriented shenanigans of Hoot Gibson and Buck Jones.

By the mid-twenties Bill Hart's Westerns had lost their box-office appeal. Paramount head Adolph Zukor told Bill he would have to make streamlined Westerns, compete with Mix, chiefly, to raise his box-office standing. But Bill refused and Zukor terminated his contract.

Believing strongly in the type of film fare he had been making, Hart formed his own company to produce *Tumbleweeds*. This 1925 feature was to be his final major screen assignment. When United Artists, who had contracted to release the film, decided it did not care for the thrust of *Tumbleweeds* and attempted to recut the footage, Hart gained a court order to prevent them from doing so. The studio retaliated by delaying the picture's release, eventually pushing it out for a minor distribution. Bill estimated he lost a fortune due to the studio's tactics. In disgust, he abandoned his movie-making career.

Alone, he settled down on his Horseshoe Ranch in Los Angeles County (his marriage to former costar Winifred Westover had terminated in 1927). There he wrote a series of books including *Injun and Whitey* and his autobiography *My Life East and West*.

Frequent rumors persisted that Bill Hart would make a screen comeback. RKO ventured to prepare two properties, but Hart was not completely satisfied with them and both were dropped.

Occasionally Hart served as technical coach, as in the case of MGM's *Billy The Kid* (1930) starring Johnny Mack Brown. For the 1939 reissue of *Tumbleweeds,* which boasted special sound effects, Hart filmed an eight-minute prologue. In the poignant sound short, Bill related the happiness and joy he had experienced making Western films, demonstrating what an asset his stage-trained voice and acting presence would have been to talking pictures. Highlighted by its marvelous landrush sequences, *Tumbleweeds* was a big hit and it recouped the funds Hart had invested in this tremendously personal project.

Bill Hart died on June 23, 1946, in Los Angeles, but was buried in Brooklyn beside his family. He left an estate of over one million dollars, and today his ranch is a public park and his home a museum.

Hart's legacy, however, went far beyond material wealth: he carefully provided future generations with an accurate picture of the Old West and a way of life that was hard and unyielding to everything but the passage of time.

Western Film Credits

The Bargain (Ince, 1914)
The Sheriff's Streak of Yellow (Ince, 1915)

On the Night Stage (Ince, 1915)
The Darkening Trail (Ince, 1915)
Between Men (Tri., 1916)

The Aryan (Tri, 1916)
The Primal Lure (Tri., 1916)
The Apostle of Vengeance (Tri., 1916)
Hell's Hinges (Tri., 1916)
Truthful Tulliver (Tri., 1916)
The Return of Draw Egan (Tri., 1916)
The Gunfighter (Tri., 1917)
The Desert Man (Tri., 1917)
The Square Deal Man (Tri., 1917)
The Cold Deck (Tri., 1917)
Wolf Lowry (Tri., 1917)
The Silent Man (Par., 1917)
The Narrow Trail (Par., 1917)
Wolves of the Trail (Par., 1918)
Blue Blazes Rawden (Par., 1918)
The Tiger Man (Par., 1918)
Selfish Yates (Par., 1918)
Shark Monroe (Par., 1918)
Riddle Gawne (Par., 1918)

The Border Wireless (Par., 1918)
Branding Broadway (Par., 1918)
Breed of Men (Par., 1919)
The Money Corral (Par., 1919)
Square Deal Sanderson (Par., 1919)
Wagon Tracks (Par., 1919)
Sand (Par., 1920)
The Testing Block (Par., 1920)
The Toll Gate (Par., 1920)
O'Malley of the Mounted (Par., 1921)
White Oak (Par., 1921)
Three Word Brand (Par., 1921)
Travelin' On (Par., 1921)
Wild Bill Hickok (Par., 1923)
Singer Jim McKee (Par., 1924)
Tumbleweeds (UA, 1925)
Tumbleweeds (sound prologue for reissue) (Astor, 1939)

Harry Carey, great Western character actor.

Harry Carey

(They called him "Old Lightnin'")

Born: January 16, 1878, New York, N.Y.
Married: Olive Golden; child: Harry, Jr., Ellen
Died: September 21, 1947

BEGINNING HIS MOVIE career in 1909 for D. W. Griffith (the classic film director who laid the foundation for cinema art), Harry Carey became one of the grandest stars of the silent Western. In the Bill Hart tradition, Harry portrayed the serious, intelligent, rugged man engaged in moral struggles. *Prairie Pirate* (1925) had him turning good-guy outlaw to hunt down the murderer of his sister, and *Satan Town* (1926) was a thinly disguised reworking of one of Hart's best and most successful films, *Hell's Hinges.*

Carey first gained fame as a cowboy star, but his portrayals on the screen were not based on any real-life experience as in the case of Tom Mix, Hoot Gibson, or Buck Jones. Henry DeWitt Carey, the son of a judge, was born in The Bronx and grew up in New York City. He attended Hamilton Academy and New York University where he prepared to be a lawyer.

His interests were diverted to the theatre when he authored a play, *Montana,* in which he appeared as the lead in the stage production. His motion picture career really got under way when D. W. Griffith gave him a role in *The Unseen Enemy,* a film which also launched Lillian and Dorothy Gish.

Carey made a number of pictures for Griffith and Biograph before moving on to other studios. In 1917 he appeared with Hoot Gibson in one of John Ford's first feature films, *Straight Shooting,* produced for Universal. Hoot Gibson and Harry Carey were to be Ford's initial big stars. Carey made twenty-six films for John Ford who has been quoted as acknowledging that he had learned how to make pictures "from Harry Carey mostly. He was actually my tutor."

The films Carey made in the next few years established him as one of Universal's most valuable properties. He continued his career as a cowboy star by appearing throughout the twenties in Westerns for such studios as Film Booking Office, Producers Distributing Corp., and Pathé.

The transition of silents to talkies saw him temporarily retired

267

from the screen, but his impressive comeback in *Trader Horn* (1930), filmed in Africa and Mexico, rooted him firmly in the era of talking motion pictures.

Carey was always more an actor than an athlete. With the introduction of talkies, his career gradually evolved from serials and independent Westerns to character acting. In 1932 he portrayed Doc Holliday in the fine Western *Law and Order,* with Walter Huston as Wyatt Earp. Based on the novel by W. R. Barnett, the film ended with a rousing presentation of the famous O.K. Corral gun duel. In the role of Tucson Smith, Carey was one of the all-star cast of *Powdersmoke Range* (1935).

His later films often saw him displaying his acting talents in pictures other than Westerns. For his performance as the Senate President in the classic *Mr. Smith Goes to Washington* (1939), starring James Stewart and directed by Frank Capra, Carey was nominated for an Oscar as Best Supporting Actor. That year, however, the Award went to an actor in a Western, to Thomas Mitchell for his work in *Stagecoach.*

Other highlights of Carey's career in Westerns were his roles as Dextry in *The Spoilers* (1942) with Marlene Dietrich and as Lem Smoot in *Duel in the Sun* (1946).

Harry Carey's final films, *So Dear to My Heart* and *Red River,* were released in 1948, the year after his death in Brentwood, California. The great screen career of a much-beloved actor had come to an end. His son, Harry, Jr., who appeared in *Red River* also, continued to bring the family name before the movie public.

John Ford prefaced his production of *Three Godfathers* (1949) with a film clip of Harry Carey on horseback and a statement that the feature was dedicated to his memory. The leading roles in the film were played by John Wayne, Pedro Armendariz, and Harry Carey, Jr.

Western Film Credits

Knight of the Range (Univ., 1916)
Cheyenne's Pal (Univ. short, 1917)
Straight Shooting (Univ., 1917)
The Secret Man (Univ., 1917)
A Marked Man (Univ., 1917)
Fighting Gringo (Univ., 1917)
Wild Women (Univ., 1918)
Thieves' Gold (Univ., 1918)
The Scarlet Drop (Univ., 1918)
Hell Bent (Univ., 1918)
Phantom Riders (Univ., 1918)
3 Mounted Men (Univ., 1918)
Bare Fists (Univ., 1919)
Gun Fighting Gentleman (Univ., 1919)
Roped (Univ., 1919)
A Fight for Love (Univ., 1919)
Riders of Vengeance (Univ., 1919)
The Outcasts of Poker Flat (Univ., 1919)
The Ace of the Saddle (Univ., 1919)
The Rider of the Law (Univ., 1919)
Marked Men (Univ., 1919)
Sure Shot Morgan (Univ., 1919)
Overland Red (Univ., 1920)
West Is West (Univ., 1920)
Sundown Slim (Univ., 1920)
Bluestreak McCoy (Univ., 1920)
Bullet Proof (Univ., 1920)
Desperate Trails (Univ., 1921)
The Wallop (Univ., 1921)
The Freeze Out (Univ., 1921)
Man to Man (Univ., 1922)
Canyon of the Fools (FBO, 1923)
Crashin' Thru (FBO, 1923)
Desert Driven (FBO, 1923)
Naked Fists (Univ. short, 1923)
Lightning Rider (PDC, 1924)
Night Hawk (PDC, 1924)
Roaring Rails (PDC, 1924)
The Man from Texas (PDC, 1924)
Flaming Frontiers (PDC, 1924)

Beyond the Border (PDC, 1925)
Silent Sanderson (PDC, 1925)
Bad Lands (PDC, 1925)
Man from Red Gulch (PDC, 1925)
Prairie Pirate (PDC, 1925)
Frontier Trail (Pathé, 1926)
Satan Town (Pathé, 1926)
Seventh Bandit (Pathé, 1926)
Driftin' Thru (Pathé, 1926)
The Texas Trail (PDC, 1926)
Border Patrol (Pathé, 1928)
Burning Bridges (Pathé, 1928)
The Trail of '98 (MGM, 1928)
Cavalier of the West (Artclass, 1931)
The Vanishing Legion (serial) (Mas., 1931)
Border Devils (Artclass, 1932)
The Devil Horse (serial) (Mas., 1932)
The Last of the Mohicans (serial) (Mas., 1932)
Night Rider (Artclass, 1932)
Cavalier of the West (Artclass, 1932)
Without Honors (Artclass, 1932)
Law and Order (Univ., 1932)
Sunset Pass (Par., 1933)
The Thundering Herd (Par., 1933)
Powdersmoke Range (RKO, 1935)
Last of the Clintons (Ajax, 1935)
Rustler's Paradise (Ajax, 1935)
Wagon Trail (Ajax, 1935)
Wild Mustang (Ajax, 1935)
Ghost Town (Commodore, 1936)
The Last Outlaw (RKO, 1936)
Aces Wild (Commodore, 1937)
Border Cafe (RKO, 1937)
Law West of Tombstone (RKO, 1938)
The Shepherd of the Hills (Par., 1941)
The Spoilers (Univ., 1942)
Duel in the Sun (Selznick, 1946)
Angel and the Badman (Rep., 1947)
The Sea of Grass (MGM, 1947)
Red River (UA, 1948)

Hoot Gibson, in 1934.

Hoot Gibson

(The Gamblin' Fool)

Born: August 6, 1892, Tekamah, Neb.
Married: Helen Winger (1917); divorced
   (1921); remarried: Helen Johnson (1921);
   divorced (1927); remarried: Sally Eilers
   (1930); divorced (1933); remarried:
   Dorothy Dunstan (1941); child: Lois
Died: August 23, 1962

OF ALL THE rags-to-riches stories in the movie industry, perhaps none is more poignant than Hoot Gibson's.

A drifter, Hoot developed into a rodeo champion and broke into movies as a stuntman extraordinaire. With the success of his first starring vehicle, *Action* (1921), he soon developed into one of the most popular children's idols of the madcap twenties, and he earned many thousands of dollars a week.

The sound era and the breakup of his second and third marriages, however, brought an end to his big-time career. He spent the thirties at "poverty row" studios and touring with a circus. Despite a slight resurgence when he appeared in the "Trail Blazers" series in the early forties (with old pals Bob Steele and Ken Maynard), Hoot's film career had ended. His unwise dabbling in real estate had depleted the remainder of his fortune and he spent his last years as a greeter in a hotel on the famous Las Vegas "Strip."

It all began for Edmund Richard Gibson in Tekamah, Nebraska, where as a youth he earned the nickname "Hoot" because he loved to hunt owls. At age thirteen, Hoot ran away from home and joined a circus, and later he was a cowpuncher in Colorado and Wyoming. In 1906 he joined the Miller 101 Ranch at Fort Bliss, Oklahoma. The next year the adventurous youth signed a four-year contract with the Dick Stanley-Bud Atkinson Wild West Show and toured the U.S. and Australia.

In 1919, when Hoot was not touring with the show, he worked in the movie industry in California. Years later, on the Groucho Marx "You Bet Your Life" program in the late fifties, he would recollect that he had been the movies' first stuntman and that he was paid $2.50 for his services and a similar sum for those of his trained horse.

One of Hoot's first screen appearances was for D. W. Griffith in *Two Brothers* (1910). He stayed with the movies briefly at this point, in 1911 acting in William Selig's *Shotgun Jones*. Regarding his fledgling movie days, Hoot recalled: "I hired out to be an Indian in the morning and turned cowboy and chased myself all afternoon. They paid five dollars a day, then, and two-fifty extra if you'd fall off a horse." In regard to a particular stunt, he once told a screen director: "Make my price ten bucks and I'll let him [the horse] kick me to death!"

In 1912 Hoot won the award of All-Around Champion Cowboy at the Annual Roundup at Pendleton, Oregon. The next year he began living with Helen Wenger, a rodeo rider. Whether or not they were ever actually wed is still a matter for conjecture, but they remained together until 1921.

During that time Helen changed her name to Helen Gibson and began stunt work in films herself. Finally she was chosen to replace Helen Holmes in the Universal serial, *The Hazards of Helen* (1914). Hoot also appeared in later chapters of this cliffhanger.

While at Universal, Hoot became friendly with Western star Harry Carey and his director John Ford, and the duo began to cast Gibson in small roles in Carey's outdoor films such as *Straight Shooting* and *A Marked Man,* both 1917 releases.

World War I interrupted Hoot's screen career for a time when he joined the army and served in its tank corps in France. He was decorated several times for bravery in action (though he was always too modest to tell anyone about himself), and was discharged after the war, in 1919, with the rank of sergeant.

The former soldier returned to Universal where he soon became the star of two-reelers, many of them made with Pete Morrison and most of them directed by John Ford. It was also Ford who directed Hoot in *Action* (1921), which launched him toward Western superstardom.

By this time William S. Hart's popularity was failing and only Tom Mix was a reigning matinee idol. As Harry Carey's features were more literate and adult oriented, there was a great opportunity to be found in sagebrush tales which appealed to children. With his breezy manner and his capacity for light comedy, Hoot soon filled the gap with his fast, action-packed, but mainly non-violent, oaters. He rarely carried a gun oncamera (unless it was stuck in the top of his boot or in the waistband of his pants); his Palomino stallion was called "Goldie"; and his films concentrated on the lighter aspects of the genre. Thus, during the period of 1921-25, Hoot Gibson developed a screen image with an immense following. By the mid-twenties, Universal was paying Hoot the huge sum of $14,500 per week.

Hoot lived up to the image of a free-spending movie star, rivaling even Tom Mix with his overt extravagance. He owned fast cars, motorcycles, airplanes, etc. He divorced wife number two (Helen Johnson) in 1927, which forced him to split his sizable estate in half. In 1930 he wed his new love, actress Sally Eilers. That same year his Universal contract was terminated: they felt that Hoot was washed up in talkies.

*The first
cowboy star
with humor and
witty ad-libs.*

Gibson and Sally Eilers would make three films together. However, with the success of her Fox film, *Bad Girl* (1931), she went her own way professionally and privately.

By this time Hoot was signed to work for Allied Pictures and while he fought to maintain the high production standards of his Universal films, the budgets for the new oaters were curtailed. Hoot remained with Allied for two seasons, and then made a few entries for First Division Pictures.

In 1931 Hoot had won the National Air Race in his private racing plane, and in 1933 he flew a match race against Western star Ken Maynard at the Los Angeles Municipal Airport. Hoot's biplane banked too sharply around a pylon and crashed, and the badly battered star was reported to have gasped to newsmen: "You can't kill me!"

At this point it was the singing cowboys who were becoming the rage of moviedom. Particularly since Hoot had kidded music in Westerns in *The Mounted Stranger* (1930), he found himself out of place in the new era. Fortunately he was reteamed with Harry Carey at RKO for two Western specials which helped to revive his popularity. The first was *Powder-smoke Range* (1935) in which he, Carey, and Guinn "Big Boy" Williams played the "Three Mesquiteers." The film established the vogue for out-door trio stars. The second production was *The Last Outlaw* (1936) based on a John Ford story. Here Harry played an oldtime outlaw who is released from jail only to find that modern racketeers rule the range. Hoot was Harry's understanding pal in the film. As a result of these entries plus a few other roles, Hoot placed ninth in the Motion Picture Herald's poll of top moneymaking Western stars for 1936. It was the only time he ever made the national poll chart.

After his Universal successes, Hoot went to Republic to appear in his first serial work in twenty years. It was *The Painted Stallion* (1937), filmed largely at St. George, Utah. Hoot took second billing to newcomer Ray "Crash" Corrigan. After this film, Hoot toured with a circus. He temporarily retired from show business in 1939.

For a time he was employed in real estate. Then in 1943 he accepted an offer from Monogram Pictures to be teamed with old pal Ken Maynard for the "Trail Blazers" series. After three entries Bob Steele joined the duo. Then Steele went into the army; Maynard, who drank too much and became too difficult to work with, quit the series; and Hoot was forced into retirement again.

Little was heard of Hoot Gibson professionally until the fifties, when he appeared in a segment of the "I Married Joan" television show and on the Groucho Marx show. As a favor to John Ford, for $5,000, Hoot did a cameo role in John Wayne's *The Horse Soldiers* (1959) and was very impressive. As a follow-up, he was guest spotted in Frank Sinatra's *Ocean's Eleven* (1960), but it held no real hope of a comeback.

Cancer claimed Hoot Gibson on August 23, 1962, at the Motion Picture Country Home & Hospital in California. Long gone was the $6 million he had earned as one of the top children's idols of the Roaring Twenties. He once said of his profession: "I know of no other business where merit is rewarded as it is in the movies—but merit must be aided by labor, and plenty of it."

Western Film Credits

A Knight of the Range (Univ., 1916)
The Cactus Kid (Univ., 1916)
Night Riders (Univ., 1916)
Straight Shooting (Univ., 1917)
A Marked Man (Univ., 1917)
A 44-Calibre Mystery (Univ., 1917)
The Golden Bullet (Univ., 1917)
Play Straight or Fight (Univ., 1918)
The Branded Man (Univ., 1918)
The Double Holdup (Univ., 1919)
The Trail of the Holdup Man (Univ., 1919)
The Jaybird (Univ., 1919)
Black Jack Horse Bandit (Univ., 1919)
Ace High (Univ., 1919)

The Four-Bit Man (Univ., 1919)
Jack of Hearts (Univ., 1919)
The Tell-Tale Wire (Univ., 1919)
The Lone Hand (Univ., 1919)
West Is Best (Univ., 1919)
The Sheriff's Oath (Univ., 1920)
Roaring Dan (Univ., 1920)
Saddle King (Univ., 1920)
Some Shooter (Univ., 1920)
One Law for All (Univ., 1920)
A Gamblin' Fool (Univ., 1920)
The Big Catch (Univ., 1920)
The Champion Liar (Univ., 1920)
The Shootin' Kid (Univ., 1920)
The Smilin' Kid (Univ., 1920)

The Fightin' Terror (Univ., 1920)
Harmony Ranch (Univ., 1920)
Cinders (Univ., 1920)
The Rustler's Kiss (Univ., 1920)
The Texas Kid (Univ., 1920)
Wolf Tracks (Univ., 1920)
The Bronco Kid (Univ., 1920)
Action (Univ., 1921)
Sure Fire (Univ., 1921)
The Bearcat (Univ., 1922)
Headin' West (Univ., 1922)
Double Dealing (Univ., 1923)
Kindled Courage (Univ., 1923)
Out of Luck (Univ., 1923)
The Ramblin' Kid (Univ., 1923)
Shootin' for Love (Univ., 1923)
Single Handed (Univ., 1923)
Forty Horse Hawkins (Univ., 1924)
Ride for Your Life (Univ., 1924)
Ridin' Kid from Powder River (Univ., 1924)
The Sawdust Trail (Univ., 1924)
The Calgary Stampede (Univ., 1925)
The Hurricane Kid (Univ., 1925)
Let 'er Buck (Univ., 1925)
The Saddle Hawk (Univ., 1925)
Spook Ranch (Univ., 1925)
The Taming of the West (Univ., 1925)
Arizona Sweepstakes (Univ., 1926)
Chip of the Flying U (Univ., 1926)
The Flaming Frontier (Univ., 1926)
The Buckaroo Kid (Univ., 1926)
The Man in the Saddle (Univ., 1926)
The Phantom Bullet (Univ., 1926)
The Texas Streak (Univ., 1926)
The Denver Dude (Univ., 1927)
Galloping Fury (Univ., 1927)
A Hero on Horseback (Univ., 1927)
Hey! Hey! Cowboy (Univ., 1927)
Painted Ponies (Univ., 1927)
The Prairie King (Univ., 1927)
The Silent Rider (Univ., 1927)
Clearing the Trail (Univ., 1928)
The Danger Rider (Univ., 1928)
The Flyin' Cowboy (Univ., 1928)
The Rawhide Kid (Univ., 1928)
Riding for Fame (Univ., 1928)
A Trick of Hearts (Univ., 1928)
The Wild West Show (Univ., 1928)

Burning the Wind (Univ., 1929)
Courtin' Wildcats (Univ., 1929)
King of the Rodeo (Univ., 1929)
The Lariat Kid (Univ., 1929)
The Long, Long Trail (Univ., 1929)
Points West (Univ., 1929)
Smilin' Guns (Univ., 1929)
The Winged Horseman (Univ., 1929)
The Mounted Stranger (Univ., 1930)
Roaring Ranch (Univ., 1930)
Spurs (Univ., 1930)
Trailin' Trouble (Univ., 1930)
Trigger Tricks (Univ., 1930)
Clearing the Range (All., 1931)
Wild Horse (All., 1931)
Hard Hombre (All., 1931)
Gay Buckaroo (All., 1932)
Local Bad Man (All., 1932)
Spirit of the West (All., 1932)
The Boiling Point (All., 1932)
A Man's Land (All., 1932)
Cowboy Counselor (All., 1932)
Dude Bandit (All., 1933)
Fighting Parson (All., 1933)
Sunset Range (FD, 1935)
Rainbow's End (FD, 1935)
Powdersmoke Range (RKO, 1935)
The Last Outlaw (RKO, 1936)
Swifty (FD, 1936)
Frontier Justice (FD, 1936)
Feud of the West (Diversion, 1936)
The Riding Avenger (Diversion, 1936)
Cavalcade of the West (Diversion, 1936)
Lucky Terror (Diversion, 1936)
The Painted Stallion (serial) (Rep., 1937)
Wild Horse Stampede (Mon., 1943)
The Law Rides Again (Mon., 1943)
Blazing Guns (Mon., 1943)
Death Valley Rangers (Mon., 1943)
Westward Bound (Mon., 1944)
Arizona Whirlwind (Mon., 1944)
The Outlaw Trail (Mon., 1944)
Sonora Stagecoach (Mon., 1944)
The Utah Kid (Mon., 1944)
Marked Trails (Mon., 1944)
Trigger Law (Mon., 1944)
The Horse Soldiers (UA, 1959)

Tom Mix—experts agree he was the greatest cowboy film star to swing aboard a saddle.

Tom Mix

(Greatest cowboy star of all)

Born: January 6, 1880, Mix Run, Pa.
Married: Grace I. Allin (1902);
  divorced (1902); remarried: Kitty Perrine
  (1905); divorced (1906); remarried: Olive
  Stokes (1908); divorced (1917); child:
  Ruth; remarried: Victoria Forde (1918);
  divorced (1931); remarried: Mabel
  Hubbard Ward (1932); child:
  Thomasina
Died: October 12, 1940

TOM MIX APPEARED in motion pictures for a quarter of a century, and during that time he developed into one of the highest paid cowboy stars of all time. He was also the most popular of genre stars and his influence in cultural history is immense. It was Tom who single-handedly took the Western and made it into a showy and action-packed genre marked for youthful audiences. The actor's Fox films were so successful that by the twenties he was making a reputed $17,500 per week.

Above all, Tom exuded the image of the clean-living cowboy. He was a source of inspiration for the young folk of his day and thereafter. Although he had been inactive in films for five years before his untimely death in 1940, he was deeply mourned at his passing. Today his popularity continues, for he was probably *the* greatest single showman the movies ever knew.

For years publicity people churned out much misinformation about Mix, which the star himself encouraged. For example, there were frequent claims that he was born in a log cabin in Texas or that he rode with Teddy Roosevelt's Rough Riders. Such assertions were erroneous, but the actor *did* have an adventurous early life that hardly needed to be exaggerated for effect.

Of Scotch and Cherokee Indian extraction, Mix was born in rural Pennsylvania (Mix Run) in 1881, the son of a lumberjack. After completing high school, Thomas Edwin Mix followed in the family tradition and became a lumberjack too.

When the Spanish-American War broke out, however, Tom enlisted in the army. He was shipped to Cuba and was involved in the Battle of Guaymas at Christobel Hill, serving as a courier and scout. It was there in the line of duty that he was shot in the neck.

277

When he recovered, and after the war ended in 1899, he went to the Philippines. From there he embarked for China where he participated in the Boxer Rebellion. Again he was injured and hospitalized for some time.

After recovering he served the British government both in the training of horses and in the fight against the Boers in South Africa. According to some accounts, he fought with the British for a while and then switched to the side of the Boers. After the Dutch lost the fracas in 1902 he returned to the U.S. to become a deputy sheriff in Sequatchie County in East Tennessee. From there he became a law enforcement officer in Kansas, Colorado, and Oklahoma. At one time he was a federal marshal in New Mexico, Arizona, and Montana, and was also a member of the Texas Rangers.

In 1909 Tom joined the famed Miller Brothers 101 Ranch in Oklahoma as a livestock foreman. Hoot Gibson was employed there at the same time. Mix began working on his horsemanship and took part in rodeo competitions, and later in the year he won his first national riding championship in Prescott, Arizona. Two years later, he again won the same title in Canon City, Colorado.

While working for the Miller Brothers Tom was offered a part in the William Selig production "Ranch Life in the Great Southwest," and he was so impressive in this one-reeler that Selig decided to sign him to a contract at $150 a week to star in Western shorts. In these early films Tom rode his horse Old Blue, whom he retired in 1914 and replaced with his new horse, Tony. Tom Mix and Tony developed into an important screen combination under Selig during those years. They began making a type of light, breezy, action-filled Western which presented lots of colorful stunting, fights, romance, and Western scenery, in contrast to the truthful but bleak and austere productions of William S. Hart.

Tom did all of his own stunting, he and Tony comprising the most adventurous duo on the screen. A good example of the Mix work for Sèlig is *The Heart of Texas Ryan* (1917), in which Tom played a ranch foreman in love with the girl of the title. Full of action, the film had excellent chase and fight scenes. Mix does win the girl at the fadeout and, contrary to today's Westerns, no one was killed in the storyline. The bad guys are even allowed to escape!

Noting the popularity of Tom's screen work, William Fox signed the star to a lucrative contract for his Fox Films in 1918, and in the next decade Tom completely revolutionized the Western format.

By 1921 Tom Mix was "The King of the Cowboys," and his glamorized type of Westerns spawned countless imitations. When Bill Hart retired in 1925 Tom Mix was left to reign as the top-paid and most popular Western star. (He did have competition from Universal's Hoot Gibson, however, and from Fox's Buck Jones, the latter hired as a lever to control Mix at his home studio.)

During the decade he was with Fox Films, Tom turned out approximately six to eight pictures per year, all of which did very well at the box office. Although his productions were not expensive, they were consistently well made and vastly entertaining. Best of all, they showcased Tom's agility and ingratiating personality which made him "the idol of every boy and girl in America." The cowboy star's official code of ethics included no smoking or drinking, onscreen, and, during this period, Tom's fan club had over two million juvenile members.

Mix's personal life, however, was in direct contrast to his screen image. Earning thousands of dollars weekly, he lived life in a grand style at his huge Beverly Hills home. (The $40,000 mansion was emblazoned with lights which flashed his name). He drove fast, custom-made cars and had the finest, snappiest clothes of any Hollywood celebrity. Tom boasted openly that he knew more people than anyone else in the U.S.— probably a true statement since he was widely traveled and a charming conversationalist.

Despite Tom's fame and status, he persisted throughout the twenties in performing his own stunts. It has been reported that during his active career he broke or cracked ribs on twenty-three occasions, broke his right arm five times and his left one three times. He endured a broken leg on three occasions and leg fractures three times. It was said he suffered over eighty different injuries during his professional life.

To insure that his films were consistent money-earners. Tom was careful always to choose stories that would properly showcase his talents. His films exuded vitality and showmanship. The actor backed himself with a unit of professionals (John Wayne was once a prop boy in his unit; actor George O'Brien was once his double) which included some of the finest directors and scenarists in Hollywood. Towards the end of his Fox series Tom appeared in films based on the works of Zane Grey, and these productions were especially well photographed, the shooting all done on location.

At the beginning of the sound era in 1927, Tom left Fox and made a brief series for Film Booking Office (FBO) during the 1928-29 season. These pictures were non-talkies, but did contain sound effects.

By 1929, the cowboy king had grown weary of the rigors of film-making, and he was uncertain of a career in talking pictures. He accepted an offer of $10,000 per week to star with Tony in the Sells-Floto Wild West Show. He remained with the touring show until 1932 when Universal offered him the same impressive sum to star in a series of big-money Westerns. Each film had a $100,000 budget and they were among the best B-Western pictures ever produced.

Disregarding advancing age, Tom still did most of his own stunt work oncamera and he looked youthful enough in the Universal series. That his nasal voice did not record very well was generally overlooked by his many fans. *Destry Rides Again* (1932) kicked off the series and in retrospect it is much superior to the 1939 edition with Marlene Dietrich and James Stewart. In *My Pal the King* (1932) Tom included a circus for-

279

The star.

mat, much to the delight of his fans. But the bulk of the series were straight Westerns such as *The Fourth Horseman* (1932), *Hidden Gold* (1932), a contemporary story with a gangster motif, and the beautifully photographed *Riders of Death Valley* (1932).

In all likelihood, even though he was in his fifties, Tom could have continued making more Westerns for Universal or for any other Hollywood studio. But he grew tired of the discipline of sound-stage work and returned to the circus tours. He was a true showman and the circus offered him an ideal forum.

In 1934 Tom bought an interest in the Sam B. Gill Circus and renamed it the Tom Mix Circus, and he made annual tours throughout the United States, Canada, and Mexico. In 1938 he merged with the Sells-Floto organization and continued his lucrative tours. It was during this period that his autobiography *Rovin' a Million* was published.

On October 12, 1940, Tom finished a performance in Tucson, Arizona, and was getting ready to go off to another show. However, while speeding along in his custom-made Cord car, the star hit a detour obstruction and lost control of the vehicle. It overturned and Tom suffered a broken neck. When a passerby eventually stopped, Tom Mix was dead.

Today a monument stands at the site of the crash, on U.S. Highway 80-89, near Florence, about fifty miles north of Tucson. Tom was buried in Forest Lawn Memorial Park in Hollywood.

Tom Mix' contributions to the Western film cannot be overestimated, for he set standards still followed today. The inscription on the monument in Arizona reads, "To the memory of Tom Mix whose spirit left his body on this spot and whose characterizations and portrayals in life served to better fix memories of the Old West in the minds of living men."

Western Film Credits

The Heart of Texas Ryan (Selig, 1917)
Durand of the Badlands (Fox, 1917)
Cupid's Roundup (Fox, 1918)
Six-Shooter Andy (Fox, 1918)
Western Blood (Fox, 1918)
Ace High (Fox, 1918)
Mr. Logan, U.S.A. (Fox, 1918)
Fame and Fortune (Fox, 1918)
Treat 'em Rough (Fox, 1919)
Hell Roarin' Reform (Fox, 1919)
Fightin for Gold (Fox, 1919)
The Coming of the Law (Fox, 1919)
The Wilderness Trail (Fox, 1919)

The Feud (Fox, 1919)
Rough Riding Romance (Fox, 1919)
Speed Maniac (Fox, 1919)
The Cyclone (Fox, 1920)
Daredevil (Fox, 1920)
Desert Love (Fox, 1920)
The Terror (Fox, 1920)
Three Gold Coins (Fox, 1920)
Untamed (Fox, 1920)
Prairie Trails (Fox, 1920)
The Road Demon (Fox, 1921)
The Texan (Fox, 1921)
Big Town Roundup (Fox, 1921)

281

The Night Horseman (Fox, 1921)
After Your Own Heart (Fox, 1921)
The Rough Diamond (Fox, 1921)
Trailin' (Fox, 1921)
Sky High (Fox, 1921)
Chasing the Moon (Fox, 1922)
Up and Going (Fox, 1922)
The Fighting Streak (Fox, 1922)
For Big Stakes (Fox, 1922)
Just Tony (Fox, 1922)
Do and Dare (Fox, 1922)
Tom Mix in Arabia (Fox, 1922)
Catch My Smoke (Fox, 1922)
Romance Land (Fox, 1923)
Three Jumps Ahead (Fox, 1923)
Stepping Fast (Fox, 1923)
The Lone Star Ranger (Fox, 1923)
Softboiled (Fox, 1923)
Mile-a-Minute Romeo (Fox, 1923)
North of Hudson Bay (Fox, 1923)
Eyes of the Forest (Fox, 1923)
Ladies to Board (Fox, 1924)
The Trouble-Shooter (Fox, 1924)
The Heart Buster (Fox, 1924)
The Last of the Duanes (Fox, 1924)
Oh, You Tony (Fox, 1924)
Teeth (Fox, 1924)
The Deadwood Coach (Fox, 1925)
Durand of the Badlands (Fox, 1925)
Riders of the Purple Sage (Fox, 1925)
The Rainbow Trail (Fox, 1925)
The Lucky Horseshoe (Fox, 1925)
The Best Bad Man (Fox, 1925)
The Everlasting Whisper (Fox, 1925)
The Yankee Senor (Fox, 1926)
My Own Pal (Fox, 1926)

No Man's Gold (Fox, 1926)
Hard Boiled (Fox, 1926)
The Great K and A Train Robbery (Fox, 1926)
The Canyon of Light (Fox, 1926)
Tony Runs Wild (Fox, 1926)
The Circus Ace (Fox, 1927)
Outlaws of Red River (Fox, 1927)
Silver Valley (Fox, 1927)
Tumbling River (Fox, 1927)
The Arizona Wildcat (Fox, 1927)
The Bronco Twister (Fox, 1927)
The Last Trail (Fox, 1927)
A Horseman of the Plains (FBO, 1928)
Hello Cheyenne (FBO, 1928)
Daredevil's Reward (FBO, 1928)
Painted Post (FBO, 1928)
King Cowboy (FBO, 1928)
Son of the Golden West (FBO, 1928)
The Drifter (FBO, 1929)
The Big Diamond Robbery (FBO, 1929)
Outlawed (FBO, 1929)
Destry Rides Again (Univ., 1932)
Riders of Death Valley (Univ., 1932)
Texas Bad Man (Univ., 1932)
My Pal, the King (Univ., 1932)
The Fourth Horseman (Univ., 1932)
Hidden Gold (Univ., 1932)
Flaming Guns (Univ., 1933)
Terror Trail (Univ., 1933)
The Rustler's Roundup (Univ., 1933)
The Miracle Rider (serial) (Mas., 1935)

Buck Jones, ready for action.

Buck Jones

(Everybody's good friend)

Born: November 12, 1889, Vincennes, Ind.
Married: Odelle Osborne (1915);
  children: Charles, Maxine
Died: November 30, 1942

THE TRAGIC FIRE that enveloped Boston's famous Cocoanut Grove night club on the evening of November 28, 1942, claimed over three hundred victims, including one of the world's most beloved cowboy star idols, Buck Jones. It was ironic indeed that Jones should die in surroundings so far removed from his beloved Western plains.

Buck had been attending a party given in his honor by a group of New England film exhibitors on the night of the tragedy, when he was overcome by the flames which suddenly swept through the structure. His removal to the Massachusetts General Hospital was followed by his death two days later, on November 30.

Trem Carr, veteran Western producer and a close friend of Jones, who had flown in from the West Coast upon hearing of the disaster, was told by the doctors that Buck died as a result of "smoke inhalation, burned lungs, and from second and third degree burns of the face and neck." And that even had he miraculously survived the holocaust, his career would have been over, "so grotesquely was he disfigured."

Narrowly escaping death in the same fire was producer-director Scott L. Dunlap, Jones' personal representative, who had accompanied the star on his trip east. They had been close friends since Buck's early days in films, a period that was preceded by some rather adventurous pre-Hollywood years.

Born in Vincennes, Indiana, young Charles Frederick Gebhart grew up in the southern Indiana farm country, and it was during this period that he acquired his famous nickname. It happened one day, so the story goes, when "Chuck," as he was first known, was thrown from a cantankerous old mule. Circulation of the story brought gales of laughter to his neighbors and provided a new handle for him when "Chuck" became "Buck."

When he was twelve years old, his family pulled up stakes and headed for the Indian territory of Oklahoma to establish a "homestead." Locating near the town of Red Rock, they took 1,350 acres and attempted to prove up the land. These early years on the Oklahoma frontier were hard for the

Gebharts, and little spending money was seen by anyone, including teen-aged Buck.

Buck struck out on his own by getting a job on the famous Miller Brothers 101 Ranch. This was a gigantic spread located near the town of Fort Bliss, Oklahoma, and consisting of 101,000 acres; hence the term "101" Ranch. The life of a working cowboy wrought many changes in Buck, and the fourteen-year-old farm boy, who took the job at $15 a month plus board, developed into a top $30-a-month hand before he was seventeen.

Many were the topics of conversation in ranch bunkhouses during that time, and one of the most fascinating to Buck was auto racing. He became so interested, in fact, that he suddenly decided to leave the 101 and head for Indianapolis, where races were held.

"It was a big decision in my life," Buck later recalled. "I was a greenhorn, through and through. I knew absolutely nothing about towns, much less cities, but the roving fever and curiosity got the best of me. I decided it was high time I got out on my own and saw a little of the world.

"I'll never forget how big and bustling and exciting Indianapolis looked to me," Buck continued, "I couldn't get over all the racket, the noise. After an entire lifetime in the quiet of the out-of-doors, I couldn't believe that people could live in that clanking confounded racket. I spent the first night at a hotel, but I didn't sleep at all.

"The next day I made my way out to the race track. It was practically completed, and already the famous race drivers from all over the country were gathered, testing the track and looking after their precious motors. Nobody paid much attention to me, except to stare at my cowboy's outfit as though I were a creature from another world.

"But one fellow, who appeared to be working as a mechanic, was very nice to me. His name was Harry Stillman, and he later became one of the most famous race drivers in all the country. I told him I wanted to get into the racing racket in some way or other, and his first remark to me in this regard was: 'These are automobiles, son, not horses.' Even though I knew he was kidding me, we became close friends."

After his experiences in Indianapolis, Buck enlisted in the army and saw action on the Mexican border with the cavalry. He was later sent to the Philippines where he was wounded in action. The 101 Ranch beckoned to Buck once more following his discharge from the army, but after the exciting events he experienced in the intervening years, life on the range seemed rather tame indeed. So it was with great enthusiasm that he heard the ranch was going to send a Wild West Show out on the road. Signing on for exhibitions of bronc riding and trick roping, Buck traveled with the Miller Bros. 101 Ranch Wild West Show to New York, where the troupe played their first important date.

It was also in New York, this spring of 1914, in Madison Square Garden, that Buck played *his* first important date. For it was here that he met

The star.

Odelle Osborne, a circus rider from Philadelphia, who soon became his wife.

"We got married in Lima, Ohio," according to Buck, "a year after we'd met, on horseback in the center of the circus ring with half the town applauding us and the other half scandalized. But we didn't care. We were in love, and we wanted to do what we loved best, ride."

Hearing there was big money to be made in Chicago breaking horses being purchased for the French cavalry, Buck and "Dell" headed there where they managed to accumulate quite a roll. This was used to finance their own small, riding exhibition circus which proved to be a profitable idea as they toured the tank towns of the Dakotas and Montana.

The big-time finally beckoned when Buck received an offer from Ringling Bros. Circus. Accepting, he and Dell traveled with the circus to California where they were forced to leave in 1917 because Dell was expecting a baby. Settling in Los Angeles, Buck was seeking steady employment when a chance meeting with an old circus pal, who was working as an "extra" in Western films at Universal, led him to his first encounter with cameras. There, on the old Universal City lot, Buck made his motion picture debut as a sheepherder, for the magnificent sum of five dollars a day.

The money from these first movie jobs enabled the Joneses to establish a home in the film capital where their daughter, Maxine, was born. Buck always had the best interests of his family at heart and it was with great pride that he later saw Maxine married to Noah Beery, Jr.

Eventually Buck graduated from extra work to featured parts in films such as the two-reelers made by Frank Farnum for Canyon Pictures

With Silver.

(*Brother Bill, Uphill Climb,* and *Desert Rat*) and later to the higher salaried position of stuntman. Here, his range-riding background proved a boon. So expert did he become at this phase of moviemaking that he was soon offered a $40-a-week contract as permanent year-round stuntman at Fox Studios.

Fox executives were at that time having plenty of trouble with their main breadwinner, Tom Mix. Tom was insisting on more money and threatening to stop making pictures unless he got it. So as a kind of threat to him, Fox decided to build up another Western star (one who had ironically stunted a few times for Mix, though the latter did nearly all of his own stunts) to scare Mix into line. Buck was selected to be that future Western star, receiving a salary increase to $150 a week, and was put to work in his first silent starrer, *The Last Straw,* (1920). This picture proved an immediate hit and "Buck Jones," the embryo cowboy star, drew enthusiastic praise from critics and moviegoers everywhere. Thus Buck was plunged into one of Hollywood's most amazing film careers.

It was at Fox that Buck formed his close association with "Scotty" Dunlap, who directed some of his early films. In the eight years he starred for Fox, Buck became that company's second largest money-earner and was reportedly earning $3,500 a week in the later years of his contract. Such affluence was, perhaps, Buck's temporary downfall, for this accumulation of capital prompted him to sever relations with Fox and embark on two financially disastrous ventures of his own.

The earliest of these was his attempt at independent filmmaking in 1928. The first of his "Buck Jones Productions," *The Big Hop,* received bad reviews, proved a box-office failure, and ultimately resulted in a loss of $50,000 for Buck.

The novelty of sound was just coming to the fore at the time of *The Big Hop*'s release and, while actually a silent film with titles, it was issued with "Synchronized Music and Sound Effects," using the Cortella Phone disc system. Placed into States Rights distribution channels, the film did not get the promotion and circulation it might have had if properly handled by a major company.

Buck's second catastrophe occurred when he put together his Buck Jones' Wild West Show. A few years previously a group of youthful admirers known as the "Buck Jones Rangers" had been organized, chiefly as a promotional stunt; the idea had mushroomed to the point where the club once boasted over 4,000,000 members. Buck had always wanted to return to the world of outside show business, and what better idea was there than bringing his wild west show to towns supporting large concentrations of "Rangers"?

It was a sound idea all right, but Buck had not reckoned with a few unscrupulous tricks sometimes practiced in the circus world. After the posting of show bills or "paper" by his advance man, rival shows would either destroy or cover up these notices, so that by the time Buck's wild west show arrived in town hardly anybody knew they were there. At the end of thirty days on the road Buck's show folded, leaving him sad and disheartened and some $300,000 poorer.

In desperate straits financially Buck returned to the West Coast, where eventually Dunlap, now his manager, was able to arrange a contract for Buck to make a series of eight Westerns for producer Sol Lesser's Beverly Pictures. There was a big difference between this pact and the one he'd had at Fox, however, for Buck's salary now was only $300 a week.

Released by Columbia in July 1930, the first of this new series was *The Lone Rider,* Buck's first talkie. Enthusiastically received and acclaimed "one of the best Western talking pictures of the season," it was followed in 1930-31 by top-notch action efforts: *Shadow Ranch, Men Without Law, The Dawn Trail, Desert Vengeance,* etc. Columbia then took over the actual production of Jones' pictures, and from late 1931 through 1934 released twenty-one.

Leaving Columbia, Buck reactivated his Buck Jones Corp. and produced a series of twenty-two action dramas for Universal release. Buck had a very active hand in this operation and, in addition to his starring and front-office activities, performed such behind-the-camera functions as scriptwriter and, upon occasion, director.

A dispute with Universal in mid-1937 (the studio wanted him to increase his annual film output) resulted in a transfer of Buck's activities to Columbia for which he provided six starrers in 1937-38.

In keeping with the trend of the times, Universal filled Buck's shoes with a singing cowboy, Bob Baker.

Old-school cowboys were naturally bitter about the musical intrusion and Buck was no exception. He was quoted as saying: "They [singing cowboys] use songs to save money on horses, riders, and ammunition. Why, you take Gene Autry and lean him up against a tree with his guitar and let him sing three songs and you can fill up a whole reel without spending any money. That's why they've overdone the singing cowboy, and that's why they're on the way out!"

Buck predicted the death of Western singing cowboy stars, all right, but many years were to pass before it became true.

No regular series of pictures was to come Buck's way for the next couple of years, so Buck appeared in two very nontypical Jones roles. The first was *Unmarried,* a 1939 Paramount Picture in which he played a broken-down prizefighter, and the other was *Wagons Westward* (1940). His role of a crooked sheriff in the Chester Morris starrer for Republic brought shrieks of angry protest from Buck's admirers: *how could they do such a cruel thing to our beloved Buck Jones?*

With Jones' star very much on the decline, Scott Dunlap came to the rescue with a Monogram contract in 1941. This pact united Buck with oldtimers and friends Tim McCoy and Raymond Hatton in that studio's "Rough Riders" series.

Buck was to star in his last film for Monogram, *Dawn on the Great Divide*, the last he would ever make on this earth. Buck crammed a rich, full life into his fifty-three years, doing the things he most loved to do. He was completely dedicated to frontier filmmaking and would quickly come to the defense of his art.

"Drop around to some neighborhood theater on a Saturday afternoon," he would say. "Then you'll see why Westerns are going to be here for a very long time to come, and why your old pal Buck is going to keep on making them as long as he can climb into the saddle."

Which is exactly what he did.

Western Film Credits

The Last Straw (Fox, 1920)
Forbidden Trails (Fox, 1920)
Firebrand Trevison (Fox, 1920)
The Square Shooter (Fox, 1920)
Sunset Sprague (Fox, 1920)
Just Pals (Fox, 1920)
Two Moons (Fox, 1921)
The Big Punch (Fox, 1921)
The One-Man Trail (Fox, 1921)
Get Your Man (Fox, 1921)
Straight from the Shoulder (Fox, 1921)
Bar Nothin' (Fox, 1921)
Riding with Death (Fox, 1921)
Western Speed (Fox, 1922)
To a Finish (Fox, 1922)
Roughshod (Fox, 1922)
The Fast Mail (Fox, 1922)
Trooper O'Neil (Fox, 1922)
West of Chicago (Fox, 1922)
Bells of San Juan (Fox, 1922)
Boss of Camp Four (Fox, 1922)
The Footlight Ranger (Fox, 1923)
Snowdrift (Fox, 1923)
Hell's Hole (Fox, 1923)
Not a Drum Was Heard (Fox, 1924)
The Vagabond Trail (Fox, 1924)
The Arizona Express (Fox, 1924)
The Circus Cowboy (Fox, 1924)

Western Luck (Fox, 1924)
Against All Odds (Fox, 1924)
The Desert Outlaw (Fox, 1924)
Winner Take All (Fox, 1924)
The Man Who Played Square (Fox, 1924)
The Arizona Romeo (Fox, 1925)
The Trail Rider (Fox, 1925)
Gold and the Girl (Fox, 1925)
The Timber Wolf (Fox, 1925)
Durand of the Badlands (Fox, 1925)
The Desert's Price (Fox, 1925)
The Cowboy and the Countess (Fox, 1926)
The Fighting Buckaroo (Fox, 1926)
A Man Four-Square (Fox, 1926)
The Gentle Cyclone (Fox, 1926)
The Flying Horseman (Fox, 1926)
30 Below Zero (Fox, 1926)
Desert Valley (Fox, 1927)
The War Horse (Fox, 1927)
Whispering Sage (Fox, 1927)
Hills of Peril (Fox, 1927)
Good as Gold (Fox, 1927)
Chain Lightning (Fox, 1927)
Blackjack (Fox, 1927)
Silver Valley (Fox, 1927)
Blood Will Tell (Fox, 1927)

The Branded Sombrero (Fox, 1928)
The Lone Rider (Col., 1930)
Shadow Ranch (Col., 1930)
Men Without Law (Col., 1930)
The Dawn Trail (Col., 1930)
Desert Vengeance (Col., 1931)
The Avenger (Col., 1931)
The Texas Ranger (Col., 1931)
The Fighting Sheriff (Col., 1931)
Branded (Col., 1931)
Border Law (Col., 1931)
Range Feud (Col., 1931)
The Deadline (Col., 1931)
Ridin' for Justice (Col., 1932)
One Man Law (Col., 1932)
South of the Rio Grande (Col., 1932)
White Eagle (Col., 1932)
Hello Trouble (Col., 1932)
McKenna of the Mounted (Col., 1932)
Forbidden Trail (Col., 1932)
Treason (Col., 1933)
Sundown Rider (Col., 1933)
California Trail (Col., 1933)
Unknown Valley (Col., 1933)
Gordon of Ghost City (serial) (Univ., 1933)
The Thrill Hunter (Col., 1933)
The Fighting Code (Col., 1933)
The Fighting Ranger (Col., 1934)
Man Trailer (Col., 1934)
Rocky Rhodes (Univ., 1934)
When a Man Sees Red (Univ., 1934)
The Red Rider (serial) (Univ., 1934)
The Crimson Trail (Univ., 1935)
Stone of Silver Creek (Univ., 1935)
Border Brigands (Univ., 1935)
Outlawed Guns (Univ., 1935)
The Throwback (Univ., 1935)
The Roaring West (serial) (Univ., 1935)
The Ivory-Handled Gun (Univ., 1935)
Sunset of Power (Univ., 1936)

Silver Spurs (Univ., 1936)
For the Service (Univ., 1936)
The Cowboy and the Kid (Univ., 1936)
Ride 'Em Cowboy (Univ., 1936)
Boss Rider of Gun Creek (Univ., 1936)
Empty Saddles (Univ., 1936)
The Phantom Rider (serial) (Univ., 1936)
Sandflow (Univ., 1937)
Left-Handed Law (Univ., 1937)
Smoke Tree Range (Univ., 1937)
Black Aces (Univ., 1937)
Law for Tombstone (Univ., 1937)
Boss of Lonely Valley (Univ., 1937)
Sudden Bill Dorn (Univ., 1937)
Hollywood Roundup (Col., 1937)
Headin' East (Col., 1937)
California Frontier (Col., 1938)
The Overland Express (Col., 1938)
The Stranger from Arizona (Col., 1938)
Law of the Texan (Col., 1938)
Wagons Westward (Rep., 1940)
White Eagle (serial) (Col., 1941)
Riders of Death Valley (serial) (Univ., 1941)

"Rough Riders" series:

Arizona Bound (Mon., 1941)
The Gunman from Bodie (Mon., 1941)
Forbidden Trails (Mon., 1941)
Below the Border (Mon., 1942)
Ghost Town Law (Mon., 1942)
Down Texas Way (Mon., 1942)
Riders of the West (Mon., 1942)
West of the Law (Mon., 1942)
Dawn on the Great Divide (Mon., 1942)

Lloyd Bridges, Katy Jurado, Gary Cooper, and Grace Kelly in High Noon *(1952).*

Gary Cooper

("Yup" said it all)

Born: May 7, 1901, Helena, Mont.
Married: Veronica Balfe (1933); child: Maria
Died: May 13, 1961

HE WAS PERHAPS the supreme Westerner: cool, courageous, and fair; quick on the draw when he had to be, but reluctant to shoot; kind, dignified and rather shy; the idol of men as well as women. He was at his very best in *High Noon,* as the prototype of the strong, just lawman fighting alone against the treacherous forces of evil. What most set him apart from his Western colleagues was his superb acting ability, which could have matched that of almost any actor in the world. Cooper began his film career as an extra in 1925, but his solid role in *The Winning of Barbara Worth* (1926) zoomed him to an uninterrupted stardom. He magnetized audiences with his sexy drawl, handsomely sculptured face, and tall lean body. He won three Academy Awards (Best Actor in 1942 for *Sergeant York*, Best Actor in 1953 for *High Noon,* and a Special Award in 1961) before he died of cancer in 1961.

Western Film Credits

The Thundering Herd (Par., 1925)
The Lucky Horseshoe (Fox, 1925)
Wild Horse Mesa (Par., 1925)
The Enchanted Hill (Par., 1926)
The Winning of Barbara Worth (UA, 1926)
Arizona Bound (Par., 1927)
Nevada (Par., 1927)
The Last Outlaw (Par., 1927)
Wolf Song (Par., 1929)
The Virginian (Par., 1929)
The Texan (Par., 1930)
Only the Brave (Par., 1930)
The Spoilers (Par., 1930)
Fighting Caravans (Par., 1931)
Operator 13 (MGM, 1934)

The Plainsman (Par., 1936)
The Cowboy and the Lady (UA, 1938)
The Westerner (UA, 1940)
Northwest Mounted Police (Par., 1940)
Along Came Jones (RKO, 1945)
Dallas (WB, 1950)
Distant Drums (WB, 1951)
High Noon (UA, 1952)
Springfield Rifle (WB, 1952)
Vera Cruz (UA, 1954)
Garden of Evil (20th, 1954)
Man of the West (UA, 1958)
The Hanging Tree (WB, 1959)
Alias Jesse James (UA, 1959)
They Came to Cordura (Col., 1959)

Tom Tyler, in 1939.

Tom Tyler

(Hero of the plains)

Born: August 9, 1903, Port Henry, N.Y.
Married: Jeanne Martel
Died: May 1, 1954

ACTING WAS IN Tom Tyler's blood from a very early age. Born Vincent Markowski in Port Henry, New York, his family later moved to Detroit, Michigan, where Tom as a teenager used all of his spending money to buy theatrical makeup kits. His father, a factory worker, thought Tom's theatrical ambitions foolish and a waste of time. So it was without his consent that Tom left home, determined to reach Hollywood and to try for a career in the movies.

Working his way across country, Tom landed in Los Angeles in 1924. Laying siege to the studios, he first worked in the film capital as a prop boy and a muscular extra. He had developed a powerful body through weight lifting, and when he heard MGM was planning to make *Ben-Hur* Tom figured this was his big break. As he later would recall: "I knew that they'd need men with good physiques in that picture, and since I'd been interested in athletics all my life it seemed a possible big chance for me." So, armed with suitable photos, Tom managed to see the casting director and was hired immediately.

A good role in Elinor Glyn's *The Only Thing* followed, and then Tom heard that there might be work for him at the FBO studios (later to be RKO). It turned out to be true, but the first question asked of him was "Can you ride a horse?" Tom told them he could, even though he'd never been on a horse, and got the job. A friend taught him how to ride effectively enough, fortunately, before he had to perform. In fact, he learned to ride so well the studio executives thought he was a genuine cowboy.

The film was *Let's Go, Gallagher* (1925). An instant hit, it was immediately followed that same year with *Wyoming Wildcat*. A brand new career was born—Tom Tyler, Western star!

Tom continued making Western features for FBO until 1929. Sharing honors with Tyler in many of these early entries was young Frankie Darro, himself slated to become a popular adventure star in the thirties.

Tom then signed with Syndicate Pictures for a series of eight silent sagebrushers in the 1929-30 season: *Law of the Plains, Man from Nevada, The Lone Horseman, The Phantom Rider, 'Neath Western Skies, Pioneers of the West, Canyon of Missing Men,* and *Call of the Desert.*

297

Mascot's *The Phantom of the West* (1930) was Tyler's first serial and also his first all-talking picture. Heretofore some of his silents had been released with music and/or sound effects. A pleasant speaking voice assured him success in the sound era and this ten-episode chapter play featured him with Dorothy Gulliver, Tom Santschi, Kermit Maynard, Joe Bonomo, and comic Tom Dugan who, of all people, turned out to be the mysterious phantom.

West of Cheyenne for Syndicate in early 1931 was soon followed by *Rider of the Plains, God's Country and the Man,* and the Universal serial, *Battling with Buffalo Bill,* in which Rex Bell was featured. Monogram then signed Tom for a series of eight Tyler starrers: *Galloping Thru, Man from Death Valley, Two-Fisted Justice, Vanishing Men, Single-Handed Sanders, Man from New Mexico, Partners of the Trail,* and *Honor of the Mounted* (1931-32). All were top-notch stanzas containing some very novel plots and were followed on the busy Tyler schedule by *Jungle Mystery,* with Cecilia Parker, a Universal serial which had Tom temporarily trading his sombrero for a Frank Buck pith helmet.

Tom really didn't have any need for gymnasium workouts during these years, for he got plenty of exercise in the action scenes on the sound stages and back lots of Hollywood. Late 1932 and most of 1933 saw him busy on four Monarch productions for Freuler Film Associates: *The Forty-Niners, When a Man Rides Alone, Deadwood Pass,* and *War on the Range*; and two more serials for Universal: *Clancy of the Mounted,* with Jacqueline Wells, and *Phantom of the Air* with Gloria Shea.

During the next three years (1933-36), producer Bernard B. Ray kept Tom toiling for his Reliable Pictures Corp. in a string of eighteen six-reelers. While making these, Tom also managed to squeeze in two features for RKO. First was 1935's *Powdersmoke Range,* the all-star production featuring him with big stars like Harry Carey, Bob Steele, and Hoot Gibson, among others. The success of this one prompted a follow-up, *The Last Outlaw* (1936), again with Harry and Hoot. These two films provided Tom with his first opportunities to play villainous roles. In the former he was Sundown Saunders, a hired gun who later reforms, and in the latter he played Al Goss, an eastern racketeer on the lam out West.

In the late thirties producer Sam Katzman needed cowboy stars for his newly organized Viceroy Pictures Corp. He chose two of the most popular names in the field: Colonel Tim McCoy and Tim Tyler. Each made eight Westerns for Katzman's company. Completing his quota, Tom then went on tour with the Wallace Bros. Circus, proving himself a popular draw under the big top.

Tom's longing to play more demanding roles than his regular cowboy parts then began to come true. His performance as Luke Plummer, John Wayne's arch enemy in *Stagecoach* (1939), started Tom on a long series of offbeat characterizations. Historical extravaganzas like *Gone with the Wind* (1939), modern dramas such as *Brother Orchid* (1940) and

The Talk of the Town (1942), his role as Geronimo in *Valley of the Sun* (1942), and especially his sensational appearance as Kharis, the living mummy, in *The Mummy's Hand* (1940)—all proved that Tom Tyler need not be confined to boots and saddle exclusively. His last two serials, *The Adventures of Captain Marvel* (1941) and *The Phantom* (1943), showed Tom to be both adept at and visually suited to transferring these famous comic-strip heroes to celluloid.

Captain Marvel proved so successful for Republic Pictures that they soon had Tom back in his Western outfit as a member of their "Three Mesquiteer" series. He made thirteen Mesquiteer installments with his old pal Bob Steele, and a lucky thirteen they were too; for the Mesquiteers were always among the top moneymakers. Comic Rufe Davis rounded out this 3-M trio in the first seven installments: *Outlaws of the Cherokee Trail, Gauchos of El Dorado, West of Cimarron, Code of the Outlaw, Raiders of the Range, Westward Ho!, The Phantom Plainsman*—and was replaced by Jimmy Dodd in the last six: *Shadows of the Sage, Valley of Hunted Men, Thundering Trails, The Blocked Trail, Santa Fe Scouts,*

Riders of the Rio Grande. The last of the series was released in late 1943.

Then tragedy began to overtake Tom Tyler in the late forties. Despite failing health, he continued to make pictures: *San Antonio, Cheyenne, Red River, The Younger Brothers, The Great Missouri Raid, Trail of Robin Hood*, etc. But the crippling arthritis that ravaged his once powerful body forced him to quit making films, and he returned to Detroit in late 1952 to stay with his sister Katherine. There on May 1, 1954, he suffered a fatal heart attack.

Throngs of Tyler's old fans attended his funeral and many more mourned his passing throughout the world. A great Western star was gone, but his memory will live on forever.

Western Film Credits

Let's Go Gallagher (FBO, 1925)
Wyoming Wildcat (FBO, 1925)
The Cowboy Musketeer (FBO, 1926)
Born to Battle (FBO, 1926)
Wild to Go (FBO, 1926)
The Masquerade Bandit (FBO, 1926)
The Cowboy Cop (FBO, 1926)
The Arizona Streak (FBO, 1926)
Red Hot Hoofs (FBO, 1926)
Out of the West (FBO, 1926)
Lightning Lariats (FBO, 1927)
The Sonora Kid (FBO, 1927)
Splitting the Breeze (FBO, 1927)
Cyclone of the Range (FBO, 1927)
Tom and His Pals (FBO, 1927)
The Cherokee Kid (FBO, 1927)
Desert Pirate (FBO, 1927)
The Flying U Ranch (FBO, 1927)
When the Law Rides (FBO, 1928)
Phantom of the Range (FBO, 1928)
The Texas Tornado (FBO, 1928)
Terror Mountain (FBO, 1928)
Tyrant of Red Gulch (FBO, 1928)
The Avenging Rider (FBO, 1928)
Trail of the Horse Thieves (FBO, 1929)
Gun Law (FBO, 1929)
Idaho Red (FBO, 1929)
Pride of Pawnee (FBO, 1929)

Law of the Plains (Syn., 1930)
Man from Nevada (Syn., 1930)
The Lone Horseman (Syn., 1930)
The Phantom Rider (Syn., 1930)
'Neath Western Skies (Syn., 1930)
Pioneers of the West (Syn., 1930)
Canyon of Missing Men (Syn., 1930)
Call of the Desert (Syn., 1930)
The Phantom of the West (serial) (Mas., 1930)
West of Cheyenne (Syn., 1931)
Rider of the Plains (Syn., 1931)
God's Country and the Man (Syn., 1931)
Battling with Buffalo Bill (serial) (Univ., 1931)
Galloping Thru (Mon., 1931)
Man from Death Valley (Mon., 1932)
Two-Fisted Justice (Mon., 1932)
Vanishing Men (Mon., 1932)
Single-Handed Sanders (Mon., 1932)
Man from New Mexico (Mon., 1932)
Partners of the Trail (Mon., 1932)
Honor of the Mounted (Mon., 1932)
The Forty-Niners (Freuler, 1933)
When a Man Rides Alone (Freuler, 1933)
Deadwood Pass (Freuler, 1933)
War on the Range (Freuler, 1933)

Clancy of the Mounted (serial) (Univ., 1933)
Tracy Rides (Rel., 1934)
Mystery Ranch (Rel., 1934)
Fighting Hero (Rel., 1934)
Unconquered Bandit (Rel., 1934)
Terror of the Plains (Rel., 1934)
Powdersmoke Range (RKO, 1935)
Silver Bullet (Rel., 1935)
Ridin' Thru (Rel., 1935)
Rio Rattler (Rel., 1935)
Coyote Trails (Rel., 1935)
Laramie Kid (Rel., 1935)
Born to Battle (Rel., 1935)
The Last Outlaw (RKO, 1936)
Silent Valley (Rel., 1936)
Fast Bullets (Rel., 1936)
Santa Fe Bound (Rel., 1936)
Riding On (Rel., 1936)
Roamin' Wild (Rel., 1936)
Pinto Rustlers (Rel., 1936)
Trigger Tom (Rel., 1936)
Rip Roarin' Buckaroo (Vic., 1936)
Phantom of the Range (Vic., 1937)
Cheyenne Rides Again (Vic., 1937)
Feud of the Trail (Vic., 1937)
Mystery Range (Vic., 1937)
Brothers of the West (Vic., 1937)
Lost Ranch (Vic., 1937)
Orphan of the Pecos (Vic., 1937)
Stagecoach (UA, 1939)
Frontier Marshal (20th, 1939)
Drums Along the Mohawk (20th, 1939)
The Westerner (UA, 1940)
Cherokee Strip (Par., 1940)
The Light of Western Stars (Par., 1940)

Outlaws of the Cherokee Trail (Rep., 1941)
Gauchos of El Dorado (Rep., 1941)
West of Cimarron (Rep., 1941)
Code of the Outlaw (Rep., 1942)
Raiders of the Range (Rep., 1942)
Westward Ho! (Rep., 1942)
Valley of the Sun (RKO, 1942)
The Phantom Plainsman (Rep., 1942)
Shadows of the Sage (Rep., 1942)
Valley of Hunted Men (Rep., 1943)
Thundering Trails (Rep., 1943)
The Blocked Trail (Rep., 1943)
Santa Fe Scouts (Rep., 1943)
Riders of the Rio Grande (Rep., 1943)
San Antonio (WB, 1945)
Badman's Territory (RKO, 1946)
Cheyenne (WB, 1947)
Red River (UA, 1948)
Return of the Badmen (RKO, 1948)
Lust for Gold (Col., 1949)
The Younger Brothers (WB, 1949)
I Shot Jesse James (Lip., 1949)
She Wore a Yellow Ribbon (RKO, 1949)
The Great Missouri Raid (Par., 1950)
Trail of Robin Hood (Rep., 1950)
Hostile Country (Lip., 1950)
Marshal of Heldorado (Lip., 1950)
Colorado Ranger (Lip., 1950)
West of the Brazos (Lip., 1950)
Crooked River (Lip., 1950)
Fast on the Draw (Lip., 1950)
The Great Missouri Raid (Par., 1950)
Best of the Badmen (RKO, 1951)
Road Agent (RKO, 1952)
Cow Country (AA, 1953)

William "Hopalong Cassidy" Boyd in 1945.

William Boyd

(Hopalong Cassidy)

Born: June 5, 1895, Hendrysburg, Ohio
Married: Diana Ruth Miller (1921);
   divorced (1924); remarried: Elinor Fair
   (1925); divorced (1930); remarried:
   Dorothy Sebastian (1930); divorced (1936);
   remarried: Grace Bradley (1937)
Died: September 12, 1972

WHEREAS TELEVISION'S arrival spelled doom for B-Westerns in the early fifties, television spelled fortune for William Boyd, better known to millions of fans as "Hopalong Cassidy." It also made him a national idol to a new generation of youngsters almost overnight.

Although wealth and fame came to William Boyd in his later years, he had known almost abject poverty as a boy. He was born William Lawrence Boyd, son of a laborer. He was one of five children. When his father was killed in a mining accident in Tulsa, Oklahoma, Bill was twelve years old. He left school to find work to help support his mother and family. Working at all types of jobs, he soon became a wanderer. In Arizona he was employed at a lumber camp, and in California he picked oranges and drove a grocery truck, among other jobs. Later he sold automobiles. He became a chauffeur to a Boston heiress, Diana Ruth Miller, whom he married in 1921.

Meanwhile, in 1918 Boyd had made a trip east. On the train he met movie idol Bryant Washburn. The latter urged him to try films because he would "photograph well." In Hollywood, the young man with prematurely white hair was given a $30-a-week player's contract with Cecil B. DeMille and cast in bits in *Old Wives for New* (1918) and *Why Change Your Wife?* (1919).

At Famous Players-Lasky (later to become known as Paramount Studios), Boyd was cast in featured roles in various films. Occasionally he worked in DeMille's lush productions, and he even supported Rudolph Valentino in *The Young Rajah* (1922). As the Roaring Twenties wore on, Boyd starred in such he-man epics as *The Midshipman* (1925) and *The Volga Boatman* (1926). For DeMille he was one of the stars of *The Road to Yesterday* (1925) and *The King of Kings* (1927). Bill also developed a way with celluloid farce in films such as *Two Arabian Knights* (1927).

Trying to calm down a spirited horse during the shooting of one of his many "Hoppy" films.

As talkies became the way of Hollywood life, Boyd became a star on the Paramount lot. He had a resonant and well-modulated speaking voice and so he had no trouble breaking into sound films. One of his first sound productions was the part-talkie *Lady of the Pavements* (1929) for D. W. Griffith. If the twenties brought Boyd screen prominence, these years did little for his personal happiness.

By 1930, Bill was divorced from Ruth Miller *and* Elinor Fair and married to Dorothy Sebastian, wife number three. They would divorce six years later. His only child, a son by his first wife, died when only nine months old.

Like Tom Mix and Hoot Gibson, Boyd was famous for his expansive living. He owned a Beverly Hills mansion, a beach home at Malibu, and a ranch, and he had a penchant for drinking and gambling.

By the early thirties, Bill had transferred to the smaller Pathé studios, working in such films as *The Painted Desert* (1931), which featured new-comer Clark Gable as the villain, and RKO's *Lucky Devils* (1933) in which he starred as the leader of a group of Hollywood stuntmen.

Then in 1932 fate played a cruel trick on William Boyd. Another film performer with the name of Bill Boyd, but who was usually billed as William "Stage" Boyd, was arrested for taking part in a scandalous beach party. The next day's newspapers across the nation carried William "Hoppy" Boyd's photo as the arrested celebrity, and, although retractions were later printed, the public began to shy away from his films. For the next two years, Boyd found very little work in feature films.

In 1935, however, Bill was offered $5,000 per film to make six Westerns for producer Harry "Pop" Sherman. It was to be a series based on Clarence E. Mulford's pulp Western hero, Hopalong Cassidy. Among others, James Gleason had originally been considered for the part of the ill-kempt, hard-drinking hell-raiser who walked with a limp due to an old bullet injury.

For the screen, Bill Boyd laundered the character into a good guy role, and after the initial entry, *Hopalong Cassidy* (1935), Bill eliminated the limp from his character. His white mount in all Hoppy pictures was named Topper.

Although Bill made a few features besides the Hoppy series, he was soon typed as a Western series star. From 1936 to 1948 he was rated high in the Motion Picture Herald poll of top Western stars. By 1938 he was earning a $100,000 annual salary, and he would make a total of sixty-six Hopalong Cassidy pictures for Sherman.

At least onscreen, Boyd took the character of Cassidy seriously, and he developed a code of ethics for his character. Hoppy did not drink, smoke, swear, and rarely kissed the heroine. He preferred to capture the villain rather than kill him, and his scenarios emphasized the picturesque rather than violence.

As typical of the genre, Boyd's features contained two sidekicks: the romantic, althletic young pal (James Ellison, first, and then Russell Hayden) and the grimy, cantankerous, rascally old buddy (George "Gabby" Hayes, who created the role of Windy Halliday in 1936; then Andy Clyde, who played the part of California Carlson from 1940 to 1948). Unlike most other Western series, the Hoppy films used different locales for each picture, and the films remain timeless because they did not depict their own time and thus became dated.

In the mid-forties, Boyd and his lucrative series transferred from Paramount to United Artists. After managerial differences with Harry Sherman, Boyd became the producer of his own films, partnered with Benedict Bogeaus and Carl Lesserman. The quality of the final dozen Cassidy films noticeably lessened.

By 1948 there was no further demand for the Hoppy series. Boyd gambled on the replay value of his pictures by mortgaging his home and cars to buy the television rights to the Cassidy character from author Clarence Mulford. Within a few months, the old Cassidy films were playing on sixty-six TV stations.

William Boyd became one of the first Western heroes of the new video medium. In 1950 he began performing the Hopalong role over Mutual radio. He also made phonograph records, reading from the Mulford stories. He made personal appearance tours as Hoppy all over the Western Hemisphere (sometimes failing to hide from fans that he was in real life a heavy drinker). Although Boyd was never too fond of children, he appreciated their role in his success. "The way I figure it," he said, "if it weren't for the kids, I'd be a damn bum today. They're the ones who've made my success as Hoppy possible."

After making 106 TV "Hopalong Cassidy" shows and some more personal appearances, Boyd retired from show business in 1953. Ironically his final cinema job was for the man who gave him his first screen role, Cecil B. DeMille. This time Boyd did a cameo appearance as himself in *The Greatest Show on Earth* (1952). Thereafter the cowboy star dabbled in real estate, and in 1958 he sold William Boyd Enterprises for $8 million. Looking back on his career, he would say, "It's a great life if you don't weaken, this motion picture business. I'm certainly glad I had a try at it."

In the late sixties, still wed to wife number four, Grace Bradley, Boyd suffered from ill health, including Parkinson's disease and cancer. He refused interviews, saying the public would be "shocked at the difference" in his appearance. His health continued to fail until his death at South Coast Community Hospital in Laguna Beach, California, on September 12, 1972. At the time, most of his Westerns were being re-issued to a new generation of upcoming Hoppy fans.

During his boots-and-saddle years Boyd tried to bring a relatively sane cinema Western character to the screen. "I avoid the stupid type of cowhand. . . . I try to speak intelligently. The minute I start acting I'm out of character. I'm like the kid's uncle and the wife's brother."

Of "Hoppy" he fondly said, "He's part philosopher, part doctor, part minister—he's everything."

Western Film Credits

The Painted Desert (RKO-Pathé, 1931)
Hopalong Cassidy (Par., 1935)
The Eagle's Brood (Par., 1935)
Bar 20 Rides Again (Par., 1935)
Call of the Prairie (Par., 1936)
Three on the Trail (Par., 1936)
Heart of the West (Par., 1936)
Trail Dust (Par., 1936)

Hopalong Cassidy Returns (Par., 1936)
Borderland (Par., 1937)
Hills of Old Wyoming (Par., 1937)
North of the Rio Grande (Par., 1937)
Rustler's Valley (Par., 1937)
Hopalong Rides Again (Par., 1937)
Texas Trail (Par., 1937)
Partners of the Plains (Par., 1938)

Cassidy of Bar 20 (Par., 1938)
Heart of Arizona (Par., 1938)
Bar 20 Justice (Par., 1938)
Pride of the West (Par., 1938)
In Old Mexico (Par., 1938)
Sunset Trail (Par., 1938)
The Frontiersman (Par., 1938)
Silver on the Sage (Par., 1939)
Renegade Trail (Par., 1939)
Range War (Par., 1939)
Law of the Pampas (Par., 1939)
Santa Fe Marshal (Par., 1940)
The Showdown (Par., 1940)
Hidden Gold (Par., 1940)
Stagecoach War (Par., 1940)
Three Men from Texas (Par., 1940)
Doomed Caravan (Par., 1941)
In Old Colorado (Par., 1941)
Border Vigilantes (Par., 1941)
Pirates on Horseback (Par., 1941)
Wide Open Town (Par., 1941)
Outlaws of the Desert (Par., 1941)
Riders of the Timberline (Par., 1941)
Secrets of the Wasteland (Par., 1941)
Stick to Your Guns (Par., 1941)
Twilight on the Trail (Par., 1941)

Undercover Man (UA, 1942)
Lost Canyon (UA, 1942)
Hoppy Serves a Writ (UA, 1943)
Border Patrol (UA, 1943)
The Leather Burners (UA, 1943)
Colt Comrades (UA, 1943)
Bar 20 (UA, 1943)
False Colors (UA, 1943)
Riders of the Deadline (UA, 1943)
Texas Masquerade (UA, 1944)
Lumberjack (UA, 1944)
Mystery Man (UA, 1944)
Forty Thieves (UA, 1944)
The Devil's Playground (UA, 1946)
Fool's Gold (UA, 1946)
Unexpected Guest (UA, 1947)
Dangerous Venture (UA, 1947)
Hoppy's Holiday (UA, 1947)
The Marauders (UA, 1947)
Sinister Journey (UA, 1948)
Silent Conflict (UA, 1948)
The Dead Don't Dream (UA, 1948)
False Paradise (UA, 1948)
Strange Gamble (UA, 1948)
Borrowed Trouble (UA, 1948)

Richard Dix, with Patricia Morison in The Round Up *(1941).*

Richard Dix

(The Western matinee idol)

Born: July 18, 1894, St. Paul, Minn.
Married: Winifred Coe (1931); divorced
   (1933); remarried: Virginia Webster (1934);
   children: Martha May Ellen, Richard Jr.,
   Robert, Sara Sue
Died: September 20, 1949

STALWART, RESOLUTE, MANLY—these are some of the appropriate adjectives to describe Richard Dix, the square-jawed matinee idol of the silent-talkie screens who became a superstar. Interestingly, since his popularity and box-office draw were so great, he never had to appear in low-budget series Westerns.

Richard Dix' vehicles were always individual starring roles in which he characterized a staunch, heroic figure, much like the earlier portrayals of William S. Hart.

Born Ernest Carlton Brimmer, Dix came from a family whose ancestry dated back to the *Mayflower*. While attending the University of Minnesota Medical School, he began to dabble in amateur theatrics and was offered a role in a touring company of *Richelieu*. Although he declined this bid (to appease his family), he later accepted work in a St. Paul stock company. Eventually the family gave him their blessings and, with the new stage name of Richard Dix, he set forth to begin a career in front of the footlights.

Acting jobs took him to New York and then to stock companies in Pittsburgh, Dallas, and Montreal. He enlisted in the army during World War I, but the Armistice came before he was to ship overseas.

Dix made his Broadway debut in *The Hawk* with William Faversham and appeared in four more New York stage shows before traveling to Los Angeles with a touring company. There he made a film test in 1919. But after seeing himself onscreen as a villain in *One of the Finest* (1919), he so disliked his celluloid image that he rejected several film bids.

Friends finally convinced Dix to take a second screen test and it resulted in his being hired for a dual-role lead in *Not Guilty* (1921). Thereafter he signed a contract with Samuel Goldwyn and soon became an important film star.

Socially inclined, Dix dated some of Hollywood's loveliest ladies, and his no-nonsense talk made good grist for fan magazines. When actor

Wallace Reid died in 1923, Dix signed with Paramount as his replacement. While at the new studio he made Zane Grey Westerns, including *To the Last Man* (1923). Then he went east to Paramount's Astoria, Long Island, studio where he found his forte in the dramas and comedies typical of the flapper era.

Always a considerate performer, Dix was constantly on the lookout for new talent and he helped numerous young performers, including Ramon Novarro and Jeanette MacDonald, to win better film roles.

By 1927 Richard Dix was Paramount's top money-making star earning a $4,500 weekly salary. However, he eventually grew tired of the company's new regime and, when his contract expired in 1929, he left Paramount to work for RKO.

Dix made his all-talking film debut in 1929 in Earl Derr Biggers' mystery *Seven Keys to Baldpate*. In 1928, he had made *Redskin* (an early '29 release). He followed with his finest screen role, that of Yancey Cravat in Edna Ferber's *Cimarron* (1931). This elaborate feature proved to be one of the best Westerns of the early sound period. For this film Dix insisted that screen newcomer Irene Dunne be given the lead opposite him.

RKO provided Dix with a wide variety of features. Among his best were *The Lost Squadron* (1932), in which he played a movie stuntman; *Roar of the Dragon* (1932), an Oriental melodrama; and *The Conquerors* (1932), a *Cimarron*-type outdoor epic. At Columbia, he did *Devil's Squadron* (1936), wherein he portrayed a test pilot. Like other Hollywood players, he found it lucrative to try his cinematic luck in England, where he made *Trans-Atlantic Tunnel* (1935). Dix was never a conventional male lead of the thirties, and he often appeared in rugged Westerns, such as *West of the Pecos* (1934). *It Happened in Hollywood* (1937) was an amusing satire with Dix as a faded cowboy star who makes a screen comeback by shooting three real-life holdup men.

During his RKO years Dix married for a second time and settled on his large ranch near Topanga, California, where he raised hogs and turkeys. In 1939 he went to Republic to star as Sam Houston in that studio's big-budget *Man of Conquest*. The film showcased Richard Dix at his finest, portraying a great American.

The early forties found the very mature Dix working out of various studios, usually cast in strongly scripted Westerns. In *Badlands of Dakota* (1941) he received special billing as Wild Bill Hickok. The next year he portrayed Wyatt Earp in *Tombstone, the Town Too Tough to Die*. *Buckskin Frontier* and *The Kansan*, both 1943 releases, were his final entries in the sagebrush genre, which by now had become the territory of singing cowboys like Gene Autry and Roy Rogers, and masked riders like Charles Starrett's Durango Kid.

In the mid-forties, Dix played in the Columbia Pictures detective series *The Whistler*, which was based on the radio show. By 1948, his health had begun to fail seriously and he suffered from recurring heart attacks. On September 20, 1949, he expired from acute cardiac collapse. He left behind an estate of over $2 million. One son, Robert, became a film actor and for a while headed a production company besides writing movie scripts.

Richard Dix always loved his profession and always gave himself unstintingly to it. He once commented that he sometimes wished he "had the drive to continue in both films and the theater," but he remained with the former.

Today it is Richard Dix' Westerns which still receive the most television exposure. Through them the masculine charm of the star remains alive. While never a truly inspired performer, Dix was always sincere and self-sufficient, qualities beloved by all his Western fans.

Western Film Credits

To the Last Man (Par., 1923)
Call of the Canyon (Par., 1923)
The Vanishing American (Par., 1925)
Redskin (Par., 1929)
Shooting Straight (RKO, 1930)
Cimarron (RKO, 1931)
The Conquerors (RKO, 1932)
Stingaree (RKO, 1934)
West of the Pecos (RKO, 1934)
The Arizonian (RKO, 1935)

Yellow Dust (RKO, 1936)
Man of Conquest (Rep., 1939)
Cherokee Strip (Par., 1940)
The Round Up (Par., 1941)
Badlands of Dakota (Univ., 1941)
Tombstone, the Town Too Tough to Die (Par., 1942)
American Empire (UA, 1942)
Buckskin Frontier (UA, 1943)
The Kansan (UA, 1943)

William "Wild Bill" Elliott, ready for action.

William "Wild Bill" Elliott

(Two-gun action hero)

Born: October 16, 1903, Pattonsburg, Mo.
Married: Helen Myer (1927); divorced (1961);
   child: Barbara; remarried: Dolly
   Moore (1962)
Died: November 26, 1965

THE WESTERN MOVIES have been glutted with a wide variety of lead players, from superstars like John Wayne to quickly fading cowpokes such as Tex Fletcher and Art Davis. Most of the cowboy star notables have been personalities rather than thespians; in fact, most of them had only a limited, if appealing, acting range. One major exception was William Elliott, better known as Wild Bill Elliott, who provided some of the finest Western performances in the motion picture business.

Elliott was one of the few Hollywood players to graduate from B-Westerns to high-budget productions. Most critics agree it was William Elliott in the sound era who best preserved the frontier tradition established in films by William S. Hart during the silent period.

Cowboy pictures turned out to be a natural vocation for Elliott. Bill, christened Gordon Nance, was the son of a Kansas City stockyard commission man. Young Gordon fell in love with horses and began riding when he was five, learning to rope, bulldog, and bust broncs soon thereafter. At age sixteen he won first place in rodeo riding in the American Royal Horse and Livestock Show in Kansas City.

Throughout his teenage years, Gordon participated in rodeos. After attending Rockhurst College, he decided to give show business a try and headed for Hollywood. His inspiration had been the William S. Hart action films, which, next to horses, were the entertainment he most enjoyed.

Gordon wisely decided to enroll at the famed Pasadena Community Playhouse. Here he gained practical stage experience while being tutored in the rudiments of his chosen craft. Here also the tall, rangy young man was spotted by a talent scout and placed in films. This was the first step in fulfilling a prophecy made by his mother years before that her son would be a movie star. Fourteen years would pass before his mother's words came true.

Upon entering films the young man changed his name to Gordon Elliott. His first film of record was *The Plastic Age* (1925), which starred

Clara Bow, and which also featured Gilbert Roland and spotted Clark Gable in a minute role. From there Gordon moved on to a number of Hollywood photoplays, including *The Drop Kick* (1927) in which John Wayne appeared as an extra.

By the late twenties Elliott was getting good-sized roles in such pictures as *The Private Life of Helen of Troy* (1927) and *Valley of Hunted Men* (1928). But the chaos that hit the movie industry when sound took over the medium set his career back. Lost in the shuffle, he was forced to play bit and extra parts.

For the bulk of the thirties Gordon was constantly busy as a bit player. He was occupied at various studios in the early depression years, and in 1933 signed a player's contract with Warner Bros. where he was employed in dozens of films—strolling through a scene here, being a party guest there, or a dance extra in some other project at the Burbank production mill. In 1935 he appeared in over twenty films for the studio, as a bit player and without mass recognition.

In 1937 he was loaned to 20th Century-Fox for the Smith Ballew Western *Roll Along, Cowboy*. Elliott was impressive enough in the part for Columbia Pictures to recognize him and give him the leading role in the serial *The Great Adventures of Wild Bill Hickok* in 1938. The exciting chapter play proved to be one of the best cliffhangers of the sound era. Harry Cohn, head of Columbia Pictures, immediately signed Elliott to a contract as a Western star and changed his name officially to Bill Elliott.

The Elliott cowboy series at Columbia were produced relatively well. Many were directed by Bill Hart's old director, Lambert Hillyer. In these entries, as in his later motion pictures, earnest Elliott projected the image of the strong, brave, and compassionate Westerner, similar to the one Hart had made famous in the silent-movie days.

Elliott's oncamera wardrobe was far more restrained than the flashy, detailed outfits of Republic's Gene Autry and Roy Rogers. Bill's only gimmick was having his guns reversed in their holsters, with the butts forward. By 1940 he had joined the ranks of *Motion Picture Herald*'s top moneymaking Western stars. And there he remained through 1954.

By 1941 Columbia was teaming Bill with Tex Ritter for an easygoing series of Westerns and continuing to use him for serials. It was almost inevitable that Bill should gravitate to Republic, *the* outstanding studio for the production of Westerns and serials. He signed a contract with it in 1943.

His new studio billed him as "Wild Bill" Elliott and immediately teamed him in a series with George "Gabby" Hayes and Anne Jeffreys. Elliott followed Don "Red" Barry in the Red Ryder role in 1943. In 1945, along with other Western stars, Bill did a guest bit as himself in Roy Rogers' *Bells of Rosarita*. By now he was a regular at Republic and a great favorite with movie audiences.

After performing in sixteen Red Ryder installments, Elliott was

With George "Gabby" Hayes in 1944.

chosen to replace unavailable Randolph Scott in the quality production *In Old Sacramento* (1946). Bill was happier making less pretentious Westerns and had no desire to become a high-budget movie star; nevertheless, he yielded to studio demands to portray Spanish Jack, a colorful highwayman in the film. He was very good indeed. The film's downbeat ending had him dying in the leading lady's arms. Later reissued as *Flame of Sacramento*, the film proved most popular.

Through 1949 Bill made ten big-budget films for Republic. All had adult themes with good production, scripts, and direction. Unfortunately, in some people's view, he was teamed with Vera Ralston (wife of Republic chief Herbert B. Yates) in *The Plainsman and the Lady* (1946) and *Wyoming* (1947), neither of which was truly suited to the European-born skating star. On the other hand, vital Marie Windsor was a good costar with her performance as the female outlaw in *Hellfire* (1949). The project was made for Ellott's own production unit, as was *The Showdown* (1949).

Sadly, by 1954 changing economics and tastes, as well as the inroads into movies made by television, had nearly finished the double-bill Western in Hollywood. Bill made a series of detective melodramas at Allied Artists, the last of which was *Footsteps in the Night* (1957). In each production Bill offered a low-key but sincere performance, showing admirable restraint in handling the sometimes banal plot situations.

315

After the demise of his motion picture career, Bill sold his Westwood, California, home and moved to a ranch near Las Vegas. He also owned a ranch near Calabasas, California, on which he raised horses and cattle. He collected Western memorabilia and studied geology as hobbies.

In the late fifties Bill was employed as national spokesman for Viceroy Cigarettes. In Las Vegas he was persuaded to host a teleseries which offered his old films. He also starred in two Western pilot films for television, but neither *The Marshal of Trail City* nor *Parson of the West* found a network sponsor.

When Elliott died of cancer on November 26, 1965, one of the true greats of Hollywood Westerns was gone. The industry had lost a powerful interpreter of realistic frontier life.

Later generations would have to settle for such genre pieces as "Bonanza" or "The Virginian." Not until the emergence of the Italian spaghetti Western in the sixties and of Clint Eastwood as the new interpreter of the bloody old West would the type again be so well represented as it was in the Wild Bill Elliott offerings.

Western Film Credits

Valley of Hunted Men (Pathé, 1928)
Arizona Wildcat (Fox, 1928)
The Great Divide (WB, 1930)
Moonlight on the Prairie (WB, 1935)
Trailin' West (WB, 1936)
Guns of the Pecos (WB, 1936)
Boots and Saddles (Rep., 1937)
Roll Along, Cowboy (20th, 1937)
The Great Adventures of Wild Bill Hickok (serial) (Col., 1938)
In Early Arizona (Col., 1938)
Frontiers of '49 (Col., 1938)
Lone Star Pioneers (Col., 1939)
The Law Comes to Texas (Col., 1939)
Taming of the West (Col., 1939)
Overland with Kit Carson (serial) (Col., 1939)
The Return of Wild Bill (Col., 1940)
Pioneers of the Frontier (Col., 1940)
The Man from Tumbleweeds (Col., 1940)
Prairie Schooners (Col., 1940)
Beyond the Sacramento (Col., 1940)

The Wildcat of Tucson (Col., 1940)
North from the Lone Star (Col., 1941)
Across the Sierras (Col., 1941)
The Return of Daniel Boone (Col., 1941)
Son of Davy Crockett (Col., 1941)
Hands Across the Rockies (Col., 1941)
King of Dodge City (Col., 1941)
Roaring Frontiers (Col., 1941)
Lone Star Vigilantes (Col., 1941)
Bullets for Bandits (Col., 1942)
North of the Rockies (Col., 1942)
The Devil's Trail (Col., 1942)
Prairie Gunsmoke (Col., 1942)
Vengeance of the West (Col., 1942)
Valley of Vanishing Men (serial) (Col., 1942)
Calling Wild Bill Elliott (Rep., 1943)
The Man from Thunder River (Rep., 1943)
Wagon Tracks West (Rep., 1943)
Death Valley Manhunt (Rep., 1943)

Bordertown Gunfighters (Rep., 1943)
Overland Mail Robbery (Rep., 1943)
Hidden Valley Outlaws (Rep., 1943)
Mojave Firebrand (Rep., 1944)
Tucson Raiders (Rep., 1944)
Marshal of Reno (Rep., 1944)
The San Antonio Kid (Rep., 1944)
Cheyenne Wildcat (Rep., 1944)
Vigilantes of Dodge City (Rep., 1944)
Sheriff of Las Vegas (Rep., 1944)
Bells of Rosarita (Rep., 1945)
Great Stagecoach Robbery (Rep., 1945)
Lone Texas Ranger (Rep., 1945)
Phantom of the Plains (Rep., 1945)
Marshal of Laredo (Rep., 1945)
Colorado Pioneers (Rep., 1945)
Wagon Wheels Westward (Rep., 1945)
California Gold Rush (Rep., 1946)
Sheriff of Redwood Valley (Rep., 1946)
Sun Valley Cyclone (Rep., 1946)

Conquest of Cheyenne (Rep., 1946)
In Old Sacramento (Rep., 1946)
The Plainsman and the Lady (Rep., 1946)
Wyoming (Rep., 1947)
The Fabulous Texan (Rep., 1947)
Old Los Angeles (Rep., 1948)
The Gallant Legion (Rep., 1948)
Hellfire (Rep., 1949)
The Last Bandit (Rep., 1949)
The Savage Horde (Rep., 1950)
The Showdown (Rep., 1950)
The Longhorn (Mon., 1952)
Waco (Mon., 1952)
Fargo (Mon., 1952)
The Maverick (Mon., 1952)
Kansas Territory (Mon., 1952)
The Homesteaders (AA, 1953)
Rebel City (AA, 1953)
Topeka (AA, 1953)
Vigilante Terror (AA, 1953)
Bitter Creek (AA, 1954)
The Forty-Niners (AA, 1954)

Tim Holt, Western star.

Tim Holt

(The kid with "true grit")

Born: February 5, 1918, Hollywood, Calif.
Married: Virginia Ashcroft (1938);
   divorced (1944); remarried: Alice Harrison
   (1944); divorced (1951); child: Lance;
   remarried: Berdee Stephens (1957);
   children: Jack, Bryanna, Jay
Died: February 15, 1973

BORN JOHN CHARLES HOLT, JR., young Tim was the son of actor Jack Holt—who played hero-villain roles for years—and the older brother of Jennifer Holt, an actress who also starred in Westerns for many years. When Tim was ten, he appeared in his father's Paramount feature *The Vanishing Pioneer* (1928). In the mid-twenties, Tim was crown prince of the Fresno rodeo, and he rode behind his father who was king of that rodeo parade.

After his parents separated in the twenties, Tim grew up on his father's 19,000-acre ranch near Fresno. In 1933 Tim entered Culver Military Academy in Culver, Indiana, where he participated in boxing, gymnastics, football, squash, polo, and tennis. Besides his studies and athletics, he took part in school dramatics, appearing in the Shakespearean play *Twelfth Night.* In addition to graduating *cum laude* in 1936, he won the Gold Spurs Award for good horsemanship.

Tim returned to California to pursue an acting career. He found work in the stage show *Papa Is All,* where he was spotted by producer Walter Wanger. Tim was signed to a personal contract by Wanger and featured in *History Is Made at Night* (1937). After a few other features he was loaned to RKO, and here he costarred with veteran actor Harry Carey in the solid Western *The Law West of Tombstone* (1938), offering a telling performance as a young outlaw. Next he supported George O'Brien in *The Renegade Ranger* (1938). RKO was by then impressed enough with his work to purchase his contract from Wanger. Thereafter he appeared in a number of dramas for the studio, but he was most impressive as the cavalryman in John Ford's classic *Stagecoach* (1939), which also launched John Wayne's career to top box office with his portrayal of the Ringo Kid.

In 1940 Tim joined Thomas Mitchell and Edna Best in a new rendition of *The Swiss Family Robinson,* and then began a starring series of high-caliber programmer Westerns for the studio. From 1941 to 1943 Tim

In a scene from Thundering Hoofs *(1942), with Lee "Lasses" White and Ray Whitley.*

was listed among the top moneymaking Western film stars by the *Motion Picture Herald*. Amidst his hard-riding adventure pictures, he gave a finely honed interpretation of the young rich man who gets his comeuppance in Orson Welles' *The Magnificent Ambersons* (1942).

By 1942, after completing sixty-four straight days of film shooting to meet his RKO quota for that year, Tim enlisted in the U.S. Army Air Corps. (At the time his father Jack Holt was serving as an officer in the Quartermaster Corps.)

Trained at Victorville, California, Tim was commissioned a second lieutenant and served as an instructor on the flight line and in ground school. He was then sent to the Pacific theater and flew fifty-nine combat missions as bombardier on a B-29. He received a number of decorations and citations for bravery, including the Distinguished Service Cross, before he was honorably discharged in 1945 and returned to making Westerns for RKO.

His first postwar job, however, was on loan to 20th Century-Fox for John Ford's *My Darling Clementine* (1946). A retelling of the events leading up to the famous gunfight at the O.K. Corral, the classic Western starred Henry Fonda (as Wyatt Earp), Victor Mature (Doc Holliday), Walter Brennan (Old Man Clanton), Ward Bond (Morgan Earp), and Tim as Virgil Earp. Following this major production, Tim was back on the

Holt throws a "knockout" punch at LeRoy Mason (1942).

RKO lot riding through a series of action-filled Westerns, some of which were remakes of Zane Grey-based films.

Tim's finest role in the Western field came in 1948 when he worked at Warner Bros. for John Huston in the film version of B. Traven's novel *The Treasure of the Sierra Madre*. He was cast as Curtin, the man who joins Humphrey Bogart and Walter Huston in their furious search for gold in the windy Sierra Madre of Mexico.

The *New York Times* commended Tim for being "quietly appealing." After this prestigious picture, which took eighteen months to complete, Tim was again back in the saddle for RKO.

The RKO Western entries were budgeted at a figure somewhere between $80,000 and $100,000 and usually grossed five times their costs. At this time Tim was earning about $70,000 a year and rated high with the filmgoing public. In his RKO films the comedy relief was often handled by Richard Martin, as sidekick Chito, and the leading ladies of the oaters ranged from Marjorie Lord (Jack's sister) to Dorothy Malone to Jane Nigh.

In 1951 Tim appeared with Robert Mitchum and Jane Russell in the gangster film *His Kind of Woman*. About two years later he made *Desert Passage* (1952), which ended his RKO tenure.

After the demise of his long film career, Tim and his third wife Berdee

321

Stephens moved to Iowa where he completed a course in animal nutrition. Then he went to New York City to perform live with veteran actor Johnny Mack Brown; the Western sequence was telecast over Ken Murray's variety show. Next he did a short subject, *Shooting Straight with Tim Holt,* for the National Rifle Association. He also filmed a pilot for TV with Charles Bronson titled *Adventure in Java.* Although it did not sell as a series, the segment was telecast on NBC-TV in 1954. Three years later Tim could be seen in the science-fiction entry *The Monster That Challenged the World.*

By 1959 Tim Holt had left Hollywood for good and had settled on a 1,400-acre ranch near Norman, Oklahoma. For two seasons he starred on "The Tim Holt Western Theatre" over KOCO-TV in Oklahoma City, hosting reshowings of his RKO Westerns. Later he entered the construction business and built numerous homes in the Oklahoma City area.

From 1962 to 1969 Tim was employed by radio station KOPR in that city, and then he moved to Denver where he was hired as an executive for Jamco, Inc., a multi-industrial firm. In 1971 he returned to Oklahoma City to take charge of the sales department for radio station KEBC-FM. He lived on a small ranch outside Harrah, not far from his job.

During the sixties Tim's only acting venture was in a segment of "The Virginian." In 1971 he made one more picture, starring in the poor exploitation feature *This Stuff'll Kill Ya!* The title was prophetic, for that year he suffered what was diagnosed as a heart attack. But the next year doctors discovered Tim had brain cancer. He underwent medical treatment and continued to work part-time at his job until his death on February 15, 1973.

On the night Tim Holt died a television tape, made during his final stay in the hospital, was presented over Oklahoma TV stations. The dramatic high of the showing was unplanned, and occurred when the announcer interrupted the program and sadly told the listening audience that Tim Holt had just succumbed to cancer.

Western Film Credits

The Vanishing Pioneer (Par., 1928)
The Law West of Tombstone (RKO, 1938)
Gold Is Where You Find It (WB, 1938)
The Renegade Ranger (RKO, 1938)
Stagecoach (UA, 1939)
The Fargo Kid (RKO, 1940)
Wagon Train (RKO, 1940)

Dude Cowboy (RKO, 1941)
The Bandit Trail (RKO, 1941)
Along the Rio Grande (RKO, 1941)
Robbers of the Range (RKO, 1941)
Riding the Wind (RKO, 1941)
Six-Gun Gold (RKO, 1941)
Cyclone on Horseback (RKO, 1941)
Land of the Open Range (RKO, 1942)

Come On, Danger (RKO, 1942)
Thundering Hoofs (RKO, 1942)
Bandit Ranger (RKO, 1942)
Pirates of the Prairie (RKO, 1942)
The Avenging Rider (RKO, 1943)
Red River Robin Hood (RKO, 1943)
Sagebrush Law (RKO, 1943)
Fighting Frontier (RKO, 1943)
My Darling Clementine (20th, 1946)
Thunder Mountain (RKO, 1947)
Wild Horse Mesa (RKO, 1947)
Under the Tonto Rim (RKO, 1947)
The Treasure of the Sierra Madre
   (WB, 1948)
The Arizona Ranger (RKO, 1948)
Guns of Hate (RKO, 1948)
Western Heritage (RKO, 1948)
Indian Agent (RKO, 1948)
Gun Smugglers (RKO, 1948)
The Stagecoach Kid (RKO, 1949)
Brothers in the Saddle (RKO, 1949)

Rustlers (RKO, 1949)
Masked Raiders (RKO, 1949)
The Mysterious Desperado (RKO,
   1949)
Riders of the Range (RKO, 1949)
Dynamite Pass (RKO, 1950)
Storm over Wyoming (RKO, 1950)
Rider from Tucson (RKO, 1950)
Border Treasure (RKO, 1950)
Rio Grande Patrol (RKO, 1950)
Law of the Badlands (RKO, 1950)
Saddle Legion (RKO, 1951)
Gunplay (RKO, 1951)
Pistol Harvest (RKO, 1951)
Overland Telegraph (RKO, 1951)
Hot Lead (RKO, 1951)
Trail Guide (RKO, 1952)
Target (RKO, 1952)
Road Agent (RKO, 1952)
Desert Passage (RKO, 1952)

Allan "Rocky" Lane in 1949.

Allan "Rocky" Lane

(Alias "Red Ryder")

Born: September 22, 1904, Mishawaka, Ind.
Married: Gladys Leslie (1924); divorced
   (1926); remarried: Sheila Ryan (1942);
   divorced (1946)
Died: October 27, 1973

THE ROAD TO Western superstardom was a long one for Indiana-born Harry Albershart, later to become known to his millions of fans as Allan "Rocky" Lane.

After high school in Mishawaka, Lane attended Notre Dame University where he excelled in sports, winning varsity letters in football, baseball, and basketball. But he gravitated toward the theater, and left Notre Dame before graduation to join a stock company in Cincinnati.

Lane was with the National Players one year when a road company of *Hit the Deck* came to Cincinnati minus a leading man. Now calling himself Allan Lane, he won the lead part and went with the tour to New York City. He remained in Manhattan for some time, working continually in the theater. He also became fascinated with photography and founded his own firm, specializing in advertising commercial photography. Among his customers were Wrigley's Chewing Gum, Camay Soap, Ford Motor Company, and Lucky Strike Cigarettes.

In 1929 at the real beginning of the sound era in Hollywood, Lane was discovered by a Fox talent scout and offered a contract. Gambling on becoming famous, Lane closed his photography business and went to Hollywood. He debuted in *Not Quite Decent* (1929), followed by *Forward Pass* in the same year.

With his tall, rangy frame and dark-complexioned good looks, Lane was one of numerous male-lead types in Tinseltown. However, when he realized there was no future for him at Fox he tried his luck at Warner Bros., where he was featured in a number of films. In 1932 he was in eight releases. At that point he decided to return to the theater, and also to reestablish his photography interests.

By 1936 he was back on the silver screen in Shirley Temple's *Stowaway* at Fox. For the same studio he had a leading role in *Charlie Chan at the Olympics* (1937). He continued hopscotching around the different studios, playing the part of a boxer for Republic in *The Duke Comes Back* (1937), his first starring film. He signed with RKO in 1938 as a contract

In Frontier Investigator *(1949) with Eddy Waller and Francis Ford.*

player. There he was given his best non-Western roles, starring in a number of the studio's films. Among them was *Maid's Night Out* in 1938, with Joan Fontaine his colead. He also made his Western film debut that year in RKO's *The Law West of Tombstone*, supporting Harry Carey and Tim Holt.

Seeking better parts for himself and greater screen recognition, Lane signed with Republic Studios in 1940. During the first three years of his tenure he made few films; the company already had Roy Rogers and Gene Autry as its major Western stars. Lane was thus assigned to such chapter plays as *King of the Royal Mounted* (1940), *King of the Mounties* (1942), and *Daredevils of the West* (1943). He also did minor musicals such as *Grand Ole Opry* (1940) and *All-American Co-Ed* (UA, 1941) with Frances Langford. One of his better parts was on loan to Fox for Stan Laurel and Oliver Hardy's *The Dancing Masters* (1943).

Finally, in 1944, Lane's screen career began to coalesce. Republic co-starred him in the popular serial *The Tiger Woman* with Linda Stirling, "Queen of the Serials," in the title role. Also in 1944 he began a nearly ten-year association with the moderately budgeted Western as a full-fledged cowboy star.

Beginning with *Silver City Kid*, Rocky Lane developed a Western hero who was neat, handsome, kind of heart, and quick on the trigger. His

326

pleasant emoting and action-filled films made him popular with the Western audience. It certainly didn't hurt his chances of success at Republic when Gene Autry was away in military service, leaving an opening for a new Saturday matinee idol.

Republic sometimes took advantage of Lane's photogenic looks for films like *Call of the South Seas* (1944) or *Night Train to Memphis* (1946), in which he was a leading-man contrast for country and western music star Roy Acuff. Mostly, however, Lane ground out six or seven B-Westerns a year.

In 1946 when Wild Bill Elliott was promoted to major Republic productions, Lane replaced him in the ongoing Red Ryder film series. *Santa Fe Uprising* was the first of his outings as Red Ryder, with Bobby Blake (later "Baretta") as Little Beaver and Emmett Lynn as Lane's grumpy sidekick. Western fans accepted him in the Ryder role, and he went on to make more Red Ryder entries before he was replaced in the Fred Harman creation by Jim Bannon.

In the late forties Lane worked oncamera with his wonder horse Black Jack and comic Eddy Waller in the Republic Westerns. But by this time the studio was reducing budgets of all its leading "B" oaters. *El Paso Stampede* (1953) was Lane's final series offering at Republic. The B-Western was now fast dying and being replaced by television.

Lane toured with various circuses and rodeos, an occupation which lasted until 1956. In 1958 he returned to filmdom for a supporting role in *The Saga of Hemp Brown*. He was featured in two more Westerns, *Hell Bent for Leather* (1960) and his final film *Posse from Hell* (1961).

Unlike many former cowboy superstars, Lane did not entirely fade from the entertainment world. From 1961 through 1966 he had a most lucrative and unusual job: supplying the offcamera voice for television's most popular talking horse, Mr. Ed. The series starred Alan Young, Connie Haines, and Leon Ames.

After "Mr. Ed" left prime-time television, Lane retired to a quiet life in Los Angeles. He died of cancer on October 27, 1973.

Western Film Credits

The Law West of Tombstone (RKO, 1938)

King of the Royal Mounted (serial) (Rep., 1940)

King of the Mounties (serial) (Rep., 1942)

Daredevils of the West (serial) (Rep., 1943)

Silver City Kid (Rep., 1944)

Stagecoach to Monterey (Rep., 1944)

Topeka Terror (Rep., 1945)

Corpus Christi Bandits (Rep., 1945)

Bells of Rosarita (Rep., 1945)

Trail of Kit Carson (Rep., 1945)

Out California Way (Rep., 1946)

Santa Fe Uprising (Rep., 1946)

Stagecoach to Denver (Rep., 1946)
Vigilantes of Boomtown (Rep., 1947)
Homesteaders of Paradise Valley
   (Rep., 1947)
Oregon Trail Scouts (Rep., 1947)
Rustlers of Devil's Canyon (Rep.,
   1947)
Marshal of Cripple Creek (Rep., 1947)
The Wild Frontier (Rep., 1947)
Bandits of Dark Canyon (Rep., 1947)
Oklahoma Badlands (Rep., 1948)
The Bold Frontiersman (Rep., 1948)
Carson City Raiders (Rep., 1948)
Marshal of Amarillo (Rep., 1948)
Desperadoes of Dodge City (Rep.,
   1948)
The Denver Kid (Rep., 1948)
Sundown in Santa Fe (Rep., 1948)
Renegades of Sonora (Rep., 1948)
Sheriff of Wichita (Rep., 1949)
Death Valley Gunfighters (Rep.,
   1949)
Frontier Investigator (Rep., 1949)
The Wyoming Bandit (Rep., 1949)
Bandit King of Texas (Rep., 1949)
Navajo Trail Raiders (Rep., 1949)

Powder River Rustlers (Rep., 1949)
Gunmen of Abilene (Rep., 1950)
Code of the Silver Sage (Rep., 1950)
Salt Lake Raiders (Rep., 1950)
Covered Wagon Raiders (Rep., 1950)
Vigilante Hideout (Rep., 1950)
Frisco Tornado (Rep., 1950)
Rustlers on Horseback (Rep., 1950)
Rough Riders of Durango (Rep.,
   1951)
Night Riders of Montana (Rep., 1951)
Wells Fargo Gunmaster (Rep., 1951)
Fort Dodge Stampede (Rep., 1951)
The Desert of Lost Men (Rep., 1951)
Captive of Billy the Kid (Rep., 1952)
Leadville Gunslinger (Rep., 1952)
Black Hills Ambush (Rep., 1952)
Thundering Caravans (Rep., 1952)
Desperadoes' Outpost (Rep., 1952)
Marshal of Cedar Creek (Rep., 1953)
Savage Frontier (Rep., 1953)
Bandits of the West (Rep., 1953)
El Paso Stampede (Rep., 1953)
The Saga of Hemp Brown (UI, 1958)
Hell Bent for Leather (UI, 1960)
Posse from Hell (UI, 1961)

Audie Murphy, in one of his many action Westerns.

Audie Murphy

(Cold-eyed hero with a quick gun)

Born: June 20, 1924, Kingston, Tex.
Married: Wanda Hendrix (1949); divorced
    (1950); remarried: Pamela Archer (1951);
    separated (1969); children: Terry, James
Died: May 28, 1971

ALL ONE HAD to do was look into Audie Murphy's troubled green eyes to realize that here was an emotionally tortured soul. From the depths of poverty to sudden fame as World War II's most decorated and publicized combat hero, he emerged from his wartime ordeal a tormented, frightened individual. He never learned to cope properly with his screen popularity.

Nevertheless, it was Murphy, along with Joel McCrea and Randolph Scott, who held together the last vestiges of the B-Western during the fifties and sixties. In fact, Audie was the last authentic hero of the double-bill Western picture.

Audie Leon Murphy was one of nine children born to sharecroppers near Kingston, Texas. Life for the Murphys was a variation on *Tobacco Road.* By 1939 the economics of family life had so deteriorated that Mr. Murphy abandoned his brood.

At age fifteen Audie had to quit school to find a job to help support his mother, brothers, and sisters. With a borrowed rifle he would hunt game to keep the family from starving, besides working long hours for whatever he could earn. Two years later the *only* woman Audie truly loved, his mother, died of a heart ailment.

After his mother's death, Audie tried to enlist in the Marine Corps and the paratroopers, but was rejected because he was too young and too frail of stature. He persuaded his older sister Corrine to falsify his enlistment papers, by which deception he was accepted into the National Guard. His guard unit was activated as a unit of the Third Army, and Audie went into combat. He saw action in Sicily and Italy, won a field commission as second lieutenant, then fought in France and Austria. Near the end of the war, *Life* magazine did an article on "The Most Decorated Soldier" for its July 16, 1945, issue. And it was Audie Murphy who was World War II's most decorated American GI. Wounded three times in battle and later given a fifty percent disability rating and a veteran's pension, he won twenty-four citations, including the Congressional Medal of Honor. It was estimated he had killed approximately 240 Germans in combat.

He was a national hero when he was honorably discharged from the army. He dreamed of matriculating at West Point, but his war injuries and the death of his sponsor, General Alexander Patch, ended these hopes.

It was airline stewardess Pamela Archer who sent his photo to producer William Cagney (James' brother) and suggested him for a screen test. The Cagney brothers offered Audie a screen trial and he made his movie debut in *Beyond Glory* (1948), followed by a bit in *Texas, Brooklyn and Heaven* (1948), starring Guy Madison and Diana Lynn.

Audie's first leading role was as a juvenile delinquent in *Bad Boy* (1949). He may have looked the part but his performance was embarrassingly unprofessional.

Despite the occasional movie work, Audie was ill at ease in front of the cameras and in a Hollywood setting. So poor he often slept on the floor of a gymnasium owned by a friend, he had all his service pension diverted to support his younger brothers and sisters who were still in a Texas orphanage.

In 1950 Audie appeared in the box-office success *The Kid from Texas*. A pleased Universal-International put him under contract and planned to make him a major Western picture star. On film his easygoing manner and soft Texas accent lent themselves well to the genre. His autobiography, *To Hell and Back*, had been published, and Universal planned to cash in on the new fame surrounding its property.

In 1951 prestigious producer-director John Huston borrowed Audie for his version of Stephen Crane's *The Red Badge of Courage*. Under Huston's supervision, Audie gave his finest screen performance in this MGM feature of fear and courage on the Civil War battlefield. Because of studio politics and industry crassness the feature was edited to shreds and the picture emerged a box-office flop. But the public and critics took note of Audie's presence and he was named one of the Stars of Tomorrow in 1952.

Returning to Universal—which was surviving on "Francis," the talking mule, and "Ma and Pa Kettle" entries—Audie continued to make two to three Westerns a year. Filmed in color, they were heavy on action and light on plot.

When Tony Curtis rejected the part, Audie starred as himself in the movie version of *To Hell and Back* (1955), which proved to be his most commercial screen appearance. Two years later he played James Stewart's younger brother in the well-done *Night Passage*, and in 1958 he starred in another type of cold-war film, *The Quiet American*, set in Southeast Asia. And by the end of the decade he was the number one B-Western star.

In the late fifties Audie began appearing on TV and even had a guest shot on "The Chevy Show" variety outing with Roy Rogers and Eddy Arnold. In 1961 he starred for a season in the NBC-TV series "Whispering Smith," which would be denounced by a congressional committee for excessive violence.

During these years Audie's personal life was unsettling. His short-term marriage to actress Wanda Hendrix proved a big mistake for both parties and in 1951 he wed Pam Archer, the girl who had introduced him to the movies. Rumors spread of unpleasant rows during the course of each of these marriages.

Whereas the fifties had been a period of professional success for Audie, the sixties were just the opposite. He started the decade with John Huston's all-star *The Unforgiven*. But this perceptive, psychological Western failed to make big money. Murphy was shuttled back once again to the cheaper adventure films ground out by Universal.

Unfortunately, as Audie once admitted, "I'm working with one helluva handicap. I have no talent."

As the years went on, Audie's screen characterizations became increasingly bland. In tandem with the studio's economy measures, his productions lacked their former charm. In 1962 he was reunited with Dan Duryea (his costar in 1954's *Ride Clear of Diablo*) for *Six Black Horses*. Again Duryea was the villain, but this time only Duryea's portrayal had any color.

By 1967 Audie was reduced to making quickies like *40 Guns to Apache Pass*. At the end of his lengthy career in oaters, he observed, "I've made the same Western about forty times, only each time with a different horse. I don't mind being an actor so long as I don't have to live up to a reputation I don't have."

With the conclusion of his career in movies, Audie's personal life seemed to fall apart. He and his second wife separated. The $2.5 million he had made from motion pictures was gone—either given away or lost in bad investments. The actor was heavily in debt and seemed surrounded by ill-begotten publicity.

In 1970 he was charged with assault with intent to commit murder in a squabble with a dog trainer. The man stated that Audie and a buddy beat him up when he supposedly mistreated an animal. However, Audie was eventually acquitted by a jury.

The former actor became interested in law enforcement and served as a special officer for the Port Hueneme, California, police department. He also aided the Los Angeles County district attorney's office in its fight against crime. Particularly vigilant against drug pushers, he often joined the police in raids on drug traffickers.

In the late sixties Audie served as the producer for the independently made *A Time for Dying*, in which he had a cameo appearance as Jesse James. The film was not released until 1971, however. On May 28, 1971, Audie and five other men were reported missing aboard a twin-engine Aero Commander plane that had taken off from Atlanta, Georgia. The wreckage was located in woods outside Roanoke, Virginia, and Audie's body was identified. He was buried at Arlington National Cemetery with the nation's greatest heroes. (Later there would be evidence that at the time of his death Audie was making special pleas to President Nixon to have ex-teamster head James Hoffa released from prison. It was also rumored there was a tie-in here with the supposed "assassination conspiracy" against President John F. Kennedy.)

In December 1975 the widow and two sons of war hero Audie Murphy were awarded $2.5 million in a suit filed as a result of his death. The suit maintained that the crash had occurred because of the negligence of the Colorado Aviation Company and the pilot of the plane.

While Audie's films are a reminder of the career that once was, other tangible memorials recall the war hero.

On May 17, 1975, an eight-foot, four-ton bronze statue was unveiled at the Audie L. Murphy Memorial Veterans' Hospital in San Antonio, Texas. A memorial room in the hospital contains Audie's original World War II medals.

Western Film Credits

The Kid from Texas (UI, 1950)

Sierra (UI, 1950)

Kansas Raiders (UI, 1950)

The Red Badge of Courage (MGM, 1951)

The Cimarron Kid (UI, 1951)

The Duel at Silver Creek (UI, 1952)

Gunsmoke (UI, 1953)

Column South (UI, 1953)

Tumbleweed (UI, 1953)

Ride Clear of Diablo (UI, 1954)

Drums Across the River (UI, 1954)

Destry (UI, 1954)

Walk the Proud Land (Univ., 1956)

The Guns of Fort Petticoat (Col., 1957)

Night Passage (Univ., 1957)

Ride a Crooked Trail (UI, 1958)

No Name on the Bullet (Univ., 1959)

Cast a Long Shadow (UA, 1959)

The Unforgiven (UA, 1960)

Hell Bent for Leather (UI, 1960)

Seven Ways from Sundown (UI, 1960)

Posse from Hell (UI, 1961)

Six Black Horses (UI, 1962)

Showdown (UI, 1963)

Gunfight at Comanche Creek (AA, 1963)

The Quick Gun (Col., 1964)

Bullet for a Badman (Univ., 1964)

Apache Rifles (20th, 1964)

Gunpoint (Univ., 1966)

The Texican (Col., 1966)

Arizona Raiders (Col., 1966)

40 Guns to Apache Pass (Col., 1967)

A Time for Dying (Ind., 1971)

Tex Ritter in 1942.

Tex Ritter

(The Texas Troubadour)

Born: January 12, 1904, Murvaul, Tex.
Married: Dorothy Fay (1944); children: Tom,
  Jonathan
Died: January 2, 1974

OF THE MANY cowboy singing stars in Western films, only Tex Ritter was both a true Westerner and a talented singer. (In his lifetime he would be elected to the Cowboy Hall of Fame and the Country-Western Hall of Fame.)

Tex grew up loving the lore of the West and its folk music. Although the major thrust of his features was the singing interludes, his films contained more action than those of either Gene Autry or Roy Rogers. The music used in the Ritter productions tended to be genuine American folk ballads of historical significance instead of the popular pap sung and strummed by other boots-and-saddles crooners. That Tex built for himself an important and lasting musical career after his Western picture-making days is ample proof of his talents.

Born Woodward Maurice Ritter, he came from a strong southern family background that included several lawmen. As a boy, Tex worked on his family's 400-acre farm. Here he learned the value of folk music from an elderly black farmhand. After graduating from high school in nearby Beaumont, he attended the University of Texas in Austin to study law. There he began to sing in public, and there he encountered Western folklore authority J. Frank Dobie. The meeting would have a great effect on the impressionable young Ritter.

Because of the Great Depression, Tex eventually had to drop out of college and go to work in a steel mill. Later he began to sing folk ballads over a Houston radio station. This resulted in a road tour to Chicago where he decided to try to study law again. He enrolled in Northwestern University. Tex found it impossible to support himself and attend college at the same time, so he fell back on his musical talents and tried his luck in New York City.

He understudied actor Franchot Tone in the Theatre Guild production of *Green Grow the Lilacs,* in which he also had a supporting part. In this nonmusical version of the property that was eventually to become the musical extravaganza *Oklahoma!* Tex began to receive media notice. In this show he earned the lifelong nickname "Tex," which was foisted on him by the stagehands and cast. Later came another Broadway role in *The Round-Up,* which had a short run. Then he was in the Western melodrama *Mother Lode,* which starred Melvyn Douglas. But that show also failed to please New York theatergoers.

Tex next tried radio. On "Lone Star Rangers" he sang songs and told tales of the old West. He was also the announcer for a New York City barndance program over WHN, and could be heard in dramatic roles in a variety of audio dramas, including "Gang Busters," "ENO Crime Clues," and "Death Valley Days."

In 1932 Tex played the role of Tex Mason in "Bobby Benson's Adventures" over the CBS radio network and this performance led to his being hired for the same role in the musical comedy version of the series called "Songs of the B-Bar-B." Later he created and starred in "Cowboy Tom's Roundup," which became the most popular children's radio program on the East Coast during its three-year run. During this period Tex, who had a very resonant and distinctive voice, made recordings for various independent labels.

While Tex was appearing at a New Jersey dude ranch, producer Edward Finney invited him to make pictures for Grand National release. The salary was $2,400 a film.

Thus Tex Ritter embarked on another career. *Song of the Gringo* (1936) was his initial release. Oldtime outlaw Al Jennings, who played a judge in this quickie film, taught Tex how to draw and fire a six-shooter properly. The success of this boots-and-saddles production launched Tex as a popular cowboy movie star.

From 1936 to 1938 Tex made over a dozen pictures for Grand National, most of which were shot on a five-day schedule with a budget of about $10,000 a film. Although the series varied in quality, the films were sufficiently entertaining for Tex to place sixth in the *Motion Picture Herald's* 1937 poll of top cowboy movie stars. (He was ninth in 1938 and seventh in 1939.)

When Finney switched from Grand National to Monogram in 1938, Tex went along with him and became a big moneymaker for that small studio. Under these favorable circumstances the studio agreed to double the budgets for Tex' productions.

All in all, Tex made over twenty-five bread-and-butter productions for Monogram. When Columbia Pictures offered him a substantial salary raise in 1941, he went there. The larger film factory teamed him with his old friend Gordon "Wild Bill" Elliott for eight features.

In the Columbia pictures Tex rode his horse White Flash, and he and his animal continued on the range when Universal hired him in 1942 for a series of films. In these features he was paired with not yet pudgy Johnny Mack Brown.

Tex was among the cowboy stars in *Frontier Badmen* (1943) and later joined a host of other Western favorites in *Cowboy Canteen* (1944). In each instance, the distinctive, crisp-voiced Tex Ritter personality held its own.

In Frontier Fugitives *(1945).*

With Marjorie Reynolds in Tex Rides with the Boy Scouts *(1937).*

Amidst a sagebrush series at Universal, Tex broke his leg and had to be replaced by star Russell Hayden. When he recovered, Tex moved to Producers Releasing Corp. for the "Texas Rangers" series. The eleven pictures he made for PRC in 1944 and 1945 (he was too old for military service during World War II) brought him back onto the top ten cowboy stars chart.

After starring in sixty outdoors films, Tex ended his tenure as a Western star in 1945. Thereafter he concentrated on his personal appearance tours and recording sessions.

He began with Decca Records in the 1930s and in 1942 switched to Capitol Records. By 1943 three of Tex's discs were the top three tunes on *Billboard*'s top ten jukebox favorites; he would continue turning out best-selling records for Capitol until his death.

During the 1940s Tex and Western film comedian Max Terhune toured the United States in various productions. In 1949 Tex formed his own Tex Ritter Western Festival & Circus, which he later renamed the Western Revue.

It was in 1950 that Tex returned to Hollywood films for a guest-starring role in *Holiday Rhythm*. Besides touring Europe in 1952 he sang the title theme song for the Gary Cooper film *High Noon*. His recording of the song was a bestseller and he sang it on the Academy Awards telecast that year.

Tex was an extremely busy man during the 1950s. He had a seven-year hitch on NBC radio's "Town Hall Party," sang the title themes for other films, narrated *The Cowboy* (1954), played a gunfighter in *Apache Ambush* (1955), and was oncamera in the documentary *Down Liberty Road* (1956). By the middle of the decade he was a regular performer on the long-running "Grand Ole Opry" radio program broadcast from Nashville. (He would move to Nashville permanently in the 1960s.)

Tex also could be heard on Red Foley's "Ozark Jubilee" program. In 1958 Tex was on TV's "Zane Grey Theatre," and in 1961 he guested on ABC-TV's "The Rebel." In the late fifties he cohosted television's "Five Star Jubilee," and in 1959 he started a four-year gig as a star of "Ranch Party," a syndicated country music show.

Despite his advancing years, Tex did not slow down. He continued recording and making personal appearances around the world, as well as showing up on TV specials and country and western programs.

In 1966 he narrated *What's the Country Coming To?* and starred as the preacher in *Girl from Tobacco Road*. He played himself in *What Am I Bid?* (1967) and sang the amusing ballad "I Never Got to Kiss the Girl," lamenting the fact that he never kissed any of his leading ladies in his Western pictures. He became the Nashville chairman of the National Committee for the Recording Arts and was both vice president and president of the Country Music Association. In 1970 he ran for the GOP nomination for a U.S. Senate seat from Tennessee, but was defeated.

Country music entertainer.

The seventies found Tex Ritter with such well-loved recording hits as "Green, Green Valley." He made his final film appearance in *The Nashville Story* (1972). On January 2, 1974, he died of a heart attack while visiting a friend in the Nashville city jail. That day Capitol Records issued his single "The Americans," which became a bestselling record.

Known as "America's Most Beloved Cowboy," Tex had a fun-loving attitude toward his Western picture making. Regarding his many screen roles, he once mused, "I guess I was pretty tough. Roy [Rogers] and Gene [Autry] sang more. . . . I killed more. . . . Old Charlie King, the bad guy in films, I must've killed him at least twenty times. And usually it was always behind that same old rock."

Western Film Credits

Song of the Gringo (GN, 1936)
Headin' for the Rio Grande (GN, 1936)
Arizona Days (GN, 1937)
Trouble in Texas (GN, 1937)

Hittin' the Trail (GN, 1937)
Sing, Cowboy, Sing (GN, 1937)
Riders of the Rockies (GN, 1937)
Tex Rides with the Boy Scouts (GN, 1937)

The Mystery of the Hooded Horsemen (GN, 1937)
Frontier Town (GN, 1938)
Rollin' Plains (GN, 1938)
The Utah Trail (GN, 1938)
Starlight over Texas (Mon., 1938)
Where the Buffalo Roam (Mon., 1938)
Song of the Buckaroo (Mon., 1938)
Sundown on the Prairie (Mon., 1939)
Riders of the Frontier (Mon., 1939)
Rollin' Westward (Mon., 1939)
Roll, Wagons, Roll (Mon., 1939)
Down the Wyoming Trail (Mon., 1939)
Man from Texas (Mon., 1939)
Westbound Stage (Mon., 1939)
Rhythm of the Rio Grande (Mon., 1940)
Pals of the Silver Sage (Mon., 1940)
The Golden Trail (Mon., 1940)
The Cowboy from Sundown (Mon., 1940)
Take Me Back to Oklahoma (Mon., 1940)
Rainbow over the Range (Mon., 1940)
Arizona Frontier (Mon., 1940)
Rolling Home to Texas (Mon., 1941)
Riding the Cherokee Trail (Mon., 1941)
The Pioneers (Mon., 1941)
King of Dodge City (Col., 1941)

Roaring Frontiers (Col., 1941)
Lone Star Vigilantes (Col., 1941)
Bullets for Bandits (Col., 1941)
The Devil's Trail (Col., 1942)
North of the Rockies (Col., 1942)
Prairie Gunsmoke (Col., 1942)
Vengeance of the West (Col., 1942)
Deep in the Heart of Texas (Univ., 1942)
Little Joe the Wrangler (Univ., 1942)
The Old Chisholm Trail (Univ., 1942)
Raiders of San Joaquin (Univ., 1942)
The Lone Star Trail (Univ., 1943)
Tenting Tonight on the Old Camp Ground (Univ., 1943)
Cheyenne Roundup (Univ., 1943)
Frontier Badmen (Univ., 1943)
Arizona Trail (Univ., 1944)
Marshal of Gunsmoke (Univ., 1944)
Oklahoma Raiders (Univ., 1944)
Cowboy Canteen (Col., 1944)
Gangsters of the Frontier (PRC, 1944)
Dead or Alive (PRC, 1944)
The Whispering Skull (PRC, 1944)
Marked for Murder (PRC, 1944)
Enemy of the Law (PRC, 1945)
Three in the Saddle (PRC, 1945)
Frontier Fugitives (PRC, 1945)
Flaming Bullets (PRC, 1945)
Apache Ambush (Col., 1955)

In Final, Lasting Tribute

Art Acord
Nick Adams
Ted Adams
"Broncho Billy" Anderson
Roscoe Ates
Warner Baxter
Noah Beery, Sr.
Wallace Beery
Rex Bell
Monte Blue
Ward Bond
Walter Brennan
Buffalo Bill, Jr.
Smiley Burnette
Bruce Cabot
Leo Carrillo
Edward Cassidy
Lane Chandler
Lon Chaney, Jr.
George Chesebro
Edmund Cobb
Bill Cody
Ray "Crash" Corrigan
Dick Curtis
Bob Custer
William Desmond
Eddie Dew
Andy Devine
Don Douglas
Dan Duryea
Earl Dwire
Dustin Farnum
William Farnum
Eric Fleming
Errol Flynn
Francis Ford
Jonathan Hale
Thurston Hall

Sam Hardy
George "Gabby" Hayes
Jack Holt
George Houston
Jack Hoxie
Tom Keene
Charles King
Fuzzy Knight
Fred Kohler
Robert Kortman
Rex Lease
Tom London
Jack Luden
Kenneth MacDonald
LeRoy Mason
Ray Mayer
Kermit Maynard
Lafe McKee
Art Mix
Ramon Novarro
Wayne Morris
Jack Padjan
Lee Powell
Jack Randall
Jack Rockwell
Will Rogers
Buddy Roosevelt
Reb Russell
Al "Fuzzy" St. John
Roy Stewart
Glenn Strange
Robert Taylor
Max Terhune
Fred Thomson
Slim Whitaker
Guinn "Big Boy" Williams
Harry Woods

HONORABLE MENTION
(Living)

Dick Alexander
Smith Ballew
Buzz Barton
Bruce Bennett
Rod Cameron
Eddie Dean
James Drury
Jimmy Ellison
Chad Everett
Henry Fonda
Dick Foran
William Haade
Monte Hale
Ty Hardin
Russell Hayden

Rock Hudson
Lee Majors
Doug McClure
Steve McQueen
Robert Mitchum
George Montgomery
Slim Pickens
Duncan Renaldo
Fred Scott
Tommy Scott
Jay Silverheels
James Stewart
Hal Taliaferro (Wally Wales)
Bill Williams

With my best Wishes

Rex Bell

Rex Bell, who married actress Clara Bow and later became lieutenant-governor of Nevada.

Jack Holt (right), with LeRoy Mason and Roy Barcroft in My Pal Trigger *(1946).*

Veteran Western actors Kermit Maynard, Bill "Cowboy Rambler" Boyd, Charles King, Art Davis, and John Merton in a scene from Prairie Pals *(1942).*

Lane Chandler, a fine Western character actor.

Monte Blue, a popular star who played heavy and character roles in the latter part of his long career.

Rod Cameron
and Fuzzy
Knight in Boss
of Boomtown
(1944).

Noah Beery, Sr.,
veteran actor of
silent and sound
Western films.

Ray "Crash" Corrigan, famed for his daredevil stunts.

Fred Thomson—he gave Tom Mix some competition in action Westerns.

Henry Fonda plays a bad guy this time in Once Upon a Time in the West *(1969).*

Lon Chaney, Jr., Thomas Gomez, and Arthur Loft in Frontier Badmen *(1943).*

Bill Cody, who achieved stardom rapidly and lost it the same way.

Index

366

376

377